OKLAHOMA
Historical Tour Guide

By Burnis Argo and Kent Ruth
Editor D. Ray Wilson
Photographer Jim Argo

COVER PHOTO

The Will Rogers Memorial in Claremore by Jim Argo.

DEDICATION

This book is dedicated to the late Kent Ruth, a life-long resident of Geary. He died in January, 1991, at the age of 74. Co-author of this book, Ruth was well-known as a travel writer, historian and longtime columnist for *The Oklahoman*. He was elected to the Oklahoma Hall of Fame, and served on the boards of the Oklahoma Historical Society, Southwestern Oklahoma Historical Society, Oklahoma Heritage Association and the Canadian County Historical Society. He was a charter member of the Indian Territory Posse of Westerners International. He received many commendations for his work.

Other books in this series:

Illinois Historical Tour Guide
Greater Chicago Historical Tour Guide
Iowa Historical Tour Guide
Nebraska Historical Tour Guide
Wyoming Historical Tour Guide
Colorado Historical Tour Guide
Kansas Historical Tour Guide
Missouri Historical Tour Guide

About the editor

D. Ray Wilson is author of historical tour guides for Greater Chicago, Illinois, Iowa, Nebraska, Wyoming, Colorado, Kansas, and Missouri. He is author of three other books. Wilson received his journalism degree from Northern Illinois University and is the recipient of an honorary doctorate from Judson College, Elgin, IL. He has over 40 years in the newspaper business and served more than 25 years as editor and publisher of daily newspapers. He is listed in the current edition of "Who's Who in America."

Authors: Burnis Argo and Kent Ruth
Editor: D. Ray Wilson
Photographer: Jim Argo
OKLAHOMA HISTORICAL TOUR GUIDE

1st Edition, 1992

Published by Crossroads Communications
Carpentersville, Illinois 60110-0007
Manufactured in the United States of America

Library of Congress Catalog Number: 91-70305
International Standard Book Number: 0-916445-31-3 (Soft Cover)
                                    0-916445-34-8 (Hard Cover)

Table of Contents

All photographs by Jim Argo, Edmond, OK, appearing in this book have been copyrighted by him. Publication of these photographs in this book is by permission of Mr. Argo and other considerations. The maps used in this book are through the courtesy of Preston George of Edmond, OK. Mr. George, a retired civil engineer, is a leading authority of railroading in Oklahoma and is often called upon by authors, historians, lawyers, and mapmakers for his assistance.

About the co-author, Photographer husband

Burnis Argo and her husband, Jim, have extensive experience as journalists. Burnis, a native Oklahoman, received her degree in English from Oklahoma State University, Stillwater. She worked for 10 years for *The Daily Oklahoman* and *Oklahoma City Times* and for the past several years has been a free lance writer for newspapers and magazines.

Jim Argo, a native Kansan, received his degree in journalism from Texas Tech in Lubbock, Texas. For over a quarter century he has been a member of the photo staff of *The Daily Oklahoman*. He has won a number of state and national awards for his work and his photos appear regularly in such national publications as Time, Newsweek, Business Week and others.

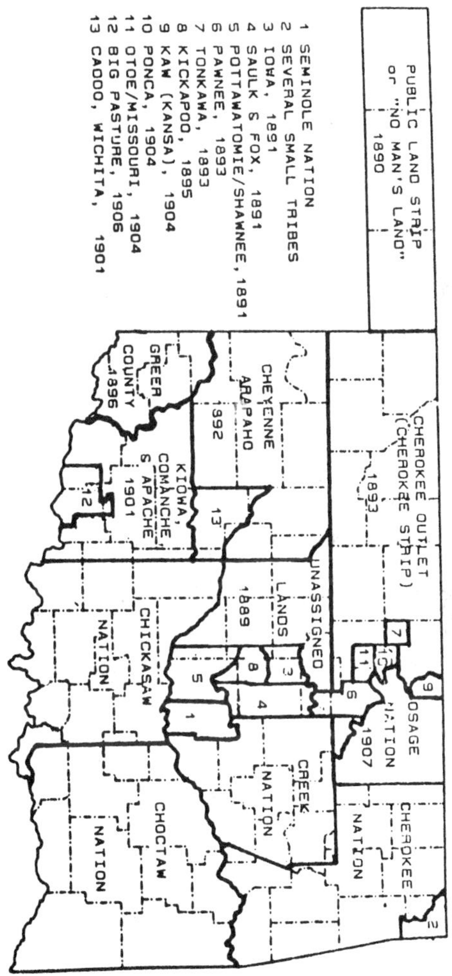

Locations of lands assigned to tribes in Indian Territory and date each area was available for non-Indian settlement. Maps used in this book were designed and produced by Preston George.

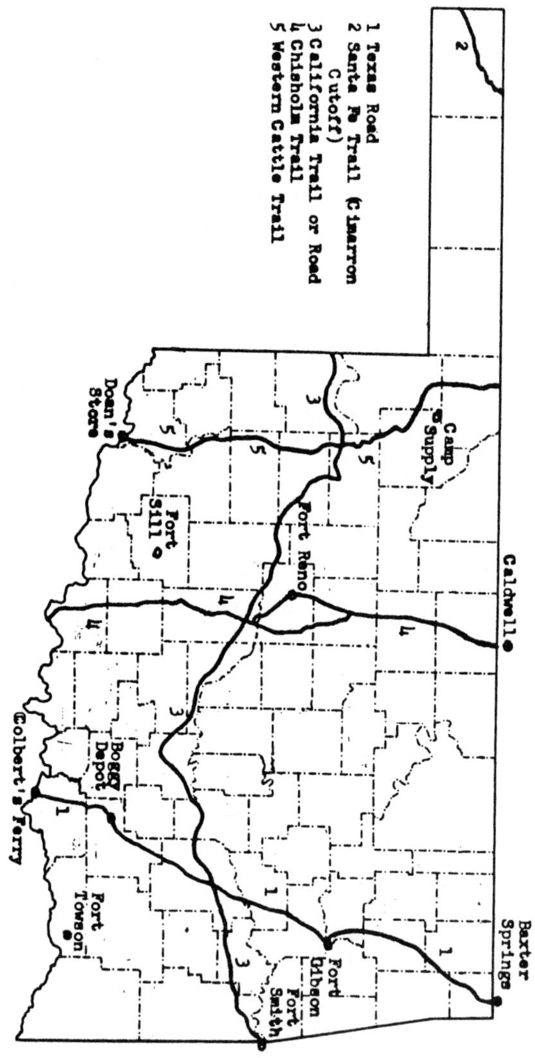

A few of the earliest trails, roads, and inhabited places in what is now Oklahoma. Map designed and produced by Preston George.

SECTION 1
An Overview

Much can be learned about a state by studying the signs and symbols, songs and slogans she considers significant enough to incorporate into her official state emblems. Oklahoma is no exception.

STATE SEAL

Inside the centered five-pointed star is a symbolic tableau—the figure of Justice holding high the balanced scale over a hand-shaking frontiersman and Indian. On November 16, 1907, in a "mock marriage" ceremony at the territorial capital of Guthrie, a cowboy representing non-Indian Oklahoma Territory was wedded to an Indian maiden representing Indian Territory. Oklahoma (from two Choctaw words: Okla meaning "people" and humma meaning "red"—literally home of red people) had become the 46th state (star) in the Union. So filling in the spaces around that centered star, nine to a section, are the 45 smaller stars of those states that came in before.

STATE FLAG

On a blue field is an Osage shield (warfare) crossed by an olive branch and a calumet (peace pipe)—again a symbol of bi-racial accord.

STATE MOTTO

"Labor Omnia Vincit" (Labor Conquers All Things) reflects the strong populist current flowing in Oklahoma when statehood was achieved. It suggests a practical modus operandi for achieving the pious goals of peace and goodwill declared by the seal and flag.

STATE SONG

"Oklahoma!" needless to say, from the enormously successful Rodgers and Hammerstein musical of the same name is the state song. Needless to say, too, it has not always been the official song, thereby signifying that Oklahoma, reflecting the buoyancy of youth, can recognize a good thing when she sees it...and break with tradition, if need be, to embrace it. It is a helpful character trait for a state to possess. Somewhat related, perhaps, is the state's readiness, when public dissatisfaction mounts to a sufficient level, to exchange governors in mid-stream. Of the seven state governors that have been successfully impeached in these United States over the years, two have been Oklahomans.

STATE NICKNAME

"Sooner" (for those participants in the state's famous land runs who took off from the starting line "sooner" than they should have) suggests yet another quirk in the Oklahoma psyche—a kind of frontier macho that sometimes leads to admiration for those who defy convention if not actually flaunt the law. This "Jesse James Syndrome" threw a certain protective Robin Hood aura around such bona fide Oklahoma outlaws as the Dalton and Doolin gangs, Belle Starr, Charles Arthur "Pretty Boy" Floyd, and Clyde Barrow and Bonnie Parker. It may have been active in the selection of a State Tree and State Floral Emblem. It obviously played a strong role in the development and perpetuation of one early-day business calling. With the sale of whiskey banned in Indian Territory, bootlegging became a curiously quasi-legal vocation. This, ironically, in a region generally considered to be solidly "Bible Belt."

STATE FLOWER

The mistletoe (phoradendron serotinum) the waxy-leafed white berry-bearing plant that allows, under certain conditions, certain public displays of affection, grows high in such native Oklahoma trees as elm and hackberry. It is, of course a parasite, hardly compatible, it would seem, to "labor omnia vincit." Yet the average Sooner, if he thinks of it at all, is inclined to smile appreciatively.

STATE TREE

Found growing wild throughout Oklahoma, but especially in the west where native flowers and blooming trees and shrubs are far from common, the redbud in April is a magnificent sight, a splash of pink-to-lavender on a still seasonally dead landscape. And yet a curious legend (although only a legend) throws something of a shadow over even such beauty as this—the suggestion that it was the redbud, for providing the cross Jesus carried to Golgotha, whose bloom turned to a blush of shame.

OTHER EMBLEMS

Oklahoma's lesser emblems are perhaps less significant as character markers. The **State Bird** is the scissor-tailed flycatcher—an acrobatic aerialist and a distinctive flash of sporty color, found almost exclusively on the Southern Plains. Also found almost exclusively in Oklahoma is the **State Rock**, a barite rose rock dug up in a small central section of the state. The **State Animal** is, predictably, the American bison—the shaggy buffalo that once roamed the plains in unbelievable numbers. As the

"Indians' Commissary," it provided Native Americans with food, shelter, clothing, tools, and implements. As for the **State Fish**, the white (or sand) bass, it is the star of countless derbies and festivals around the state. Just recently Oklahoma added some more emblems to the list, **State Wildflower**, the Indian paintbrush; and **State Reptile**, the Mountain boomer or collard lizard; and **State Grass**, Indian grass.

HOME OF THE RED PEOPLE

The "Home of Red People" has been occupied—at least roamed over—for perhaps 15,000 years, archaeologists say, perhaps even 40,000 years if evidence recently uncovered at a site in Woods County in northwestern Oklahoma proves valid.

Scattered evidence of these "presences" is continually being uncovered, analyzed, and interpreted.

First presence of European visitors came in 1541 with the appearance of Coronado searching for his Seven Cities of Cibola. (Still controversial are indications of Viking visitors more than five centuries before Coronado.) Not until the end of the 18th century and the early years of the 19th did the fur trade bring French and Spanish trappers and traders, but the wilderness that was to become Oklahoma was virtually unoccupied in 1803 when the Louisiana Purchase transferred it to the United States. Only largely nomadic Indian tribes like the Wichitas, Caddoes, Kiowas, Osages, and Comanches roamed the area until then.

Meanwhile, in the Southeast, pressure was building against the continued presence of the Five Civilized Tribes—the Cherokees, Chickasaws, Choctaws, Creeks, and Seminoles. Gradually the federal government began to encourage the Indians to give up their traditional homelands in Mississippi, Alabama, Georgia, Florida, Tennessee, and the Carolinas for extensive new holdings in the west. Several of the tribes sent representatives to check on the promised lands and some of their leaders counseled accepting the offer, feeling it might give them a better chance of maintaining their own culture.

Some bands of Indians did move westward voluntarily. Most, however, did not. For them it was a bitter, forced migration over what came to be called the "Trail of Tears." But by 1840 most of them were in Oklahoma, beginning to rebuild their towns and schools, their political, social, and economic institutions. . . their old way of life.

The Civil War interrupted their progress. Having come to

Oklahoma from the southern states, many of them with slaves, the tribes had divided loyalties and for the most part they sided with the Confederacy. For them the war brought double suffering, hardship and defeat, on top of the physical destruction from internecine warfare. Because of their support of the Confederacy the Indian Nations were stripped of their extended land holdings in western Oklahoma. It was into these lands that scores of Indian tribes in eastern and northern states were moved in the decades after the war. By 1880 more than 60 different tribes had new "homes" in Oklahoma.

But already forces were advancing rapidly to put these homes in jeopardy as well. Railroads appeared in the east as early as 1871. Coal deposits were discovered, and exploited. From Texas countless longhorn cattle were driven northward across the Indian lands to markets in Kansas. White settlers followed each development and soon there was increasing demand to open up the state. Finally, in 1889, Congress authorized opening the "Unassigned Lands"—some two million acres in the central part of the state that had not been given to any Indian tribe.

On April 22, 1889, came the first famous "run," a frenzied affair that is still celebrated annually throughout the area. Raucous tent cities like Guthrie and Oklahoma City sprang up in a day, created by those who chose town lots rather than a 160-acre homestead. The die was cast. Subsequent opening to white settlement of even more Indian lands in central and western Oklahoma was inevitable. Other notable "runs" came in 1891, 1892, 1893, and 1895. In 1901 much of southwestern Oklahoma was opened with a giant lottery.

Indian Territory felt more and more threatened. With the failure in 1905 of an attempt by the Five Civilized Tribes to form from their five nations the separate State of Sequoyah, the stage was set for the last act. Theodore Roosevelt signed the Enabling Act in 1906 and on November 16, 1907, the "wedding" of Indian Territory and Oklahoma Territory was consummated. Oklahoma had become the 46th state. Guthrie, capital of Oklahoma Territory, became the state capital. It held that position until 1910. Then it lost a bitter state wide election and Oklahoma City became the capital.

THE EARLY MILITARY POSTS

The frontier Army was called upon to protect white immigrants from the Indians and the Indians from each other in many instances. As a result several early day military posts were established in the area that would eventually become Oklahoma Territory and then the State of Oklahoma.

Fort Arbuckle, established as Camp Arbuckle on the road from Fort Smith to Santa Fe about a mile from the Canadian River near Byers, opened August 22, 1850. This camp was abandoned on April 17, 1851, and the post was moved four miles south of the Washita River, 76 miles northwest of its confluence with the Red River, seven miles west of the present city of Davis, and reestablished as a fort on April 19, 1851. It was occupied by Confederate troops in May, 1861, and reoccupied by federal troops in November, 1866. It was abandoned on June 24, 1870 (Section 6).

Fort Cobb was established on October 1, 1859, on the Washita River at the present city of Fort Cobb. It was evacuated on May 5, 1861, but was reoccupied after the Civil War in November, 1868, and served as a center for the control of the Kiowa and Comanche Indians. It was abandoned on March 12, 1869, in favor of Fort Sill.

Fort Coffee was established on June 17, 1834, on the right bank of the Arkansas River, about a dozen miles west of the present Arkansas boundary. It was an important post during the removal of the Indians, and was abandoned on October 19, 1838 (Section 11).

Fort Gibson, called Cantonment Gibson in the early years, was established in April, 1824, on the east bank of the Neosho or Grand River two and one-half miles above its confluence with the Arkansas River. It was abandoned in 1857 and reoccupied on April 5, 1863, by volunteer troops, who were replaced by federals on February 18, 1866. It was finally abandoned on September 22, 1890 (Section 8).

Cantonment on the North Fork of the Canadian River was established on March 6, 1879, on the North Fork of the Canadian River about 60 miles up the river from Fort Reno. The post was never given a formal designation. It was abandoned in June, 1882 (Section 13).

Camp Nichols was established at Cedar Bluffs or Cold Springs by Col. Kit Carson in May, 1865, to guard the immigrant trail "on the Cimarron route to the States." Camp Nichols was abandoned in November, 1865 (Section 9).

Camp Radziminski was established in September, 1858, on Otter Creek, at the base of the Wichita Mountains. It was abandoned on December 6, 1859 (Section 14).

Fort Reno, first known as the Camp near Cheyenne Agency, was established in August, 1874, on the North Fork of the Canadian River, about two miles from the Cheyenne and Arapaho Indian Agency. It was important in the campaign of 1874-75 against the Kiowa, Comanche, and Cheyenne Indians. It was officially designated Fort Reno on February 21, 1876. Fort Reno was also important in 1878-79 campaign against the northern Cheyennes. It was deactivated in 1949 and now serves as an agricultural research facility, operated jointly by Oklahoma State University and the U.S. Department of Agriculture (Section 5).

Fort Sill, originally named Camp Wichita, was established on March 4, 1869, near the foot of the Wichita Mountains at the junction of the Cache and Medicine Bluff creeks. The name was changed to Fort Sill on July 2, 1869. The fort served as an important headquarters in the wars against the southern Plains Indians. It is an active military post in 1991 (Section 4).

Fort Supply, originally called Camp Supply, was established on November 8, 1868, at the confluence of Wolf Creek and the North Fork of the Canadian River. It was designated a fort on December 30, 1878. It was abandoned on February 25, 1895 (Section 14).

Fort Towson, first called Cantonment Towson, was established in May, 1824, six miles north of the Red River and the same distance east of the Kiamichi River. Its mission was to protect the Choctaw Indians from the Plains Indians. The post was temporarily abandoned in 1829 but reestablished in 1831. It was named Fort Towson on February 8, 1832, and finally abandoned on June 8, 1854 (Section 15).

Fort Washita was established on April 23, 1842, northwest of Durant on the banks of the Washita River. Its mission was to protect the Chickasaw and Choctaw Indians from the hostile Indians of the Southwest. The fort was abandoned on May 1, 1861. It was occupied by Confederate troops during the Civil War but was never reoccupied by the federals again (Section 7).

Fort Wayne was established in 1839 east of Watts. It was moved later that year to a site on the north bank of the Spavinaw Creek, almost on the Arkansas line. It was abandoned in 1842 (Section 11).

OKLAHOMA'S MILITARY AND SPACE HEROES

Oklahoma is credited with 18 Congressional Medal of Honor

recipients. The CMH is the highest award for military valor.

SFC Tony K. Burris, Co. L, 38th Infantry Regiment, 2d Infantry Division, was awarded the CMH for heroism in the vicinity of Mundung-ni, Korea, October 8-9, 1951. He was a native of Blanchard.

2nd Lt. Ernest Childers, 45th Infantry Division, received the CMH for conspicious gallantry at Oliveto, Italy, September 22, 1943. He was born in Broken Arrow.

S/Sgt. John R. Crews, Co. F, 253d Infantry, 63d Infantry Division, was the recipient of the CMH for his heroism near Lebenbacherhof, Germany, April 8, 1945. He was born in Golden.

Commander Ernest E. Evans, commanding officer of the *U.S.S. Johnston*, received the CMH for conspicious gallantry against the Japanese fleet during the battle off Samar, October 25, 1944. He was born in Pawnee.

1st Lt. Donald J. Gott, 452d Bombardment Group, 8th Air Force, was awarded the CMH for heroism displayed after his B-17 was severely damaged during a bomb run on Saarbrucken, Germany, November 9, 1944. He was a native of Arnett.

1st Lt. George P. Hays, 10th Field Artillery, 3d Division, received the CMH for gallantry in action near Greves Farm, France, July 14-15, 1918. He entered the Army from Okarche.

1st Lt. Frederick F. Henry, Co. F, 28th Infantry Regiment, received the CMH for action beyond the call of duty near Amg Dong, Korea, September 1, 1950. He was a native of Vian.

Pvt. Harold G. Kiner, Co. F, 117th Infantry, 30th Infantry Division, was awarded the CMH for sacrificing his life by falling on a hand grenade to save two comrades near Palenburg, Germany, October 2, 1944. He was a native of Aline.

Lt. Richard M. McCool, Jr., USN, commanding officer of the *U.S.S. LSC-122*, received the CMH for his courageous action during operations against Japanese forces off Okinawa, June 10-11, 1945. He was born in Tishomingo.

Sgt. Troy A. McGill, Troop G, 5th Cavalry Regiment, 1st Cavalry Division, was awarded the CMH for his heroism in action against enemy forces on Los Negros Islands, Admiralty Group, March 4, 1944. He entered the Army from Ada.

1st Lt. Jack C. Montgomery, 45th Infantry Division, received the CMH for gallantry in action near Padiglione, Italy, February 22, 1944. He was born in Long.

Sgt. Larry D. Pierce, Hq and Hq Co., 1st Battalion, 503rd Infantry, 173rd Airborne Brigade, was awarded the CMH for saving the lives of his squad by throwing himself on a land mine near Ben Cat, Republic of Vietnam, September 20, 1965. He was a native of Wewoka.

Pfc John N. Reese, Jr., Co. B, 148th Infantry, 37th Infantry Division, received the CMH for his bravery in the attack on 300 enemy troops at Paco Railroad Station, Manila, P.I., February 9, 1945. He was a native of Muskogee.

Cpl. Samuel M. Sampler, Co. H, 142d Infantry, 36th Infantry Division, was awarded the CMH for his heroism against the enemy near St. Etienne, France, October 18, 1918. He was born in Altus.

Pfc Albert E. Schwab, USMCR, received the CMH for conspicuous gallantry and loss of life in action against Japanese forces on Okinawa Shima in the Ryukyu Islands, May 7, 1945. He joined the Marines in Oklahoma.

Major John L. Smith, USMC, Marine Fighting Squadron 223, was awarded the CMH for his heroic achievements in aerial combat and shooting down 16 Japanese planes in the Solomon Islands area, August 21 and September 15, 1942. He was born at Lexington.

Capt. Jack L. Treadwell, Co. F, 180th Infantry, 45th Infantry Division, received the CMH for singlehandedly capturing six pillboxes and 18 prisoners near Nieder-Wurzbach, Germany, March 18, 1945. He entered the Army from Snyder.

Cpl. Harold L. Turner, Co. F, 142d Infantry, 36th Infantry Division, was awarded the CMH for singlehandedly capturing 50 German soldiers and four machine guns near St. Etienne, France, October 8, 1918. He entered the Army from Seminole.

Four native-born Oklahomans have been involved in the American astronaut program.

L. Gordon Cooper, Jr., was selected as an astronaut in 1959 and flew on Mercury 9, May 15-16, 1963, and on Gemini 5, August 21-29, 1965. Born in Shawnee on March 6, 1927, Cooper retired as a colonel from the U.S. Air Force.

Owen K. Garriott was selected as an astronaut in 1965 and flew on Skylab 3, July 28-September 25, 1973, and STS-9, November 28 to December 8, 1983. Born in Enid on November 22, 1930, Garriott entered the program as a civilian.

William R. Pogue was selected for the astronaut program in 1966 and flew on Skylab 4, November 16, 1973, to February 8, 1974. Born in Okemah on January 23, 1930, Pogue retired as a colonel from the U.S. Air Force.

Born in Shawnee, L. Gordon Cooper Jr. is one of four native born Oklahoma U.S. astronauts. He was one of the first astronauts selected by NASA in 1959 and flew on Mercury 9 and Gemini 5. The others are Owen K. Garriott, from Enid; William R. Pogue, from Okemah; and Thomas P. Stafford, from Weatherford.

Thomas P. Stafford was selected for the astronaut program in 1962 and flew on Gemini 6, December 15-16, 1965; Gemini 9, June 3-6, 1966; Apollo 10, May 18-26, 1969; and the Apollo-Soyuz Test Project, July 15-24, 1975. Born in Weatherford, Stafford retired as a lieutenant general from the U.S. Air Force.

Oklahoma lays partial claim to three other astronauts.

Stuart A. Roosa, a retired Air Force colonel, attended school in Claremore and then Oklahoma State University. He became an astronaut in 1966 and was a member of the Apollo 14 crew that flew January 31 to February 9, 1971. He was born in Durango, Colorado.

Edgar D. Mitchell, a retired Navy captain, once lived in Tahlequah. He also was a member of the Apollo 14 crew with Stuart Rossa. Selected as an astronaut in 1966, Mitchell was born in Hereford, Texas.

Shannon Lucid, a civilian selected as an astronaut in 1978, was born of missionary parents in China but reared in Bethany, Oklahoma. She received her BS and PhD at the University of Oklahoma and she and her husband and children lived in Oklahoma City until she was selected for the astronaut program. She was a member of STS-51-G (Discovery) crew June 17 to 24, 1985. She went into space again in August, 1991.

WHAT OKLAHOMA REALLY IS

Oklahoma has long carried the popular image of "cowboys and Indians," an image it has tried without notable success to modify. After all, the 1990 census gives Oklahoma an Indian population of 251,000, representing 36 separate tribes, second highest of the 50 states. And cattle raising continues to be an all-important economic cornerstone. (Stockmen feed out more than half a million beef animals alone each year.) But other people and other resources have played significant roles in the state's development, too.

Discovery of rich coal deposits in the east spurred railroad building and the immigration of Italian and middle Europeans to mine them. Rich soils in the state's heartland brought successive waves of farmers with cultural ties to Germany, Czechoslovakia, Russia, and other countries. Freed slaves were joined by blacks from the south, many sponsored by railroad-linked colonizers, to form yet another sizeable minority.

Economic changes, of course, have been many over the years. Nearly a quarter of the state is considered forest and a sizeable lumbering industry has grown up in the southeast on some five million acres of commercial timber. Mineral resources have been developed in 76 of the state's 77 counties—gypsum, copper, lead, and zinc, along with granite and limestone. But oil and gas, now produced in 71 counties, has dominated the economic scene since the turn of the century. In recent years, however, manufacturing—aircraft and automobiles, machinery, electronic gear, food products, clothing—has become increasingly important.

Physically Oklahoma is as diverse—and at times obverse—as her state emblems suggest. Like neighboring Texas, she is large enough to stretch from cypress-dotted swamps in the southeast (lowest point 305 feet above sea level in McCurtain County) to dry juniper-covered headlands in the northwest corner of the Panhandle (highest point 4,973 feet atop Black Mesa in Cimarron County). Flora and fauna are dictated by an annual rainfall ranging from nearly 100 inches down to a semi-arid 15 inches over the same southeast to northwest sweep. The rest of the state is rolling for the most part, broken occasionally by eroded canyons, rocky outcroppings, and modest woods-covered hills, particularly in the east. And it can boast at least four officially designated mountain ranges.

They are the Ouachitas (wah-she-taws) in the southeast, the Arbuckles in the central south, the Ozarks in the northeast (a continuation of the more impressive mountains of northwest Arkansas and southwest Missouri), and the Wichitas in the southwest. Oklahoma's climate, finally, is also a reflection of the terrain and latitude. The southeast is low and damp, hot and humid in summer but mild in winter. The northwest is hot and dry in summer, low in humidity and quite bearable but likely to be cold and icy in January and February. But the state is hospitable—and visitable—year-round. As the unofficial state slogan has it: "Come when you can."

A Word About Super Highways:
Free and Otherwise

Let's begin, if we may, with an oxymoron. . .like "interstate-loving history buff." Need it be pointed out that today there simply is no such animal? Time was when the motorist with an interest in things historical could pull to the side of the road at will—to read a historical marker, examine an interesting old building, re-create in his mind's eye a significant scene from the past. But no longer. Today a quarter-billion of us drive too many vehicles, too fast, on too narrow roads. And short of confiscating driver licenses, the only solution seems to be the proliferation of super roads — "free" as in our fine interstate system; "toll" as in our growing web of turnpikes. Hence the oxymoron.

In Oklahoma, as elsewhere, if he has normal regard for life or limb, the history buff will gladly abandon the high speed super road for the more leisurely secondary routes. And with greater safety he will also gain more time for on-site sign reading and easier access to the sites themselves. But before we get to the byways, let's get a quick overview of the (super) highways.

Since the early 1950s when the 88-mile **Turner Turnpike** between Oklahoma City and Tulsa was opened, Oklahoma has been something of a leader among the states in the super highway building field. The Turner was the nation's first turnpike west of the Mississippi River. Its success led to the equally popular extension northeast from Tulsa into Missouri, the **Will Rogers Turnpike**. Both of these toll roads parallel old US 66, the storied "Main Street of America" (Section 5). When the Interstate Highway System was authorized these toll roads became part of I-44. Also designated I-44 is the **H.E. Bailey Turnpike** that goes southwest from Oklahoma City (Section 2) to the Lawton/Fort Sill area (Section 4), then on south to Texas. The motorist interested in the history along this stretch will follow US 62 (Section 8). Old US 66, meanwhile, turned west at Oklahoma City paralleling present I-40 to the Texas state line. East of Oklahoma City, I-40 travelers on the lookout for history will primarily travel US 62 (Section 8). Much of the **Cimarron Turnpike**, west from Tulsa (Section 3) to I-35, is paralleled by US 64 (Section 9). I-35, which runs from the northern to the southern border of the state is paralleled by US 77 (Section 6). Although **The Muskogee Expressway** from Tulsa southeast to I-40 and the **Indian Nation Turnpike** (from I-40 south to Hugo, Section 15), are not of real concern to history buffs they can be utilized as a quick way to get to an area of historic interest.

To provide readers of this book with the most helpful historical information we have tried to cover the state using 11 highway tours and three metropolitan area tours. Included in the highway tours are several side-trips and alternate routes. However, the traveler should be aware of the interstates and toll roads in Oklahoma. By planning ahead, with the help of a good road map, they can speed him through metropolitan areas or past historical sights to be left for a future date when more time is available.

SECTION 2
Oklahoma City

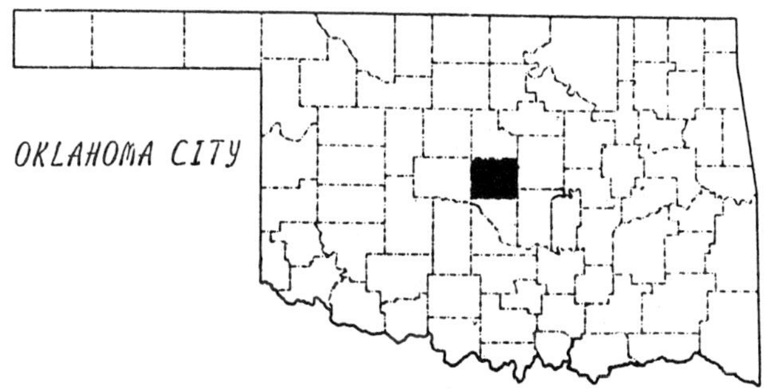

Oklahoma City as it appeared on May 22, 1889.

Oklahoma City as it looked at the turn of the century.

SECTION 2
Oklahoma City

At noon on April 22, 1889, **Arthur W. Dunham**, Santa Fe Railroad agent at **Oklahoma Station**, climbed up on a boxcar for a good view of the excitement that would not be long in coming.

This was the hour selected for the bugles to blow, signaling the start of a scramble (by foot, horse, train, wagon, even bicycle) for between two and three million acres of unclaimed land in what is now central Oklahoma.

Dunham didn't have long to wait.

"My astonishment was complete—people seemed to spring up as if by magic as far as the eye could reach. I could see them racing in every direction, some on horses, some in vehicles, and a greater number on foot," he later wrote.

One thing all of them had in common, if Dunham was able to see them so soon after noon—they were in Oklahoma Station "Sooner" than they should have been. The nearest legal starting line was 15 miles away and those who started from there were much later in arriving.

At 2:05 p.m. the first of several special trains (this one a northbound from Purcell) pulled into the station carrying eager land-seekers.

One witness described the train, loaded with passengers inside and out, as looking "like a huge centipede with arms, legs, and heads sticking out everywhere."

At daybreak on April 22 there had been only a handful of people and six structures at Oklahoma Station, including the depot, a shack being used as a post office, and the home of station agent Dunham. By nightfall an estimated 10,000 to 12,000 people were settling down in a town where none had existed 24 hours before.

On the second day (April 23) **Joseph C. Chrisney** wrote a letter to his friends and family back in Chrisney, Indiana.

"The much talked of Oklahoma country was formally opened yesterday precisely at noon....Tents and small houses cover the town site. Papers are being sold on the streets. Preaching has been announced for next Sunday.

"No whiskey is allowed....(but there is) plenty of water from a dug well. One pump here in the center of town never stops from

5 a.m. until 10 p.m....Water works and street car lines are already talked of," he wrote.

The new residents had wasted no time in beginning to build their city.

There were, however, a few problems. Two townsite companies set up headquarters and began surveying city lots. The **Seminole Land and Improvement Company** began surveying north from what is now **Sheridan Avenue** in downtown Oklahoma City. The **Oklahoma Colony Company** began surveying south of the street. Since the federal government had not made any provision for city lots, streets, or alleys there was a great deal of confusion. The two surveys didn't match, leaving a jog in all the north/south streets crossing Sheridan (at that time named Clarke). The jogs on **Robinson** and **Harvey** were finally straightened out in 1975.

Three days after the run an election was called. Here, as in the other towns settled in the land rush, almost no one knew anyone else so the elections for local leaders were as unusual as the method used to settle the area. Those who chose to run for office or were picked to run simply paraded across a platform where they were cheered or jeered by the crowd. They were truly "elected by their looks."

In June, 1889, volunteers conducted a door-to-door survey and found the new town was bounded by the Santa Fe railway on the east, Walker Street on the west with North and South Seventh forming in the other two sides. The population was 4,138; many had moved on in the days after the run. There were 1,603 occupied dwellings (most were permanent, few tents remained), three water wells, and numerous commercial establishments including seven ice cream parlors. There also were 53 doctors and two dentists in residence.

In June, 1906, President Theodore Roosevelt signed the Enabling Act which cleared the way for Oklahoma to become the 46th state in 1907. One of the provisions was that Guthrie, the territorial capital, would serve as the temporary state capital until a permanent capital was established sometime before 1913.

In June, 1910, an election was held to select Oklahoma City, Guthrie, or Shawnee for the seat of state government. Oklahoma City received, unofficially, 100,000 of the 135,000 votes cast. Upon hearing the news Governor Charles N. Haskell contacted his secretary to transport the State Seal immediately to Oklahoma City. The secret removal of the seal (according to legend, in a laundry basket during the night) caused a storm of controversy between Guthrie and Oklahoma City which occasionally pops up even today.

Contemporary Oklahoma City has a population of about 440,969 and extends into parts of Canadian and Cleveland Counties although most of the area is in Oklahoma County.

Through the years many well-known people have called Oklahoma City home. Some were born here while others moved

Oklahoma City's Civil Rights marches began from the Calvary Baptist Church in the 1950s.

17

in later. Among them, but certainly not all, are astronaut **Shannon Lucid**, test pilot **Jerrie Cobb**, actors/entertainers **Lon and Lon Chaney Jr., Dale Robertson, Ronnie Claire Edwards** (Corabeth on "The Waltons"), **G. D. Spradlin**, and **Ted Shackelford**; and the first model for Aunt Jemima, **Rosa Lee Hall.**

Also musicians/songwriters/singers **Charlie Christian, Wanda Jackson, Mason Williams, Jimmy Wakely,** and **Henson Cargill**; pioneer aviators **Paul and Thomas Braniff,** and **Clarence Page;** baseball greats **Allie Reynolds, Bobby Mercer,** and **Darrell Porter,** and ballet stars **Yvonne Chouteau** and her husband **Miguel Terekhov.**

And broadcast journalists **Frank McGee** and **Walter Cronkite,** authors **Ralph Ellison** and **Louis L'Amour,** poet **Welborn Hope,** sports reporter **Curt Gowdy,** inventors **Sylvan N. Goldman** (the shopping cart) and **Carl McGee** (parking meters) and the "hostess with the mostest" **Perle Skirvin Mesta.**

The first radio station west of the Mississippi River was **WKY** which is still broadcasting in Oklahoma City. The station went on the air in 1920 and is now the third oldest station in the U.S.

The notorious and murderous **Bonnie (Parker)** and **Clyde (Barrow)** appeared in Oklahoma City during a hot summer day in July, 1933, and for no apparent reason shot and killed a traffic officer after asking for directions. Later that month they stole a government car and raided the National Guard Armory in Enid where they stole several firearms. The Barrow gang crisscrossed Oklahoma several times during their brief but bloody crime spree during the early 1930s.

George R. "Machine-Gun" Kelly, bootlegger and kidnapper, operated a bootlegging business from Oklahoma City in the 1920s and was finally arrested for selling liquor to Indians. He received a one year sentence in Leavenworth for violating the National Prohibition Act. Upon his release from prison he returned to bootlegging until the evening of July 22, 1933, when he and Albert Bates, a small-time crook, kidnapped millionaire oilman Charles F. Urschel of Oklahoma City. They demanded and finally received $200,000 in ranson money. Urschel was released unharmed. Kelly was captured in Memphis on September 26, 1933. He was tried with his wife, Kathryn, Albert Bates and Mr. and Mrs. R. G. Shannon, Kathryn's parents who helped guard Urschel. All received life sentences. "Machine

Gun" Kelly died at Alcatraz in 1954.

Oklahoma City has seven historic districts:

Capitol—Lincoln Terrace, roughly NE 13 to NE 23 and Lincoln to Kelley.

Edgemere Park, Robinson to Walker between NW 30 and NW 36.

Heritage Hills, Robinson and Walker from NW 14 to NW 21 and Classen Drive.

Maney, 725 NW 11, 1200 and 1223 N. Shartel.

Oklahoma City University, 2501 N. Blackwelder.

Putnam Heights, between Georgia and McKinley on NW 35, 37 and 38.

A scene on the campus of Oklahoma City University. The campus is included in a historic district.

19

Stockyards City, an irregular pattern along Agnew and Exchange.

There are a number of National Register of Historic Places (NRHP) properties in Oklahoma City. A few of these are **Calvary Baptist Church**, 2nd and Walnut; **Central High School** (One Bell Central), 700 N. Robinson; **Colcord Building**, Robinson and Sheridan; **Farmers Public Market**, 311 S. Klein; **St. Joseph's Old Cathedral**, 225 W. 4th; **Union Depot**, 300 7th St.; **Oklahoma Publishing Company**, 500 N. Broadway; **Magnolia Petroleum Building**, 727 N. Broadway; **India Temple Shrine** (Journal-Record Building), 621 N. Robinson; **Goodholm House**, state fairgrounds; and **Kaisers Ice Cream Parlor**, 1039 N. Walker.

There are many museums in Oklahoma City, most located in the far northeast quadrant. Other historic properties are in the State Capitol area on NE 23.

Two house museums are near the downtown area in Heritage Hills.

OVERHOLSER MANSION (National Register of Historic Places and Oklahoma Historical Society property) is located at

The Overholser Mansion dates back to 1903.

405 NW 15. This 1903 mansion was built by early-day civic leader **Henry Overholser** for his family. Overholser, a wealthy 43-year-old, arrived by train during the Run of '89 and quickly involved himself in the business, political and cultural life of his new home. In October of '89 he married 17-year-old **Anna Ione Murphy** who soon became one of the leading socialites in the young city. This home, built on three lots, was planned to "set the pace" for other homes Overholser believed, rightly, would soon be built in the area. At the time of construction this location was "way out in the country" surrounded by corn fields. The house has original furnishings. It is open from 10 a.m. to 4 p.m. Tuesday through Friday and from 2 to 4 p.m. weekends. Tours begin on the hour. Admission is free.

OKLAHOMA HERITAGE CENTER is located at 201 NW 14. The center is housed in the former home of **Judge and Mrs. Robert A. Hefner**. Judge Hefner was a justice of the state supreme court and mayor of Oklahoma City for eight years. The mansion was built in 1917; the first two floors have been restored with original furnishings and are maintained as the Hefner family lived in them between 1927 and 1970. It is open from 9 a.m. to 5 p.m. Monday through Saturday and from 1 to 5 p.m. Sundays. An admission is charged.

The state capitol complex is located a few blocks north and east at NE 23 and Lincoln Boulevard.

OKLAHOMA STATE CAPITOL (NRHP) is one of the few state capitols without a dome and the only one with oil wells on the grounds. The building was designed originally to have a dome but World War I interfered. Periodically it is suggested a dome be built and the residents of the state immediately form two rather vocal camps; those who think the building should have its dome and those who think it is just fine the way it is. It is open daily from 8 a.m. to 7 p.m. with guided tours between the hours of 8 a.m. and 4:30 p.m. Admission is free.

GOVERNOR'S MANSION is located at 820 NE 23. This Dutch Colonial home with a Spanish-style red tile roof was begun in 1927 and completed in 1928. Governor Henry Johnston and his family were the first residents and the first families of the state have resided here since. It is open from 1 to 3 p.m. on Wednesdays. Admission is free.

OKLAHOMA HISTORICAL SOCIETY MUSEUM is located at 2100 Lincoln Blvd. The Oklahoma Historical Society began in 1893 in Kingfisher, moved to Norman, and then to Oklahoma

The south front of the Oklahoma State Capitol Building.

City where the society was given a spot in the basement of the capitol building. In 1929-30, this limestone building was constructed. Extensive displays depict the history of the state from the days of the prehistoric Indians to the present. It is open from 8 a.m. to 5 p.m. Monday through Saturday. Admission is free.

CAPITOL COMPLEX GROUNDS is site of several historical markers. Among those located near the OHS building are for **King Charles Grant** and for **Solomon Andrew Layton**, pioneer architect. Near the latter marker is the cupola from the **Baum Building** which once stood in downtown Oklahoma City. Also in this vicinity, and marked, are the **Liberty Bell Replica**, a **Civil War Ten-Pounder** used by the New Jersey Volunteer Artillery and still in operating condition, and a descendant of the first trees planted in present-day Oklahoma by **Col. A.P. Chouteau** at **Salina** (Section 7). On the north side of the museum is the **Oklahoma Veterans Memorial** dedicated to all state men and women who have served in the armed forces, designed by Oklahoma artists **Bill Sowell**, Pawhuska, and **Jay**

The first oil well in the Oklahoma City Field came in on December 4, 1928. This stone marks the site of the well.

The Oklahoma Historical Society Building in Oklahoma City. The Baum building cupola sits on the lawn in front of the building.

O'Meilia, Tulsa. Near the south door of the capitol is the **Petunia Number One** (OHS), the oil well drilled under the building in the early 1940s. When this particular well finally ran dry, 44 years later, it was plugged and left in place as if it were still a working well.

1889er HARN HOUSE MUSEUM is located at 313 NE 16. This is part of an '89 homestead claim bought by **William Fremont Harn**, a special agent of the General Land Office sent to Oklahoma Territory in 1891. Harn and adjacent landowner **John James Culbertson** each donated 40 acres of land to be used for the state capitol building which was started in 1914. Harn died in 1944 but his niece, Miss Florence Wilson, continued to live in the house with its collection of farm buildings and a few acres of farm land until 1967. She donated the house and some land to Oklahoma City, which by then completely surrounded this urban farm.

Featured here are three homes, two barns, restored schoolhouse, and garden all designed to give visitors a feeling of

The Harn House Museum in Oklahoma City.

how the pioneers of Oklahoma lived. It is open from 10 a.m. to 4 p.m. Monday, Tuesday, Friday, and Saturday and from 1 to 4 p.m. Sunday. An admission is charged.

MUSEUM OF THE UNASSIGNED LANDS is located at 4300 N. Sewell, north and a little west of the capitol off of Santa Fe. This museum depicts the history of central Oklahoma and Oklahoma County in particular. It is open from 10 a.m. to 3 p.m. Monday, Wednesday, and Friday. Admission is free.

North and east of the capitol complex are a number of other

A statue of Buffalo Bill Cody is located on the grounds of the National Cowboy Hall of Fame in Oklahoma City.

museums of interest to history buffs. Also in this area is the **Lincoln Park Zoo,** oldest zoo in the southwest, established in 1904 in **Wheeler Park,** moved to the present location, NE 50 and Lincoln, in 1926.

FORTY-FIFTH INFANTRY MUSEUM is located at 2145 NE 36. The history of Oklahoma's citizen-soldier is detailed here

This statue, titled "Safe at Home," marks the site of the National Softball Hall of Fame in Oklahoma City.

from the days of the Five Civilized Tribes to the present. It is open from 10 a.m. to 4 p.m. Tuesday through Saturday. The last tour is at 3 p.m. An admission is charged.

NATIONAL SOFTBALL HALL OF FAME is located at 2801 NE 50. Presented are the history and memorabilia of the sport. It is open from 9 a.m. to 4:30 p.m. Monday through Saturday

This marker honors Oklahoman Clarence Tinker for whom Tinker Air Force Base is named.

The Sheriffs & Peace Officers monument at Highway Patrol headquarters, 36th and Eastern, in Oklahoma City. It memorializes three of the famous U.S. deputy marshals, Bill Tilghman, Heck Thomas, and Chris Madson (also spelled Madsen), who kept a somewhat quiet peace in the Oklahoma Territory.

from March through October. An admission is charged.

OKLAHOMA FIREFIGHTERS MUSEUM is located at 2716 NE 50. On display are an extensive collection of historic firefighter apparatus, memorabilia, and a shoulder patch collection. It is open from 10 a.m. to 5 p.m. daily. An admission is charged.

KIRKPATRICK CENTER is located at 2100 NE 52. In this complex is the **Air and Space Museum** which preserves the history of flight from balloons to Kitty Hawk to the space shuttle. Also located here is the Center of the American Indian, International Photography Hall of Fame and Museum, Omniplex (a hands on) Science Museum, a planetarium and gardens. It is open from 9:30 a.m. to 6 p.m. Monday through Saturday and from noon to 6 p.m. Sunday from Memorial Day to Labor Day. Weekend hours are the same in the winter. It is closed at 5 p.m. the rest of the week. An admission is charged..

NATIONAL COWBOY HALL OF FAME/WESTERN HERITAGE CENTER is located at 1700 NE 63. This museum, sponsored by 17 western states, contains the world's largest collection of western lore. It is open from 8:30 a.m. to 6 p.m. daily Memorial Day to Labor Day; from 9 a.m. to 5 p.m. during the winter months. An admission is charged.

Bordering Oklahoma City on the east is **Midwest City**, home of **Tinker Air Force Base**, home of AWACS (America's early warning system). The base is named for Oklahoman and Osage Indian, **Maj. Gen. Clarence Tinker** (1887-1942).

TINKER AIR FORCE BASE, Gate 20, is located on S. Douglas Blvd. A two hour tour is available the first and third Fridays of each month, beginning at 9 a.m. This includes a drive along the flightline where aircraft can be seen. Reservations are required, 2854 Air Base Group, Office of Public Affairs, Tinker AFB 73145. Amission is free.

For information on other attractions and museums in Oklahoma City, visit the Convention and Visitor's Bureau, 4 Santa Fe Plaza, downtown.

SECTION 3
Tulsa

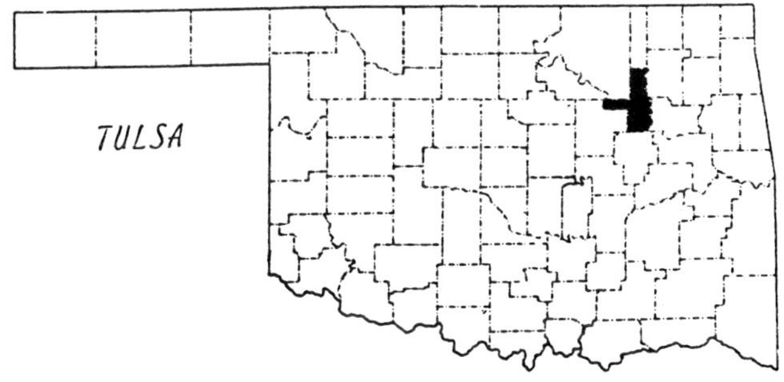

The Creek Indians held a Council under this oak tree at the site of Tulsa in 1836.

SECTION 3
Tulsa

In late 1834, the **Lochapoka Clan** (the Turtle People) of the Creek Nation voluntarily began removal from their home in Alabama to Indian Territory. The journey was difficult, especially after they reached Arkansas. Low water in the rivers made it impossible to continue by boat so they loaded their few possessions on pack ponies and walked the remaining 300 miles. The mortality rate was very high.

The group arrived in 1836 at the present day site of Tulsa. They chose to settle in an area now bounded by 17th and 18th Streets, Cheyenne, and Denver. Here they placed the ashes they had brought from Alabama and kindled a new ceremonial fire under an oak tree on a hill overlooking the Arkansas River.

The tree, called the **Creek Council Oak** (National Register of Historic Places) is still standing. Credit for this goes first to local DAR members who found and marked it in the 1920s. Second to be thanked are four Tulsa citizens who bought the plot of land on which the tree stands in 1973 to save it from being sacrificed for a proposed housing development. The resulting small park is now owned and maintained by the Tulsa County Historical Society.

In 1848, a mixed-blood named **Lewis Perryman** established the first known business in the area, a trading store. His son George eventually became the largest land holder in the Creek Nation. In the 1870s the younger Perryman built a large home, called the "White House," near present 41st St. between Peoria and Utica Aves. March 25, 1879, the house was designated a post office with George Perryman's brother, Josiah, as postmaster. It was named Tulsa.

Tulsa is believed to be a variant spelling for a tribal town in Alabama known as Tallasi, probably meaning "Old Town." Early spellings of Tulsa were Tulsee and Tulsey, the latter often with the word Town tacked on the end.

In 1882, the **Atlantic and Pacific Railroad** came to "Tulsey-Town" along with some whites who wanted to settle in the area. In the Creek Nation it was possible for non-Indians to obtain a traders license so they could live in the area to conduct business. This was unlike the other Indian Nations which required settlers to be married to a member of the tribe. Soon a town began to form between Main Street and Boston near the present **Union Station**.

By 1900 Tulsa was well on its way to becoming an important city in Indian Territory. In 1901 something happened to insure Tulsa's future as a metropolitan center. Oil was discovered four miles west across the Arkansas River at **Red Fork**. Although this was not a big strike, one was not long in coming.

November 22, 1905, 15 miles south of town, the **Ida Glenn No. 1**, a real gusher, came in. It produced 85 barrels of oil a day. The second well produced 700 barrels a day. By mid-1907, the **Glenn Pool** was the most productive oilfield anywhere and Tulsa was the "Oil Capital of the World."

Today Tulsa has a population of 364,535. While a little of the city is in Osage County, most of the area is in Tulsa County.

A number of well-known people were born in Tulsa including radio and newspaper commentator **Paul Harvey**; show business personalities **Jennifer Jones, Tony Randall, Mary Kay Place, Alfre Wood**, and **Blake Edwards**. Also born here was **Daniel P. Moynihan**, a U.S. Senator from the state of New York and a former ambassador to the United Nations.

Others who have called Tulsa home are musicians **David Gates, Leon McAulife, Leon Russell, Bob Wills, Johnnie Lee Wills**, and **Roy Clark**; actors **William S. "Hopalong Cassidy" Boyd, Donna Reed, Gary Busey**, and **Gaylord Sartin**, and two of Oklahoma's five internationally-known Indian ballerinas, **Moscelyne Larkin** and **Rosella Hightower**.

Also financier **J. Paul Getty**, TV newsman **Jim Hartz**, statesman **J. Patrick Hurley**, author **R. A. Lafferty**, golf pro **Nancy Lopez-Melton**, oilmen **William Skelly** and **Waite Phillips**, Miss America of 1926 **Norma Smallwood**, and cartoonist **Russell Myers**.

The infamous **Kate "Ma" Barker** planned several bank robberies in the mid-1920s and ran a hideout in Tulsa during this period for escaped convicts and bank robbers on the run. It was also where her four sons Arthur "Doc", Fred, Herman and Lloyd became involved in crime as youngsters. **"Doc" Barker** was arrested for killing a night watchman at St. John's Hospital in Tulsa while attempting to steal a drug shipment. He was sentenced to life in the Oklahoma State Penitentiary and served 13 years before being paroled in 1932. **Fred Barker** was arrested for a burglary in Claremore in 1931 but escaped. In

August , 1932, he and two others robbed the Citizen's Security Bank in Bixby. **Herman Barker** became a member of the Kimes-Terrill gang in the early 1920's that robbed banks in Texas, Oklahoma, and Missouri. **Lloyd Barker** was the only brother who did not join the family gang. He was arrested for robbing a post office in rural Oklahoma in 1922 and served a 25-year sentence at Leavenworth. The Barkers teamed up with **Alvin "Creepy" Karpis** and robbed banks and kidnapped two Minnesota businessmen. "Ma" and her son, Fred, were killed in a 45-minute gun battle with FBI agents at Lake Weir, Florida, January 16, 1935. "Doc" was killed in an attempt to escape from Alcatraz on June 13, 1939. Herman committed suicide September 19, 1927 after being trapped by lawmen in Kansas. Lloyd was killed by his wife in 1949. All are buried in **Welch** in Craig County, Oklahoma.

There are four historic districts in Tulsa.

Tracy Park is in an area bounded by Norfolk and Peoria and 11th and 13th Sts.

Maple Ridge is located between Hazel Blvd. and S. Peoria Ave. and between 14th St. and Railroad.

Gillette Historic District boundaries are S. Yorktown and S. Lewis Aves. and E. 15th and E. 17th Sts.

Brady Heights is outlined by Marshall and Easton Sts. and Denver and Cheyenne Aves.

Tulsa has a number of National Register of Historic Places properties. Some of them are **Boston Avenue Methodist Church**, Boston Ave. and 13th; **Mayo Hotel**, 115 W. 5th; **Oklahoma Natural Gas Building**, 624 Boston Ave., and **Petroleum Building**, 420 S. Boulder.

Also **Philcade Building**, 511 S. Boulder; **Philtower**, 427 S. Boston; **Public Service of Oklahoma**, 600 S. Main; **Tribune Building**, 20 E. Archer, and **William G. Skelly** house, 2101 S. Madison..

There are two homes of interest to tour.

HARWELDEN MANSION (NRHP) is located at 2210 S. Main. Oil baron **Earl Palmer Harwell** built this 30-room, four level Tudor Gothic mansion which he named Harwelden in the early 1920s. It is open weekdays from 9 a.m. to 5 p.m. Admission is free.

MABLE LITTLE HERITAGE HOUSE. This is a replication of the **Prince-Mackey** home which originally stood at the corner of Easton and N. Greenwood. This house was rebuilt by a

Tulsa's Boston Avenue Methodist Church is listed on the NRHP.

black Tulsa couple after the Tulsa race riot in 1921. Wanting to be sure the house could never be burned again, the owners used very little wood relying instead on bricks and cinder blocks. It is now restored after years of neglect. It is open from 1 to 4 p.m. Tuesday, Thursday, and Sunday An admission is charged.

A popular landmark in Tulsa is the 76-foot tall figure made of steel and concrete named "The Golden Driller," a replica of an

The Golden Driller statue at the fairgrounds complex in Tulsa is a tribute to those involved in Oklahoma's oil industry. Oil was discovered near Tulsa in 1901 followed by other strikes and in 1907 the Glenn Pool was the most productive oilfield anywhere.

Exhibits in the Fenster Museum of Jewish art and historic objects in Tulsa.

oil field roustabout. This statue is in the Expo Square Complex, 21st and Yale. On the south side of the Exposition Building, near the front door, is a historical marker honoring the International Petroleum Exposition and Congress begun in October of 1923 in Tulsa. The exposition was originated to create an international forum to share knowledge among oil-producing areas of the world.

There are several museums in Tulsa.

FENSTER MUSEUM OF JEWISH ART, 1223 E. 17th Pl.,

contains the third largest collection of objects of ceremonial and aesthetic Judaica in the United States, some dating back to 5000 B.C. Exhibits reflect the art, history, and customs of the Jewish faith. It is open from 1 to 4 p.m. Tuesday through Friday and from 10 a.m. to 4 p.m. Sunday. Admission is free.

GILCREASE MUSEUM, Newton and Gilcrease Museum Rd., features, in addition to a treasury of western art, Indian artifacts, rare books, and documents, an original certified copy of the Declaration of Independence. It is open from 9 a.m. to 5 p.m. Monday through Saturday and from 1 to 5 p.m. Sunday Admission is free.

TULSA COUNTY HISTORICAL MUSEUM is located on the grounds of Gilcrease. The museum is located in the former home of oilman/art collector **Thomas Gilcrease**. This house was purchased in 1914 by Gilcrease for his family. Eighteen months

These statues by Frederic Remington appear in a section of the Gilcrease Museum.

The former home of Waite Phillips is home of the Philbrook Art Center in Tulsa.

later the couple and their two sons moved to California. In 1926, following a divorce, Gilcrease moved back to Tulsa and this house. In 1928 he married **Norma Smallwood**, a former Miss Tulsa and Miss America of 1926. The couple lived here with their daughter until 1933 when they separated and later divorced. Gilcrease lived in San Antonio, Texas, for several years but once again returned to this house (1948) where he stayed until his death in 1962.

Several of the rooms have been restored to the early 1920s

period. Rotating exhibits of a historical nature also are featured here. It is open from 11 a.m. to 4 p.m. Tuesday through Thursday and Saturday and from 1 to 5 p.m. Sunday. Admission is free.

PHILBROOK ART CENTER/MUSEUM (NRHP) is located at 2727 S. Rockford Rd. In the late 1920s oilman **Waite Phillips** commissioned a home for his family and cost was no object. This Italian Renaissance villa, with formal gardens on 23 acres of

Gargoyles appear on the face of Mincks Adams Hotel. This Tulsa hotel is listed on the NRHP.

land, was the result. Ten years later, Phillips donated the home to be used as a fine arts museum. In addition to the fine art collection, there are collections of Indian pottery, basketry, and artifacts. It is open from 10 a.m. to 5 p.m., Tuesday through Saturday and from 1 to 5 p.m. Sunday. An admission is charged.

While not strictly a museum, there is one other attraction in the Tulsa area which should be considered as something to see because it is tied so closely to Oklahoma and its history at the time of statehood.

DISCOVERYLAND! is a 2,000-seat outdoor amphitheatre several miles west of downtown Tulsa on W. 41st St. Nightly from early June to late August the musical play "Oklahoma!" is presented here, complete with horses in the cast. The actual area in which the play is set is not too many miles away in the Claremore area (Section 5). For information, contact Discoveryland Business Office, 2502 E. 71st St., Tulsa 74136. An admission is charged.

For other things to see in Tulsa visit the Convention and Visitor's Bureau, 616 S. Boston.

SECTION 4
Lawton/Fort Sill

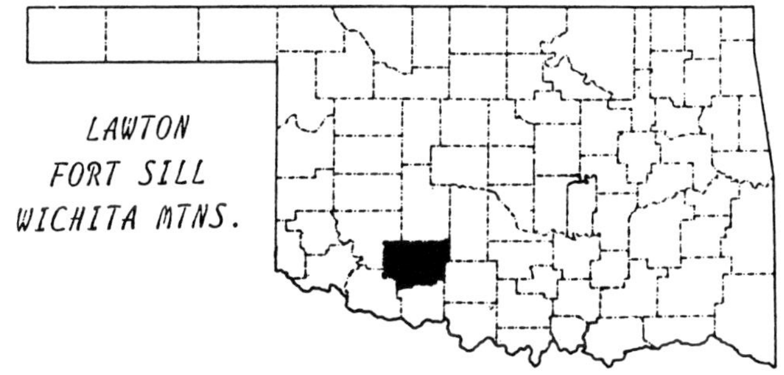

Geronimo (c. 1829-1909) was the leader of a Chiricahua band of Apache Indians. After the Chiricahua reservation was closed in 1881, Geronimo led a renegade band in Mexico and terrorized Arizona and Sonora, Mexico, until 1886 when he surrendered to the authorities. He was imprisoned in Alabama and then allowed to go to Fort Sill where he lived out his life.

SECTION 4
Lawton/Fort Sill

Like many towns in Oklahoma, Lawton was settled in a single day. This time, however, it was not by a "run" where land-seekers lined up at a starting point and at a signal hurried off to try and be first to stake a claim. Land runs were becoming rather rowdy and there were many proven instances of unfairness in this method so it was decided to settle the southwest part of Oklahoma Territory by lottery.

This area contained surplus reservation land left after each Indian man, woman, and child in the **Comanche, Kiowa, Apache, Wichita**, and **Caddo** tribes was allotted 160 acres. The tribes had agreed to sell the remaining two million acres to homesteaders and the land was divided into 13,000 homestead farms of 160 acres each.

The area was divided into two districts, the northern being the El Reno district and the southern, Lawton. Registration was held at Fort Sill and El Reno.

According to an account written in 1924, each person who registered "had to state under oath that he was 21 years of age, or head of a family, that he did not own more than 160 acres of land in any state or territory, and that he was a citizen of the United States or had declared his intention of becoming one.

"(The registrant's) name, address, birthplace, height, weight, and color of hair and eyes were then noted on a small card which was sealed in a plain envelope. These were later placed in four large boxes, two for each district. Everyone who registered (and about 170,000 people did) had to choose to be in the drawing for either the northern or southern district."

Women who were unmarried, for whatever reason, also were allowed to register. As the names were drawn out of the hoppers at El Reno the lucky winners selected their claims, in order drawn, and these were plotted on a large map. The drawing was August 1, 1901.

The 360 acre townsites laid out for the three proposed counties were **Lawton, Hobart,** and **Anadarko** and settlement for them was to be by auction August 6, 1901. The lottery had been held six days earlier and many of the losers in El Reno hurried off to be on hand for the bidding in one of the three townsites. Because of rumors of gold in the nearby Wichita Mountains, good farmland, and the promise two railroads would cross in the townsite, Lawton became a prime target for the would-be settlers. Lots were sold to the highest bidder for cash to be paid within 30 minutes of the bidding. When the day was over, $414,845 had been paid for the 1,422 town lots.

Lawton was named for Civil War major general **Henry W. Lawton**. The county was named **Comanche** for the Indian tribe. By March of 1902 there were five banks in Lawton, a railroad was coming through from the north and most of the 1,119 residents were adequately housed. Lawton has enjoyed a steady growth through the years because of its close proximity to **Fort Sill**. Today the population is 79,544.

Local properties listed on the National Register of Historic Places include the **Carnegie Library**, B Ave. and 5th, and three churches. **First Christian**, 701 D Ave.; **First Presbyterian**, 8th and D Ave., and **Methodist Episcopal South**, 702 D Ave.

Among the well-known who have lived in Lawton are actresses **Candice Earley** and **Joan Crawford**; early-day lawman **Henry "Heck" Thomas**, and Pulitzer Prize winning author **N. Scott Momaday**.

Police chief of Lawton for seven years was **Henry A. "Heck" Thomas**, of the more famous lawmen who worked in Oklahoma. Thomas, **Bill Tilghman** and **Chris Madsen** were known as the "Three Guardsmen." A memorial to them is located in front of the Department of Public Safety Building, 3600 Martin Luther King, in Oklahoma City. During the three-year period from 1893 to 1896, Thomas was responsible for the arrest of over 300 men. He died in Lawton in 1912.

Among the places to visit in Lawton are these three.

MATTIE BEAL HOUSE (NRHP) located at 1006 SW 5, built by Mattie Beal and her husband, Charles Payne. Miss Beal was the second name drawn in the lottery at El Reno for land. The publicity surrounding the luck of the 23-year-old Wichita telephone operator brought her 500 proposals of marriage. She eventually married the Lawton lumberman she met while buying material to prove up her claim. This 14-room mansion built by them in the early 1900s was almost torn down in 1973, but a group of Lawton fourth-graders wrote letters to the local Arts and Humanities Council asking that this bit of Lawton history be saved. They sent along $5.54 to begin a fund to buy the property. It is open the second Sunday of each month and by appointment. An admission is charged.

FIRE, TRANSPORTATION, FARM MUSEUM is located at 816 SE 1. Featured are antique Rolls Royces, fire trucks, buggies, saddles, Army and Navy relics, and an African spear collection. It is open by appointment, 405/248-7707. Admission is free.

MUSEUM OF THE GREAT PLAINS is located at 601 Ferris Ave. in Elmer Thomas Park. History, archaeology and anthropology of the Great Plains are detailed from prehistoric times through the early 1900s. Special attraction is an outdoor prairie dog village and a replica of an 1840s fortified trading post featuring a living history interpretive program. It is open from 8 a.m. to 5 p.m. weekdays, from 10 a.m. to 5:30 p.m. Saturday and from 1:30 to 5:30 p.m. Sunday. An admission is charged.

FORT SILL

Five miles north of Lawton is Fort Sill, established by **Gen. Phillip A. Sheridan** as a cavalry post in Indian Territory January 8, 1869. At first the post was referred to as **Camp Wichita** or **Camp Medicine Bluff** but Sheridan later suggested the garrison be named Sill to honor a West Point classmate who had been killed in the Civil War, **Brig. Gen. Joshua W. Sill**.

Constructed in 1872-73, Fort Sill's Old Post Guardhouse is known as the Geronimo Guardhouse.

Cannon Row at Fort Sill is located behind the Geronimo Guardhouse.

Located just east of today's main post is the old post with many of its original buildings. Part of this area is a museum. Visitors are advised to pick up a map from the visitor center in the old post area or from one of the map boxes outside the center.

OLD POST MUSEUM (NRHP) includes eight period buildings, a stone corral and Cannon Walk which features historic artillery field weapons from around the world. Included in the self-guided tour are the **Old Post Headquarters**, built in 1870, and the **Geronimo Guardhouse** (sometimes called the Geronimo Hotel) where the old Apache chief spent many years as a prisoner of war. The Museum complex is open from 9:30 a.m. to 4:30 p.m. daily. Admission is free.

Also nearby are two cemeteries.

APACHE PRISONER CEMETERY contains the grave of Geronimo, the fierce Apache warlord who fought white settlers and soldiers in some of the bloodiest battles between the races for more than 30 years. He finally surrendered to Gen. Nelson Miles in 1886 and was sent into exile in Florida. In 1894, he was transferred to Fort Sill, Indian Territory, where he died in 1909.

CHIEF'S KNOLL/OLD POST CEMETERY (NRHP), sometimes called the "Indian Arlington," contains the graves of many Indian leaders including those of Comanche chief **Quanah**

Geronimo is buried in the Apache Cemetery at Fort Sill.

Parker, Kiowa peace chief **Kicking Bird**, and Kiowa war leader **Satanta.** Also buried here is **Cynthia Ann Parker**, mother of Quanah Parker. This white woman was captured by Comanches in May, 1836, when she was nine years old. In her teens she became the wife of an up and coming young chief, Peta Nocona, and bore him three children, Quanah, Pecos, and

49

Quanah Parker, noted Comanche chief, is buried in Chief's Knoll/Post Cemetery at Fort Sill.

Prairie Flower. She didn't rejoin her white relatives until she was 34 years old and then only under protest as she had become a Comanche, at least in spirit. Cynthia and her daughter died in east Texas in 1864. Her Comanche husband and son, Pecos, both died a short time later.

It was believed Quanah went on his first raid, in which he killed an enemy, when he was only 15 years old. He joined the most radical band of Apaches and proved to be a fearless warrior and eventually became their chief. In December, 1860, Quanah's band was attacked, after numerous raids throughout Texas, by Texas Rangers and a detachment of cavalry led by Ranger Capt. Sul Ross. It was here that Cynthia Ann and Prairie Flower were captured and returned to her white relatives.

After years of bloody warfare Quanah surrendered at Fort Sill on June 2, 1875. From that time he lived a peaceful life but always worked on behalf of the Comanches. He also became a friend and hunting companion of President Theodore Roosevelt. He died in February, 1911.

Kiowa Chief **Kicking Bird** led the more conservative faction of his tribe, believing the Kiowas would be best served by cooperating with the whites coming westward in great tides. He preached peace to his people to such an extent that he was called a coward in public in 1870. As a result, in July, he led a raiding party into Texas where he encountered a 53-man detachment of the 6th Cavalry, led by Capt. Curwen McClellan, out of Fort Richardson. In the fight that ensued, Kicking Bird proved his fighting skills and courage and regained his stature as a warrior and chief when he returned to the Kiowa-Comanche Agency near Fort Sill. Born in 1835, Kicking Bird died in April, 1875, poisoned by his own people it is believed.

Kiowa Chief **Satanta, or White Bear**, signed the Medicine Lodge Treaty in 1867 in which the tribes agreed to cede their homelands, go to a reservation in Indian Territory and accept government guaranteed land, rations and protection from whites and hostile Indians. He continued to lead raiding parties against the white settlements but was eventually captured by Gen. William T. Sherman. He was tried and sentenced to death but was later pardoned and released. After leading another raid, he was arrested, tried and sentenced to prison. He committed suicide to escape his sentence.

Exit Fort Sill to the east onto US 62 heading north. Take the turnoff west on SH 49 and follow it to Medicine Park.

MEDICINE PARK was a fashionable resort in the early 1900s. The name came from **Medicine Creek** which flows through here and which the Indians believed had medicinal, healing powers. The idea for a resort was first thought of by lawyer (later U.S. Senator) **Elmer Thomas** in 1901. It was in 1908 before he could get clear title to all the land he needed. The resort opened July 4, 1908. During the 1920s and '30s this was

The Meers General Store/Cafe features the locally famous cheeseburger, the "Meersburger," and it is of such size it is usually shared by two or more people.

a popular vacation spot for people from Oklahoma and northern Texas. The old rock hotel (NRHP), built in 1906, is currently the Old Plantation Restaurant and open.

MOUNT SCOTT. Continue west on SH 49 to the base of this peak to pick up a three-mile long paved road to the top. There is a parking area at the top and an unforgettable panoramic view.

Capt. Randolph B. Marcy camped at the base of the mountain on his 1852 trip through the area. He believe it to be the tallest peak in the range but **Mt. Pinchot** is actually 12-feet taller. Marcy named the peak after Gen. Winfield Scott.

MEERS, an old mining town, is west of here. Follow SH 49, then turn north on SH 115. This was one of the many towns that began during gold rush days in the Wichitas between 1901 and 1905. Meers was originally established about half a mile south but was moved when it was found to be in the Wichita Forest Reserve. The town was named for Col. A. J. Meers who had been seeking both gold and silver in the Wichitas (illegally) since the late 1880s. Oddly enough he never lived here but at Wildman, another mining town due west about 25 miles (Section 14). Today the main center of activity is the Meers General Store/ Post Office/Cafe (NRHP) where travelers line up to buy one of the locally famous "Meersburgers."

HOLY CITY site can be reached by returning to the SH 49/ 115 junction, then go west to the grounds. The buildings for the annual Easter Pageant held here were constructed in the 1930s by the CCC workers. This is supposedly a replica of the ancient city of Jerusalem and is open to visitors all year.

Continue west on SH 115 through the wildlife refuge watching for bison, longhorn cattle, elk, and prairie dog town. Just south of US 62 near Cache is Eagle Park.

EAGLE PARK is a complex of 17 historical buildings, all moved here to preserve them. Oldest is the "Picket House" built at Fort Sill by the Buffalo Soldiers of the 10th Cavalry in the 1870s. Also here is the Star House (NRHP) of Quanah Parker which originally was about two miles north.

Parker added the 14 white stars to the outside of his house when he noticed the generals at Fort Sill wore stars to denote their high rank. This was his signal to them that he, too, was a "big chief." In spite of government pressure to do otherwise Parker held on to one Indian tradition. He had seven wives, although not more than five at one time. It is reported all Star House bedrooms were furnished alike so there could be no complaints. Parker outlived all but two of his wives.

Eagle Park is open from 10 a.m. to 4 p.m. Monday through Saturday and from 1 to 4 p.m. Sunday in June, July, and August. At other times open by appointment, 405/429-3238. An admission is charged.

Quanah Parker's house in Eagle Park in Cache is called "The Star House."

SECTION 5
Historic US 66

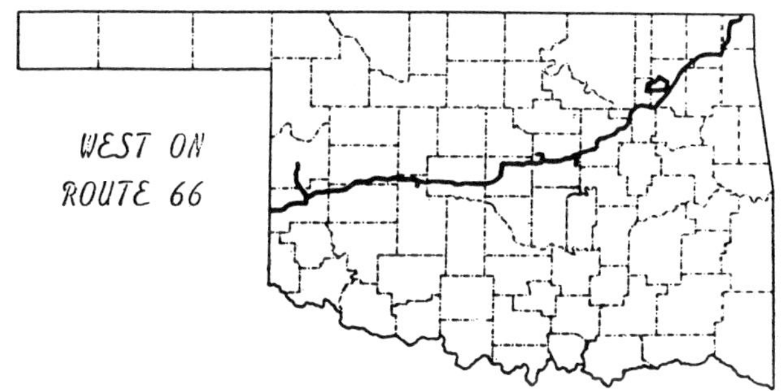

This statue of Oklahoma's favorite son, Will Rogers, is in the entrance of the Will Rogers Memorial Building in Claremore. Rogers was actually born near Oologah, a dozen miles west of Claremore. He was killed in a plane crash in Alaska with aviator Wiley Post, who had lived in Oklahoma since the age of five.

SECTION 5
Historic US 66

"A legend in its own time that needs no introduction" may be a hoary cliche but in the case of Route 66 a claim could certainly be made for the validity of the statement. How else could one understand the nostalgia boom that has sprung up embracing Historic Route 66, a.k.a. US 66-Gateway to the West; the Mother Road; Main Street of America; the Glory Road. Route 66 was born in 1926 and officially decertified in 1985. In those six decades it saw America grow up, survive its greatest depression, shift mightily from northeast to southwest demographically, and go through significant change socially and technologically. It also contributed the drive-up window, a massive Bunion Derby, and countless similar divertissements to the pleasure of roadside living. Radio, then television spread the word to the diminishing few lacking first-hand experience with the road. The mystique built up, expanded, solidified. Gradually it assumed a life of its own. Within days of the official demise of the road an "Old US Route 66 Association" was organized. As state highway crews were busily removing the obsolete US 66 signs, one state was ordering replacements to meet the demand of souvenir hunters. All of Route 66 is fun today, but it's most fun in Oklahoma. Just don't forget to pick up a copy of "Discover Oklahoma...Route US 66" at the nearest state tourism center.

WEST ON 66

Almost all of this trip will follow the historic highway, as much as the modern traveler is able. From the Kansas State line to Oklahoma City it is possible to follow the road almost in its entirety. From Oklahoma City to the Texas State line, it is not so easy as much of I-40 was built on top of old US 66 or so near as to have chopped it into many small, unjoined segments.

For much of the way on this western leg, bits of the road can be seen as access road for local use most often on the north, sometimes on the south side of the interstate and running parallel to it. A traveler with some extra time and lots of patience can try to follow the old road. Watch for the concrete, stained pink from the red soil of Oklahoma, usually with a raised, sloped edge. Watch also for the white and brown Historic Route 66 signs which are beginning to go up along the old route all the way

57

across the state. In most of the towns along the highway, US 66 went right down the main street so the interstate traveler from Oklahoma City west, getting off to see the sights in each of these population centers, will be able to travel on the original 66 at least a part of the time.

OTTAWA COUNTY

Oklahoma's portion of what is now SH 66 begins at the Kansas line in **Ottawa County** (named for the tribe, an Algonquian word "adawe" meaning to trade or to buy and sell). Just inside the line is a historical marker welcoming travelers to **Indian Territory**. This region was unique as a territory because it had no territorial government, just the governments of the various Indian nations along with federal law administered by the U.S. Marshals operating within its borders. At one time an attempt was made to make this a separate state called **Sequoyah** but in 1907 the twin territories (Oklahoma and Indian) were joined to make the 46th state—Oklahoma.

Ottawa County is part of the **Tri-State Mining District**, a 1,188 square mile lead and zinc mining area in Missouri, Kansas, and Oklahoma. By the mid-1920s the Oklahoma portion was producing almost $50 million of lead and zinc

This historical marker in the Tri-State Mining Area near Commerce indicates lead was discovered in the district in 1848.

58

annually. At **Pitcher** (pop. 1,714) was the largest lead and zinc mining complex in the world in 1931. Mining had declined to almost nothing by 1960.

Four miles inside the state line is **Quapaw** (pop. 928). It is six miles to **Commerce** (pop. 2,426), another mining town and the hometown of baseball great **Mickey Mantle.**

Bonnie (Parker) and **Clyde (Barrow)** with Henry Methvin, a small time crook, were driving on a road between Commerce and Miami on April 6, 1934 when their stolen car got stuck in the mud. They forced a trucker at gunpoint to pull their car out but a passing motorist noticed the bullet holes in the car's windshield and notified officials in Commerce. Chief of Police Percy Boyd and Constable Cal Campbell found the weary trio in their car still on the roadside. In the shoot out that followed, Campbell was killed and the wounded Boyd taken captive. Boyd was finally released near Fort Scott, Kansas.

The county seat town of **Miami** is five miles south of Commerce.

MIAMI

MIAMI (pop. 13,071), named for the tribe, traces its beginnings to a trading post named **Jimtown** for the four nearby farmers all named Jim. Twenty small Indian tribes were settled in this area including the **Quapaw, Peoria, Ottawa, Shawnee, Modoc, Miami, Wyandotte,** and **Seneca.** About 12 miles east of Miami on SH 10/10C then .5 mile south is the **Modoc Mission Church** of the Society of Friends and the **Modoc Cemetery** (both NRHP).

Miami is the hometown of artist **Charles Banks Wilson.** Among his portraits are those of famous Oklahomans **Sequoyah, Will Rogers, Robert S. Kerr,** and **Jim Thorpe** in the state capitol.

COLEMAN THEATER (NRHP) is located on Main. Recently restored is this theater where Will Rogers used to perform. **George Coleman Sr.** lived at 1001 Rockdale listed on the NRHP as is the **Commerce/Hancock Building,** 103 S. Central.

DODSON MUSEUM CENTER, 110 A St. SW, includes the home of a local merchant named Dodson who operated an ice plant and lumberyard and was engaged in mining activities in the early 1900s. The museum contains Indian art, a mining display, tools, toys, and furniture. It is open from 1 to 4 p.m. Sunday, Wednesday, and Friday. Admission is free.

Modoc Mission Church, built circa 1891 some 12 miles east of Miami, has been restored.

Twelve miles south of Miami (follow US 69) is **Afton** (pop. 915) named for **Afton Aires** whose father named her for the river in his Scottish homeland. It is 15 miles south, then west on US 60 to **Vinita**, seat of **Craig County** (named for prominent Cherokee **Granville Craig**). From Vinita to Oklahoma City follow the SH 66 and Historic Route 66 markers.

VINITA

In 1871 the **Atlantic and Pacific** (Frisco) and the **Missouri, Kansas, and Texas** (MK&T) railroads met here and the town of VINITA (pop. 5,768) began under the name Downingville. One of the town promoters was **Col. Elias C. Boudinot,** a Cherokee attorney, who chose to name the new settlement after sculptor **Vinnie Ream** (1850-1914) who did the life-size statue of **Abraham Lincoln** in the U.S. Capitol Building in Washington, D.C. The town of Vinita often was mentioned by Will Rogers who called it his "college town" though this was where he attended secondary school at **Willie Halsell Institute**. He was said to have felt more at home here (1892-1895) than at any other school he ever attended. The next two years he spent at Scarret College, then Kemper Military Academy, both in Missouri. Although he was not a bad student Rogers just never cared for the regimen or confining atmosphere of the traditional schoolroom.

COURTHOUSE (NRHP) completed in 1920 features cut-stone trim and a distinctive half-story on the roof.

EASTERN TRAILS MUSEUM, 215 W. Illinois, has displays of pioneer and historical artifacts. It is open from 1:30 to 4 p.m. Monday through Saturday. Admission is free.

HISTORIC HOMES map can be obtained at the Chamber of Commerce, 104 E. Illinois. A driving tour of town is outlined on the map.

It is 17 miles to **Chelsea** in **Rogers County** (named for **Clem V. Rogers**, oldest member of the Oklahoma Constitutional Convention and father of Will Rogers).

CHELSEA

In 1889 oil was discovered west of CHELSEA (pop. 1,616), named for the town in England. This well only had to be drilled to a depth of 36 feet.

HISTORIC OIL WELL is located one mile south on SH 66, then four miles east. This is a replica of one of the oldest oil wells in Oklahoma, believed to be the oldest non-commercial well in the state. It is open daily. Admission is free.

HOUGH HOUSE (NRHP), 1001 S. Olive, was built in 1912, the first "ordered from Sears and Roebuck" pre-cut house constructed in Oklahoma and one of the first west of the Mississippi River.

It is six miles to **Bushyhead** (named for Cherokee Chief

Totem Pole Park contains many unusual sculptures.

Dennis W. Bushyhead). Three miles further is **Foyil**.
FOYIL
Named for Alfred Foyil, first postmaster, FOYIL (pop. 86) was established in 1890. Born near here was **Andy Payne**, the young Cherokee Indian who won "The Bunion Derby," a 3,400-mile foot race in 1928 from Los Angeles to New York City. The

route followed US 66 from LA to Chicago, then went east to New York. Top prize was $25,000.

Payne was just 19 years old and an unknown athlete when he entered this race which attracted professional runners from all over the world. The race began March 4, 1928, with almost 300 participants. When New York was reached on May 26, 55 were left. Payne's actual running time from Los Angeles was 573 hours, 4 minutes, 34 seconds, all the more remarkable considering he was slowed down for 16 days with tonsillitis.

Mr. Payne traveled east to cheer his son along the last few days of the race leaving Mrs. Payne and the six younger children to run the farm. When news of Andy's victory reached the Claremore/Foyil area residents celebrated for two days before someone remembered Andy's mother didn't know about it. A group was dispatched to the farm with the news. Mrs. Payne promptly fainted.

Turn east on SH 28A and it is 4.5 miles to the **Totem Pole Park**, called the best example of folk art left in Oklahoma. Although NRHP listing has been sought for this site in the past it has only recently been old enough to be considered. It is on the Oklahoma Landmarks Inventory.

TOTEM POLE PARK contains sculptures of concrete and reinforcing steel in the side yard of Ed Galloway's rural home. The late manual arts teacher made these sculptures between 1937 and 1962. These took the form of trees, birds, tables and chairs, totem poles, fencing, even a building, all with an Indian motif which he then painted with lead-based house paint. In recent years the Kansas Grassroots Art Association has been stabilizing and restoring this unusual roadside park as funds permit. It is open daily. Admission is free.

Back on 66 it is 11 miles to **Claremore**, seat of **Rogers County**.

CLAREMORE

In 1842 **Elijah Hicks** established a trading post at the site of present CLAREMORE (pop. 13,225). The site had been a settlement even prior to this when Osage Chief **Black Dog** had a village here. A post office was added in 1874 and the name selected honored Osage Chief **Clermont** (or Clermos) who had moved his people into this area in 1802. Many people believe Claremore is the birthplace of Will Rogers; it is not, but it is closely tied to him. It also is a good starting point for a short circle tour of "Will Rogers Country."

The Will Rogers Memorial is located in Claremore. Will, his wife, Betty, and two children are buried on the east side of the building.

Claremore is the birthplace of playwright **Lynn Riggs**. One of his plays, "Green Grow the Lilacs," was adapted as a musical for the Broadway stage and renamed "Oklahoma!". Also from Claremore is singer **Patti Page**. Astronaut **Stuart Roosa** attended school here.

LYNN RIGGS MEMORIAL, W. Will Rogers Blvd., is located in the library on the **Rogers State College** campus. Exhibits include memorabilia from his professional life. On display is the "surrey with the fringe on top" used in the original production of "Oklahoma!". It is open from 8 a.m. to 10 p.m. Monday through Thursday; from 8 a.m. to 4:30 p.m. Friday, and from 2 to 6 p.m. Saturday. Admission is free.

OKLAHOMA MILITARY ACADEMY MEMORIAL is located on the RSC campus in Maurice Meyer Hall, listed on the NRHP. Before it became a co-educational institution and changed its name, Rogers State was **Oklahoma Military Academy**. Housed here is memorabilia of the Corps of Cadets. It is open from 8 a.m. to 5 p.m. weekdays. Admission is free.

TREASURE HOUSE DOLL MUSEUM, 1215 W. Will Rogers Blvd., features rooms of antique and character dolls. It is open from 9 a.m. to 5:30 p.m. Monday through Saturday; from 1 to 4:30 p.m. Sunday from April through December. Admission is free.

J.M. DAVIS GUN MUSEUM is located at 333 Lynn Riggs Rd. On display are firearms covering a 700-year span. Also displayed are saddles, musical instruments, a statuary collection, World War I posters, animal horns, and trophy heads. It is open from 8:30 a.m. to 5 p.m. Monday through Saturday and from 1 to 5 p.m. Sunday. Admission is free.

WILL ROGERS MEMORIAL is located on W. Will Rogers Blvd. This 20-acre hillside was bought by Rogers in 1911 with the intention to someday build a home "overlooking Claremore." It was used instead as a memorial following his death in a plane crash with fellow Oklahoman **Wiley Post** on August 15, 1935, at Point Barrow, Alaska.

Oklahoma's favorite son was born November 4, 1879, about 12 miles north of here. In his lifetime he was a philosopher, writer, broadcaster, commentator, humorist, cowboy, showman, screen actor, superb roper, and polo player. He was also a dedicated family man. Rogers was an early supporter of aviation and was constantly trying to get people to try it for themselves. The purpose of the final trip he and Post took was to find a new passenger route for the airlines across the top of the world.

Rogers, his wife, Betty; daughter Mary Rogers Brook (who died in 1989) and an infant son, Fred, are buried here on the east side of the memorial building. Exhibits fill the many rooms of this museum. His films are shown daily (twice daily in summer) in the 178-seat theater. It is open from 8 a.m. to 5 p.m. daily. Admission is free.

A SIDE-TRIP

Leave the memorial and go north on SH 88 for four miles. Here is a historical marker for **Claremore Mound**, site of a battle in 1817. A band of western Cherokees, armed with rifles, wiped out a village of Osage, armed only with bows, arrows, and a few smooth bore muskets.

After crossing an arm of **Lake Oologah**, about seven miles, look for the turn, north to the **Will Rogers Birthplace**.

WHITE HOUSE ON THE VERDIGRIS (NRHP) was completed in 1875 on the 60,000-acre ranch and was a well-known center of frontier hospitality. The house no longer stands on the **Verdigris River** as it had to be moved in 1959, less than one mile west, to make way for Oologah Lake. At that time members of the Rogers family, who had lived in the house for three generations, deeded it to the state of Oklahoma. To get an

Will Rogers birthplace near Oologah.

idea of where the house used to be, walk through the front yard to the north gate. Straight ahead is a point of land. The house was originally just on the other side of this point.

Clem Rogers started this house in 1870. It began as a two-room log cabin and ended as a two-story, seven-room ranch house. A portion of the white weather-board has been removed from the outside of the house to show the hand-hewn logs. Plaster has been removed from the inside to reveal the original log walls.

At the time of his death Rogers had started restoring the house and out-buildings and repurchasing some of his father's old cattle range and farmland. Today the house is filled with family furnishings of the period as much of the original furniture from this house was lost in a fire many years ago. There are, however, a couple of original pieces. It is open from 8 a.m. to 5 p.m. daily. Admission is free.

Return to SH 88 and go west into **Oologah**.

OOLOGAH

Will Rogers said he always told people he was from Claremore because "no one but an Indian could pronounce Oologah." The word means "Dark Cloud," the name of a Cherokee chief. The town wasn't settled until 1890 when the Kansas and Arkansas Valley railroad came through. The residents (pop. 731) of the town recently have been restoring the tiny business district. Brick sidewalks have been uncovered and facade work has been done on almost every building, all with private funds, no public money.

OOLOGAH PUMP (NRHP) is located at Maple and Cooweescoowee Sts. This pump, installed in 1920, is important as the first public water system in Oologah and the only remaining town pump in northeastern Oklahoma. Nearby is a replica of the Will Rogers birthplace. Another replica is between the railroad and the highway. It was built in 1931 as an Eagle Scout project and restored in 1986.

BANK OF OOLAGAH (NRHP) is at the same intersection. The correct spelling of Oologah is "Oolagah." Sometime around statehood the name was misspelled as it has been ever since. This bank building was finished in 1906 (before the town name was misspelled) and served the community for 20 years. In 1983, it was bought by a local couple and restored to the 1906-1932 period. The owners have had to rely on authentic fixtures from other places. The Chamber of Commerce now uses the building for offices. It is open from 9 a.m. to 5 p.m. weekdays and weekends by appointment, 918/443-2790. Admission is free.

OOLAGAH HISTORICAL MUSEUM is across from bank. This is believed to be the oldest building in downtown. Exhibits include antiques from the local area. It is open from 9 a.m. to 1 p.m. weekdays and by appointment. Admission is free.

Eleven miles southwest of Oologah on US 169 is Collinsville.

COLLINSVILLE

In 1899 when it was anticipated the Santa Fe railroad would come through the area, this community was incorporated and named COLLINSVILLE (pop. 3,600) in honor of prominent citizen **Dr. H. H. Collins**.

COLLINSVILLE DEPOT MUSEUM is located at 115 S. 10. Exhibits include turn-of-the-century room settings and railroad memorabilia. It is open from 1 to 5 p.m. Sunday. Admission is free.

It is 17 miles back to Claremore and Historic 66, then 12 miles on to **Catoosa**.

CATOOSA

An old Cherokee town founded in 1882 at the temporary terminus of the then **Atlantic & Pacific Railroad**, CATOOSA (pop. 2,930) was named for nearby **Catoos Hill**. The word is from the Cherokee "gatv gitse" meaning new settlement place. Another source believes it is from "Gi-tu-zi" meaning here live the people of the light. It is said the "people of the light clan" used to meet on the summit of Catoos Hill. Today, Catoosa is not a terminus but a beginning—of the 440-mile long **Arkansas Navigation System** completed in 1971 giving Tulsa access to the Gulf of Mexico via the Arkansas and Mississippi Rivers.

PORT OF CATOOSA/ARKANSAS WATERWAY MUSEUM is at 5350 Cimarron Rd. Watch for signs to the port. Featured are artifacts and other memorabilia representative of the development of the waterway. It is open from 8 a.m. to 4:30 p.m. weekdays. Admission is free.

Historic 66 is now routed through Tulsa (Section 3) on I-244. The old road followed 11th Street, a little over a mile south. Near the Turner Turnpike Gate SH 66 leaves I-244 and heads south to **Sapulpa**, eight miles.

SAPULPA

As is often the case when dealing with history—those who really know the answer to a question are gone and it is up to those remaining to puzzle it out to the best of their ability. So it is with the name of SAPULPA (pop. 18,041), seat of **Creek County** (it is definite the county was named for the Indian tribe).

For years it has been said Sapulpa was named for a man called **Jim Sapulpa** who established a combination store/home here about 1850. His name, it has been further stated, means "sweet potato" in the Creek language. Along comes another historian who says there is no truth to the word meaning sweet potato or to the town being named after Jim Sapulpa who is only the son of the man the town was really named for. He believes the town took its name from a Creek Indian from Alabama named "Sepulcher" (from the bible) and that the word gradually evolved into "Sapulpa." This Sepulcher/Sapulpa has also been given the title of "chief" which our historian says also isn't true. However, a statue of "Chief Sapulpa" does stand in front of the Sapulpa City Hall.

The origin of the name of Sapulpa may be in doubt but not the origin of the **Frankoma Pottery** company which moved here in 1938 from **Norman** and which, under the guidance of the late **John Frank** and his family, has produced from Oklahoma clay a product known round the world.

The COUNTY COURTHOUSE (NRHP) is located at 222 E. Dewey. This ornate building was started in 1912 and completed in 1914. It is one of 17 in the state designed by the firm of architect **Solomon Layton.**

SAPULPA HISTORICAL MUSEUM is located at 100 E. Lee. On display are turn-of-the-century clothing, kitchen items, and room settings. It is open from 1 to 5 p.m. Tuesday through Sunday. Admission is free.

Just west of the Sapulpa Golf Course, west side of town on SH 66, look for a sign reading "Old US 66." Turn right, up and over the railroad track and down a winding road over the **Rock Creek Bridge** with its brick floor, one of the original sections of old US 66. This road will lead back into SH 66 shortly.

Between Sapulpa and **Arcadia**, 58 miles west, SH 66 and Historic 66 will cross over and under the **Turner Turnpike** (linking Oklahoma City and Tulsa) a number of times. In many areas parts of the original US 66 concrete pavement can be spotted running almost parallel to the newer-straighter SH 66. Sometimes these sections can be followed for a little distance but missing bridges and "Dead End" signs make this impractical. Watch for old cafes, signs, and abandoned tourist courts along the way.

It is 22 miles to **Bristow** from Sapulpa. Enroute is **Kelleyville** (pop. 984). On September 2, 1917, two Frisco trains collided head-on one mile west of town killing 23 people and injuring 80. This is Oklahoma's worst train disaster.

BRISTOW

The post office for BRISTOW (pop. 4,066) was established in

1898, but a Creek Nation trading post had been here for several years. The town was named for a Kansas senator, **Joseph L. Bristow**.

VFW NATIONAL WAR MEMORIAL is located in city park. **National Wake Island Memorial** contains guns used by the Wake Island defenders during World War II. Ten engraved stones tell the story of the defense and fall of the island. Signs point the way to the park.

It is 18 miles to **Stroud**, just inside the **Lincoln County** line (named for the president).

STROUD

The midway point on the Turner Turnpike is STROUD (pop. 2,594), its post office, established in 1892, was named for **James J. Stroud**, an early-day trader. As it was located just two miles inside "wet" Oklahoma Territory, Stroud prospered until statehood in 1907 on illicit whiskey traffic with "dry" Indian Territory.

Henry Starr, a horse thief and bank and train robber, a relative by marriage of bandit queen Belle Starr, led six outlaws in a simultaneous robbery of Stroud's two banks on March 27, 1915. The double holdup was held in the early morning and in a few minutes the gang had gathered their loot and five of them escaped behind human shields. A young rifleman wounded Louis Estes and Starr and both were captured. Starr had been sentenced to hang for an 1894 murder but in 1896, while his case was on appeal, disarmed fellow prisoner Crawford "Cherokee Bill" Goldsby during an attempted jail break. He was pardoned for this deed. He later served prison terms in Colorado (1909-13) and in Oklahoma (1915-19). Henry Starr is believed to be the first bank robber to use an automobile in the commission of the crime. He died on February 22, 1921, four days after being shot while robbing a bank in Harrison, Arkansas. He is buried in a cemetery in Dewey.

A number of properties in Stroud are listed on the NRHP including the **Southwestern Bell Telephone** building, 301 W. 7th, and the **Stroud Trading Company and Graham Hotel**, both at Main and 2nd. Several homes on West 5th, 6th, and 7th and North 2nd and 4th Ave. also are on the register. In 1869 a large group of **Sauk and Fox Indians, Mississippi Band,** (sometimes spelled Sac and Fox) arrived from Kansas at their new reservation in parts of present-day Payne, Lincoln, and Pottawatomie Counties. The agency is located five miles south of the SH 66/99 junction in Stroud. A historical marker one block east tells about the agency.

SAUK AND FOX AGENCY is located five miles south on SH 99. Another historical marker is at the site of the old agency and boarding school. The original buildings were clustered in the area of the **old vault** just behind the modern **Arts and Cultural Center**. Today the tribe has a recreational vehicle park, tribal center, and museum on these grounds. Among the museum displays is one honoring famous tribal member **Jim Thorpe**, the great Indian athlete (Section 6). It is open from 10 a.m. to 6 p.m. daily. Admission is free.

Back on SH 66 it is 15 miles to the county seat of **Chandler** (named for Kansan **George Chandler**, President Harrison's assistant Secretary of the Interior).

CHANDLER

Established in September, 1891, shortly after the run opening the Sauk and Fox Reservation to non-Indian settlement, was CHANDLER (pop. 2,590). It was almost completely wiped out five years later, March 30, 1897, when a tornado roared through destroying almost every building, killing 14 people, and injuring scores more.

Several commercial buildings in the business district as well as a number of homes in Chandler are listed on the NRHP including the homestead of frontier marshal **Bill Tilghman**, northwest of town. One building not saved was the county courthouse built in 1907. It burned in 1967. Information on NRHP properties can be obtained at the museum.

William M. "Bill" Tilghman, Jr. became a buffalo hunter in Kansas at the age of 16 and scouted for the Army. In 1877 he was appointed deputy sheriff of Ford County, Kansas, and in 1884, city marshal of Dodge City, Kansas. He came to Oklahoma Territory in the land run of 1889. He served as city marshal of Perry until appointed deputy U.S. marshal in 1892. In 1910 he was elected to the state senate but resigned to become Oklahoma City chief of police. He was killed November 1, 1924, while taking a prisoner to jail at Cromwell where he was city marshal.

MUSEUM OF PIONEER HISTORY is located at 717 Manvel Ave. Exhibits and displays of pioneer life in Lincoln County can be found here including collections for Marshal Tilghman and for **Benny Kent,** a pioneer movie news photographer from Chandler. It is open from 9 a.m. to 4 p.m. Monday through Thursday and from 9 a.m. to 3 p.m. Friday and Saturday.

Admission is free.

In 1915 Kent, Tilghman, Chris Madsen, and two other former U.S. Marshals formed the Eagle Film Company. The group wanted to tell the true story of the outlaws to counteract the glamorized versions of their exploits as depicted in Hollywood movies and in magazines of the day. Their film was called "The Passing of the Oklahoma Outlaw." As they concluded filming at Tilghman's ranch, word came of the robbery of two banks in Stroud. Kent and Tilghman hurried to the neighboring town to film the captured bandits being patched up by the doctor and then being transported to jail. This unexpected bit of real-life drama was added to the movie.

INDIAN SPRINGS is located on Iowa St., southeast of the business district. In this small park, now owned and maintained by the local DAR chapter, is an early landmark called Indian Springs. Cowboys herding up the **West Shawnee Trail** stopped here as did travelers between the Iowa village near **Fallis** and the Sauk and Fox Agency south of Stroud.

There are two structures in Chandler identified with Route 66 days. One is at the north end of the business district: the restored, cottage-style service station with its tile roof (Westfall Texaco). These stations were built all over the midwest in the 1920s by the Oklahoma-based **Phillips Petroleum Co.** and the style was chosen to blend in with residential areas where most were located. The Seaba Garage is a few miles west of town on SH 66. The red brick machine shop, built in 1920, once was a filling station along old 66.

It is 11 miles from Chandler to the turn on 66B to **Wellston,** then 3.5 miles north and three miles west on blacktop to **Fallis.** At Wellston the present SH 66 is a cut-off to miss the town. Present SH 66B is the original US 66. Until this cut off was established all highways in Oklahoma went right through all towns enroute. Wellston sued the state to stop the bypass but lost. This historic decision resulted in many more of the state's towns being "bypassed" by a main road to keep the traffic moving.

A SIDE-TRIP

The village of FALLIS (pop. 49) was established December 28, 1892, as **Mission,** taken from the nearby **Iowa Indian Mission.** In 1894 the name was changed to honor **William H. Fallis,** first postmaster. At statehood the town had two railroads and a population of 350; it is doubtful it was ever much

This Indian statue, entitled "A Friend" is at the site of Indian Springs.

larger. Visiting this tiny settlement today with its few scattered homes, it is difficult to imagine this apparently was once a literary mecca. Five nationally recognized authors and two well-known state poets lived here.

Blanche C. Hunt was a writer of children's stories, in particular the "Little Brown KoKo" series. Her home, called **KoKo Knoll,** still retains its iron entrance gate, with the name, over the drive.

Beulah Rhodes Overman wrote detective short stories.

Vingie E. Roe wrote western novels including "West of Abilene," "Guns of Round Stone Valley," and "Dust Above the Sage." One of her novels "Divine Egotist," has Fallis as the setting .

Jenny Harris Oliver was Poet Laureate of Oklahoma in 1940 and published short stories as well.

Aletha Caldwell Conner was a novelist ("Pices's Child" was her most noted) and editor of the annual "Anthology of Poetry" written by Oklahoma authors in the 1930s.

Cecil Brown was a poet. "Journey's End," his most important book, was published in 1948.

Delbert Davis was Poet Laureate of Oklahoma in 1963.

Back on SH 66 at Wellston, it is 17 miles to **Arcadia** in Oklahoma County.

ARCADIA

The post office for this hamlet was established in 1890, a year after the area was settled in the land run opening the Unassigned Lands of central Oklahoma to settlement. The word means "ideal, rustic contentment."

ARCADIA ROUND BARN (NRHP) is a still-remembered

The Arcadia Historic Round Barn Association was restoring William Odor's 1898 round barn in 1990.

74

landmark on old 66. This distinctive barn was built in 1898 by **William Harrison Odor**. Exactly why Odor chose to make the barn round is not known but one story says it is because he believed if tornadic winds (common in Oklahoma) hit it they would just slide around the curved, unobstructed sides of the structure and the barn wouldn't be damaged. Odor's brother-in-law also built a round barn about the same time nearby but his had a refinement. A roof overhang was added several yards above the ground and completely encircling the barn. This was to shelter cattle when they came to feed. This barn was destroyed in 1912 by a tornado. Odor's barn, without the overhang, is still standing, a fact he was said to have often noted.

Residents say cars still stop every day to take photographs. Many of these are people who remember the barn from Route 66 days and are back to see if it is still there. The barn almost was lost to time and the elements but has recently been restored by the **Arcadia Historic Round Barn Association**. Funds are now being raised to establish a museum in the barn.

RINGING THE WILD HORSES dates back to 1832. The evening of October 27, 1832, **Washington Irving** and his party camped in the Arcadia area while on "A Tour on the Prairies." A historic marker on SH 66 just east of town is near what Irving called "the buffalo camp" because a buffalo was shot along **Coffee Creek**, a little south. The next day the group moved south to a valley on the **North Canadian River** now known as **Nine Mile Flats** (site listed on the NRHP). Here they found a large herd of wild horses and spent the day trying to encircle and capture some of them. Irving's chapter on "Ringing the Wild Horses" was reprinted in countless school text and exercise books in the mid-1800s and was a familiar story to schoolchildren of that time.

It is 10 miles to **Edmond**. SH 66 does not go through Edmond now but US 66 did so we will go that way.

EDMOND

This small city of 52,315 is one of the state's "instant cities" settled in one day, April 22, 1889. The fuel and water stop along the Santa Fe had been named **Summit** in 1887 by the railroad because it was believed to be the highest point on the Santa Fe grade between Kansas City and Galveston (or between Arkansas City and Fort Worth or between the Cimarron and North Canadian Rivers; opinion varies). The townsite committee in 1889 was planning to name the new settlement **Birge City** but when the papers were filed at the land office in Guthrie, Birge City had been crossed off and the word Edmond written above. Nobody knows who did the crossing out and for 101 years no one knew who "Edmond" was. Recent (1991) information uncovered indicates the town may have been named for Santa Fe freight agent, Edmond Burdick.

A historical plaque at the corner of 2nd and Broadway, in front of *The Edmond Sun* newspaper office, recognizes the birth of this paper, July 18, 1889, and its colorful editor, **Milton "Kicking Bird" Reynolds**. Reynolds, a well-known Kansas journalist, was an ardent supporter of the Boomers' efforts to open the Unassigned Lands to settlement. On the day of the run he was in the correspondent's car on the first train coming out of Arkansas City. He stopped in Guthrie and started a newspaper but early in July moved to Edmond and established *The Edmond Sun*. It is said the name "Kicking Bird" was a pseudonym he adopted from Kiowa chief Kicking Bird who hid him once from some angry Cheyenne Dog Soldiers.

UNIVERSITY OF CENTRAL OKLAHOMA is on the north side of Historic 66, east side of town (historical marker at the intersection with Boulevard). Originally a Normal School, this was Oklahoma Territory's first institution of higher learning open for instruction on November 9, 1891. Classes were held in the Methodist Church until what is known today as **Old North Tower** (NRHP) was built in 1892, the first structure built in the territory for a state-supported institution of higher learning.

FIRST SCHOOL BUILDING in Oklahoma Territory is at 124 E. Second. A historical marker in front of Sanders Camera Shop marks this structure built in August, 1889, as the first schoolhouse in the territory. First fund-raiser for the building was held in July, 1889. A profit of $25 was realized from the sale of blackberries, ice cream, cake, and lemonade.

FIRST CHURCH BUILDING in Oklahoma Territory was St. John's Catholic Church, completed on June 24, 1889, and used by other denominations as well until their buildings were completed. A playhouse-size replica of this building stands near present St. John's on S. Boulevard, just south of 9th.

EDMOND HISTORICAL SOCIETY MUSEUM is located at 431 S. Boulevard. Exhibits portray the history of Edmond. It is open from 10 a.m. to 4 p.m. Thursday and Friday; from 1 to 4 p.m. weekends. Admission is free.

WPA MURAL in the city building at the northeast corner

Old North Tower, University of Central Oklahoma, was the first building used for higher education in Oklahoma Territory.

of 1st and Littler was originally in the post office. When the new post office was built and this structure remodeled for city use, the mural was carefully removed from the wall, restored, and put back up. **Ila McAfee Turner** portrayed the wildlife of "Pre-settlement Days" in this mural painted in 1939 as part of the Section of Fine Arts of the Works Progress Administration (WPA). The artist also did the post office mural in **Cordell** (Section 14).

Leave Edmond south on Broadway going toward Oklahoma City (Section 2). Watch for the brown and white Historic 66 sign. At the I-44 exit turn west and follow I-44 past the May Ave. exit, continuing straight west on the 39th Street Expressway (SH 66). The Oklahoma Historic Route 66 Association office is on this road in downtown **Bethany**. Watch for the signs in front.

BETHANY HISTORICAL MUSEUM is three blocks south of NW 39 on College. It is open from 9 a.m. to 5 p.m. Monday through Saturday.

Seven miles west of Bethany is **Yukon**. Enroute the original US 66 passed across the overhead truss bridge and along the north shore of **Lake Overholser**. Somewhere in this vicinity, perhaps along the east side of the lake where the river bed of the North Canadian River lies, was the site of **Camp Alice**. This was one of several camps **David Payne** and a group of **Boomers** set up in an attempt to settle in the Unassigned Lands in February of 1883, six years before the area was opened legally. Within a month this large group had been escorted back to Kansas by federal troops.

YUKON

YUKON (pop. 20,803) actually began life as **Frisco**, a ghost town today, settled by a colony of Civil War veterans during the Run of '89. For a time the settlement was known as **Veteran City** and the first Oklahoma **Grand Army of the Republic Post** was organized here. When the Choctaw Coal and Railway (later the Choctaw Oklahoma and Gulf and after 1904 the Rock Island) came through this area enroute from El Reno to Oklahoma City, Frisco was missed by a few miles. The stores and homes of the community were jacked up and moved south to the rail line, and the new town of Yukon, named for the river in Alaska, came into existence.

Among the properties listed on the NRHP here are **Czech Hall**, south of town; **Yukon Public Library**, 512 Elm, and **Mulvey Mercantile**, 425 W. Main.

A branch of the old CHISHOLM TRAIL went through here and a cold spring used by the trail drivers is located in Yukon City Park. Located one and a half blocks east of SH 92 on Vandament St. are two site markers commemorating this trail first traveled by **Charles Goodnight** in 1866. This cattle trail ran from Montague County, Texas, to Abilene, Kansas.

Yukon is the hometown of country/western singer **Garth Brooks**.

The town of Yukon originally began as Frisco, settled by a colony of Civil War veterans. This marker tells the Frisco story.

FRISCO CEMETERY contains the grave of Denmark native **Chris Madsen**, one of Oklahoma's famous frontier deputy marshals. The cemetery can be reached 2.5 miles on a county road north of the junction of 66/SH 92.

In the 1980s a Danish film crew spent several weeks in Oklahoma making a television documentary on the adventurous life of this colorful native son of Denmark. Born in 1851, Madsen served in the Danish Army, French Foreign Legion, and the U.S.

Army. For the latter he served as a scout, then quartermaster sergeant with the Fifth Cavalry and during the Spanish-American War joined the Rough Riders.

Madsen fought Indians in several western states and territories earning a Silver Star medal and counted William F. "Buffalo Bill" Cody as a close friend. When Oklahoma opened for settlement he took a claim near El Reno but soon tired of the quiet life and was no doubt glad when he was appointed chief deputy marshal. He served as a special investigator for the Oklahoma governor from 1918 to 1922. He died in Guthrie January 9, 1944, at the age of 93.

Back on 66 it is 12 miles to **El Reno,** seat of **Canadian County,** named for the river.

EL RENO

Another "run" town is EL RENO (pop. 15,382). The name "Reno" came from nearby **Fort Reno** (named for **Maj. Gen. Jesse A. Reno)** and the "El" was to distinguish it from nearby Reno City. Reno City was soon abandoned, due to flooding on the North Canadian and the fact the Choctaw railroad was going through El Reno.

A number of El Reno buildings are listed on the NRHP including the county jail, 300 S. Evans; **Southern Hotel,** 319 S. Grand, and the **Goff House,** 506 S. Evans, now a bed and breakfast inn. North of town on US 81 is **Mennoville Church** (NRHP) built in 1894 and the oldest existing structure pertaining to the Mennonite faith in Oklahoma.

CARNEGIE LIBRARY (NRHP) is located at 215 E. Wade. This two-story structure of cream-colored brick was built in 1904-05, the fourth Carnegie Library in Oklahoma Territory. It is the oldest in the state still in use as a library.

The COURTHOUSE here was built in 1962-64 to replace an older building. The ornate courthouse built in 1901 was complete with a neo-classical dome topped with a statue of "Justice." The statue is now in the foyer of the new building. Outside is a "Doughboy" statue and memorial to those who served in World War I.

CANADIAN COUNTY HISTORICAL MUSEUM COMPLEX is at Wade and Grand. The museum is housed in the old **Rock Island Depot** (NRHP) and features exhibits pertaining to Darlington/Concho (Section 10), Fort Reno, Rock Island Railroad, and ranching. Also on site are the **El Reno Hotel** (NRHP) built in 1892, a schoolhouse, and the first **Red Cross Canteen** (NRHP),

The first Red Cross Canteen Hut in the U.S. was built in 1917 at El Reno.

built in 1917, an idea that soon spread across the nation. It is open from 10 a.m to 5 p.m. Tuesday through Friday; from 1:30 to 5 p.m. Sunday. Admission is free.

It is seven miles west from downtown El Reno to Fort Reno. One mile west on I-40 Business/SH 66 is the west boundary for the Run of '89. Near the entrance to Fort Reno is a historical marker for the fort, today the Fort Reno Livestock Research Station. Much remains to be seen of the old fort, however.

FORT RENO

This fort was established in 1874 to protect Darlington Indian School, across the North Canadian. It was a post until 1908, then a reserve remount station until 1949. During World

One of the buildings built at Fort Reno in the 1880s.

War II it served as a prisoner of war camp for German and Italian soldiers. Some earlier "prisoners of war" here were Northern Cheyenne rounded up after Custer's defeat on Little Big Horn. Many buildings dating to the 1880s are still standing on the grounds. Of special interest is the Post Cemetery. Buried here are frontier scouts **Ben Clark** (chief scout for General Custer) and **White Elk**. In a special section are several graves of German and Italian prisoners of war. It is open from 8 a.m. to 4:30 p.m. daily. Admission is free.

Return to Business I-40 which runs southwest into I-40. It is 18 miles to the **Hinton/Red Rock Canyon** exit. The town is four miles south of the interstate and the park is on the south edge of town. In Hinton stop in at the **Hobbs Drug Store** which has been restored in the downtown area.

RED ROCK CANYON

This long, narrow, tree-shaded canyon has been a stopping place for Indians, outlaws, cowboys, travelers on the gold trail to California, and today's campers and picnickers. Signs in the state park show where the **California Trail** entered and left the canyon. In 1902 the **Chicago, Rock Island, and Pacific Railway** laid a track on the west rim of the canyon along the line from **Anadarko** to Enid. The old fill can still be seen. Four miles farther west on county road is **Rock Mary** (NRHP), the prominent landmark on the California Trail first publicized by a party of gold-seekers being escorted west by soldiers under the command of **Capt. R. B. Marcy** in 1849. The red sandstone rock rises 60 feet above the prairie and could be seen for many miles before it was reached by early travelers. In the official report of this first trip, the rock was described as looking "like a pound-cake well puffed and partially broken at its center." The name honored a 17-year-old Arkansas girl who was traveling with the group, **Mary Conway**. Today this landmark is difficult to find on backroads west of Hinton.

Back on I-40 it is 19 miles to **Weatherford** in **Custer County** (named for **General Custer**).

WEATHERFORD

WEATHERFORD (pop. 10,078) began in a cornfield on August 6, 1898, with the arrival of the CO & G. This was the terminus of the railroad at that time. Anything going further west had to go by wagon. Artist **Oscar E. Berninghaus** chose to depict the depot setting in the WPA mural he did for the Weatherford Post Office in 1940.

The California Trail as it emerges west out of Red Rock Canyon.

The town was named for **William J. Weatherford**, a deputy U.S. Marshal who came here in 1892 with the opening of the Cheyenne-Arapaho Reservation to non-Indian settlement in a land run on April 19, 1892.

SOUTHWESTERN OKLAHOMA STATE UNIVERSITY, at the north end of State St., was established in 1901 as a teachers' training school. On campus the Science Building is listed on the NRHP.

Astronaut **Thomas P. Stafford** is honored by his hometown with a statue located in a small roadside park just off the west end of the I-40 Business Loop at the junction with SH 54.

GEN. THOMAS STAFFORD MUSEUM is located at the Weatherford airport, northeast side of town. The museum features memorabilia from NASA and from the Apollo 10 flight to the moon in May, 1969. It is open from 8 a.m. to 5 p.m. daily. Admission is free.

Clinton is 14 miles west.

CLINTON

Second largest town in Custer County is CLINTON (pop. 9,265), just five miles south of the tiny county seat town of **Arapaho**. Several attempts have been made to lure the county government south but none have succeeded (Section 14). Clinton began with the arrival of the railroads and to honor the crossing here of the CO & G and the **Blackwell, Enid and Southwestern** (BES), the town was to be called **Washita Junction**. The post office department, however, chose to honor **Clinton F. Irwin**, a federal judge.

POST OFFICE MURAL "Race for Land" by artist **Loren Norman Mozley** in 1938 is one of five WPA murals done in the state using Land Run as a theme. Four of these were in post offices (the other three at Drumright, Sayre and Yukon).

WESTERN TRAILS MUSEUM (OHS) is at 2229 Gary Freeway. Prehistoric artifacts and old farm equipment, household furnishings, and doctor and dental equipment dating up to 1900 are among the displays. It is open from 9 a.m. to 5 p.m. Wednesday through Saturday and from 1 to 5 p.m. Sunday, November through March. April through October it is also open Tuesday. Admission is free.

Eighteen miles west is the exit for **Canute** in **Washita County** (named for the river).

CANUTE

During US 66 days the highway went through CANUTE (pop. 538), named for the ancient King of Denmark, instead of north as the interstate does.

Always of interest to the passersby, many of whom would stop, was the Catholic Cemetery on the east edge of town. Here is a hillside rock sepulcher, built in 1928, with a glass door framing a setting of angels and Christ, and nearby a bronze statue of Christ on the cross with two kneeling Marys below.

Five miles west on I-40 is **Elk City** in **Beckham County** (named for Governor J. C. Beckham of Kentucky). Elk City is the hometown of **Susan Powell**, Miss America in 1981. Singer, songwriter **Jimmy Webb** was born here.

ELK CITY

This town of 10,419 began in 1901 when the nearby settlement of **Crowe** moved to this spot to be near the CO & G, changing its name in the process to **Busch**. The name was to honor St. Louis beer magnate **Adolphus Busch** but when an anticipated brewery for the town didn't materialize, the name was changed again, to honor nearby **Elk Creek**.

HISTORIC TRAILS includes three tours that have been outlined by a local historical group for visitors interested in a residential or commercial walking tour or a driving tour. Information is included about each historic site on a folder which may be obtained at the local museums.

DISPUTED CHISHOLM TRAIL MARKER southeast corner of Broadway and Adams, is one of the spots included on the tour. This mysterious marker should have marked the **Great Western Cattle Trail** (sometimes called **Dodge City Trail**). This trail actually ran two miles east of Canute, which is just a few miles east. The Chisholm Trail was many miles east, back in the El Reno-Yukon area.

OLD TOWN MUSEUM, 66 and Pioneer Rd., includes an authentic turn-of-the-century home, Rock Bluff schoolhouse, and replicas of a 1900s chapel and the Katy Depot. Rodeo and Indian memorabilia are displayed here, also. It is open from 10 a.m. to 5 p.m. Tuesday through Saturday and from 2 to 5 p.m. Sunday. An admission is charged.

ANADARKO BASIN MUSEUM OF NATURAL HISTORY is located at 107 E. 3rd. Western Oklahoma fossils, gas and oil exhibits, as well as natural history items are displayed. Newest addition to the museum is a 17-story high oil drilling rig which has been put in the lot next door to the museum. When this rig and two others just like it were built in the 1960s, they were the largest rigs in the world at that time. The museum is open from 10 a.m. to 5 p.m. weekdays. An admission is charged.

It is 10 miles to **Sayre**, seat of **Beckham County**, located halfway between Oklahoma City and Amarillo, Texas.

Elk City's Old Town Museum Complex displays several early buildings of the area.

SAYRE

SAYRE (pop. 2,884) is another town established with the coming of the CO & G (1901) and it was named for an official of the line, **Robert H. Sayre**. **Jess Willard**, who became the world heavyweight boxing champion in 1915, once ran a boarding house here. **Joseph Benton**, the Metropolitan Opera star, moved to Sayre as an infant.

The COURTHOUSE, built in 1911, stands at the top of Main Street overlooking the business district. Most unusual is the dome with its collonades supporting a vaulted, gable roof and above that, a smaller replica reproduced to scale.

A SIDE-TRIP

North of Sayre on US 283, 22 miles, is **Cheyenne**, site of the **Battle of the Washita** (the site is listed on the NRHP) in **Roger Mills County** (named for a Texas congressman).

CHEYENNE

The post office for the county seat town of CHEYENNE (pop. 948), named for the local tribe, was established a week before the run of 1892. The town was designated as the seat of County F, formed with the run, and the first courthouse was a tent on the northwest corner of the courthouse square. In 1907 a sandstone

This farm scene, taken in 1910, is near the site of the Battle of Washita near Cheyenne.

vault was constructed to keep the county records safe. This vault has been part of a two-story frame courthouse and a two-story concrete and brick courthouse, and when the newest courthouse and jail were built in 1986, the building was designed so the old sandstone vault could remain in its original location. It is located near the front entrance of the new facility and open for viewing. On the grounds is a stone memorial listing all of the known servicemen from Roger Mills County.

A statue of a fleeing Indian woman and child in the courthouse entrance hall is a dramatic memorial to the Cheyenne Indian men, women, and children massacred during the Battle of the Washita on November 17, 1868. Early that morning, Lt. Col. George A. Custer attacked the sleeping village of Cheyenne chief **Black Kettle** and the chief and his wife were among those killed. (They had been promised peace by other white leaders.)

BATTLE OF THE WASHITA is remembered by a monument and memorial located two miles west and north of town on SH 47 and SH 47A. This site is a National Historic Landmark. It is open daily. Admission is free.

BLACK KETTLE MUSEUM (OHS) is located on US 283 and SH 47 near the courthouse. Indian relics, 7th Cavalry items and early pioneer artifacts recount the battle. It is open from 9 a.m. to 5 p.m. Wednesday through Saturday and from 1 to 5 p.m. Sunday in the winter. It is also open on Tuesday in the summer. Admission is free.

ROLL SCHOOLHOUSE, now located in the Cheyenne City Park, was moved here in late 1990 from the nearby community of Roll. Restoration of the one-room school, built in 1903, was funded by the Cheyenne Historical Preservation Committee. During May, September, and October area 4th graders will be able to attend a special "living history" class in the building to find out what school was like for their ancestors. When classes are not being held, the school will be maintained as a museum with visitors welcome.

George "Red Buck" Weightman, a ruthless member of the Dalton-Doolin gang, spent some time in the Cheyenne Country where he organized his own gang. He was killed by a posse on March 5, 1896.

Back in Sayre, the remainder of the trip to the state line (25 miles) can easily be made on old 66. From the courthouse go west down Main Street which curves south at 8th St. into 9th St. Follow this street south out of town. Just before the entrance to I-40 is a blacktop frontage road to the right. Watch for a brown and white historic sign. Within a few miles this road becomes four-lane to the state line.

ERICK

ERICK (pop. 1,067) was established November 16, 1901, exactly six years to the day before Oklahoma became a state. This is the hometown of country singer and songwriter **Roger Miller**; actor **Sheb Wooley** (Pete Nolan on "Rawhide") who also is a singer and songwriter, and songwriter **Michael Smotherman**.

The Barrow gang held a reunion near Erick on June 11, 1933. **Bonnie (Parker)** and **Clyde (Barrow)** came here to meet his brother, Buck, and his wife, Blanche. Bonnie and Clyde had kidnapped Sheriff Dick Corey and Marshal Paul Hardy. The two handcuffed police officers were tied with fencing wire to a tree during the brief get-together of the gang. Bonnie was badly burned in a car fire here and was disabled for several weeks.

100th MERIDIAN MUSEUM is located on Main and Broadway. Exhibits relate the story of the 100th Meridian of longitude from prehistoric times to the present. The museum building (NRHP) was built in 1907 to house the **First National Bank**. It is open from 1 to 4 p.m. Friday and Saturday from April through June and from September through November. It is open from 9 to 11:30 a.m. Friday and Saturday in July and August. The rest of the year it is open by appointment, 405/526-3221.

Admission is free.

From Erick to **Texola**, on the state line, is seven miles. Watch for the old and tiny rock jail in Texola. The western boundary of the main body of the state is on the 100th Meridian, once the international boundary between the United States and Spanish territory. This area, between the North Fork of the Red River and the Red River was once **Greer County** in Texas. A supreme court decision in 1896 gave this corner of the state to Oklahoma Territory (Section 8).

SECTION 6
Along US 77

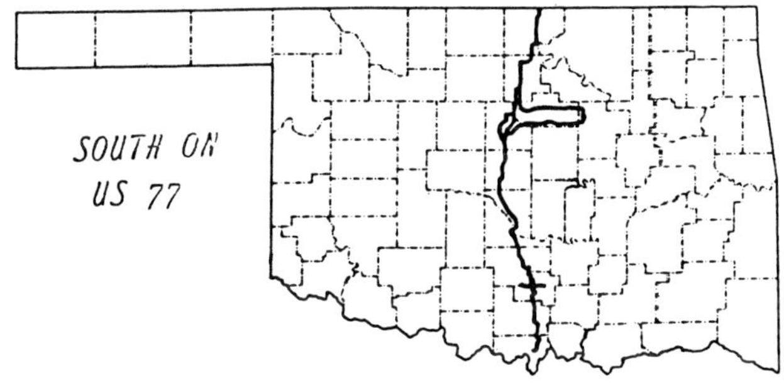

When Oklahoma became a state in 1907 there was a symbolic wedding between Mr. Oklahoma Territory and Miss Indian Territory. This statue in front of the Territorial Museum in Guthrie is a portrayal of the mock ceremony which was part of the statehood festivities.

SECTION 6
Along US 77

Officially this 254-mile-long Kansas-to-Texas route is the **Blue Star Memorial Highway**, so declared by the Oklahoma Legislature in 1951. Laid out in the early 1900s, it roughly paralleled the pioneering Santa Fe railroad built two or three years before arrival of the homesteaders in the 1889 Run for free land. One can make a strong case for naming US 77 the state's Great Divider route and at the same time, one can point to increasing evidence it is now emerging as a "Unifier Highway." Geographically US 77 is indeed the true east-west divider of the main body of the state as well as a division line between Indian Territory and Oklahoma Territory, between rolling, well-watered woodlands and semi-arid Great Plains. Paralleling it today for much of the way is Interstate 35 which brings in the "unifying" part.

I-35 provides easy access to such fine Sooner State features as the scenic and recreational facilities of the Arbuckle Mountains area, the sport and cultural activities surrounding the University of Oklahoma and Oklahoma State University, the multi-faceted lures of a major city that is also today's state capital as well as Guthrie, the territorial and first state capital.

SOUTH ON US 77

This route begins at the Kansas-Oklahoma state line north of Newkirk and ends at Marietta, some 240 miles south. Included, but optional, are an alternate route and a 100-mile side-trip through part of the old Cushing Field that once dominated the U.S. petroleum industry.

Just inside the state line is a large granite monument put up by the Ponca City Chapter of the Daughters of the American Revolution to commemorate the opening of the Cherokee Outlet (or Cherokee Strip) to settlement on September 16, 1893. This roughly 60 by 170-mile area was originally given to the Cherokees as a passage to the hunting areas in the plains to the west. The "run" for these 6.5 million acres by homesteaders was the largest opening of Indian land to settlement in the history of the United States. A historical marker to "Oklahoma, The Indian State" is located along the highway near the DAR marker.

To the southwest can be seen a water tower and a few

A Boomer Camp on the Oklahoma / Kansas state line waiting for the Unassigned Lands to open.

limestone buildings in a grove of trees, one of the Strip's most significant historical landscapes. Here, for nearly a century, stood the "Light on the Prairie"–Chilocco Indian School.

CHILOCCO

Until it closed in 1980, Chilocco was one of the largest Indian schools in the U.S. It was established by an act of Congress in 1882 as a non-reservation boarding school for children of the Plains tribes in western **Indian Territory**. Classes began in 1884 with 130 male and 56 female students from the Kiowa, Comanche, Apache, Cheyenne, and Arapaho agencies. Eventually students from 40 tribes across the U.S. attended the school for vocational and academic training. Today the old school grounds houses one of the Church of Scientology's "New Life Centers."

Eight miles south of the state line on US 77 is **Newkirk**.

NEWKIRK

The fourth largest town in **Kay County**, NEWKIRK (pop. 2,168), curiously enough is the county seat. Kay County was created in 1893, after the Outlet was opened, and first designated as County "K". The settlers kept the name, deciding simply to spell it "Kay." Newkirk, a Santa Fe railroad town, first named **Lamoureaux** then **Santa Fe**, became Newkirk to distinguish it from Kirk, another stop two miles up the line. The central business district is listed on the National Register of Historic Places (NRHP) as a collection of virtually unaltered structures of the 1894-1930 period. Most are built of locally quarried limestone.

"Dynamite Dick" Clifton, a member of Bill Doolin's "Oklahombres" gang was captured and being held in jail at Guthrie when he escaped in July, 1896. On December 4, 1896, he was confronted by marshals near Newkirk and was killed as he attempted to flee.

NEWKIRK COMMUNITY MUSEUM, 101 S. Maple, is a collection of items relating to Kay County/Cherokee Outlet. Many Indian artifacts also are on display. There is evidence Indians have lived along the Arkansas River near here for thousands of years. The first known white settlement in Oklahoma (1740-50) is believed to have been just east of town at Ferdinandina. The site of this French trading post is listed on the NRHP. The museum is open from 2 to 4 p.m. Sunday. Admission is free.

The COURTHOUSE (NRHP), on US 77, is perhaps one of the more unusual public buildings in that the countyans saved up the money first, then paid cash for the construction completed in 1926. The fountain in front of the structure was restored to working order in 1990. In 1991 a memorial consisting of bronze rifles and helmets patterned after those used by soldiers in World Wars I and II, Korea, and Vietnam was placed on the grounds. The names of all from Kay County known to have lost their lives in these wars are listed.

It is 13 miles to **Ponca City**.

PONCA CITY

By nightfall of the day of the Cherokee Outlet opening, 3,000 people had settled in the area around **Big Spring**, located near present 14th Street and South Avenue. Today, 26,359 people call **Ponca City** home. **New Ponca**, then **Ponca**, finally Ponca City, was home to two of Oklahoma's better known oil barons, **E. W. Marland** and **Lew Wentz**.

PIONEER WOMAN STATUE/MUSEUM (NRHP and OHS), is located on US 77 and Highland. In 1926, Marland asked 12 of the world's leading sculptors to submit models for a statue

This Pioneer Woman statue in Ponca City was commissioned by an Oklahoma oil baron to honor the thousands of pioneer women who endured the hazards and hardships of the frontier to establish homes in the west.

honoring the thousands of women who suffered hardships to establish homes in the west. (All of the models can be seen in the museum at Woolaroc, Section 13). Selected by a vote of viewers who saw the entries was this bronze by **Bryant Baker**. From base to top of the bonnet is 40 feet. The nearby museum exhibits antique household items, clothing, and other memorabilia of family life in the pioneer era. It is open from 9 a.m. to 5 p.m. Tuesday through Saturday; and from 1 to 5 p.m. Sunday, from April to November. It is closed on Tuesdays the rest of the year. Admission is free.

MARLAND MANSION/ESTATE (NRHP) is located just north-northeast of the Pioneer Woman statue. **Ernest Whitworth Marland** was an oilman, philanthropist, 10th governor of the state, and a U.S. Congressman. He was a wealthy man and one who enjoyed sharing it with others. He was a pioneer in providing employee benefits to his workers and the

This mansion was built by oilman E. W. Marland, 10th governor of Oklahoma. The mansion has been converted into a museum in Ponca City.

Pioneer Woman Statue was his gift to the state of Oklahoma. Many old-timers from Kay County can still recall the polo matches and fox hunts he organized, certainly exotic pursuits for the time and place.

Marland liked beauty, and it was always his desire to live in a palace. Between 1925 and 1928 his dream, modeled after the Davanzatti Palace in Florence, Italy, was constructed at a cost (including furnishings) of $5.5 million. Marland and his wife, **Lydie,** only got to enjoy their "palace" for a short time as the Depression soon ended such lavish living. The Marlands moved into the guest house and only opened the mansion on special occasions. Today it is open daily from noon to 4 p.m. September through May and from 10 a.m. to 4 p.m. the rest of year. An admission is charged.

CULTURAL CENTER MUSEUM (NRHP), 1000 E. Grand, was the first showplace home of Marland, founder of the Marland Oil Company which later merged with Continental (Conoco) Oil Company. Now an Indian/pioneer museum, its 101 Ranch room is filled with memorabilia of the famous **Miller Brothers ranch** located a few miles southwest near the town of **Marland**. It is open from 10 a.m. to 5 p.m. weekdays, except Tuesday, and from 1 to 5 p.m. Sunday. Admission is free.

The special interest traveler has a choice here. For many years US 77 proceeded southwesterly from Ponca City on the route of present SH 156. Anyone interested in the cowboy/Wild West Show heritage of Oklahoma is well advised to return to it here. The traveler more interested in the Indian/oil heritage can continue on US 77 west from Ponca City to Tonkawa, then drop south through Three Sands (both Section 12).

ALTERNATE ROUTE

The US 77/SH 156 intersection is four miles west of Ponca City. Seven miles south are the crumbling ruins of the old **101 Ranch.**

101 RANCH (NRHP), covered 100,000 acres, three towns, and was in parts of four counties. Little remains of it today. In its heyday it was a self contained community with its own churches, schools, telephone and mail service, newspaper, stores, and monetary system for the hundreds of people employed on the ranch. The ranch was also home to the famed **101 Ranch Wild West Show** which toured the United States and Europe until 1931. **Col. George W. Miller** staked his original claim with the opening of the Cherokee Outlet. After his death in 1903 the

The Old 101 Ranch Store south of Ponca City burned in recent years. The 101 Ranch was headquarters for the 101 Wild West Show. The ranch site is listed on the National Register of Historic Places.

ranch was run by his three sons, George Jr., Joe, and Zack. A historical marker stands between the cracked foundation of the **White House** (ranch headquarters) and the ranch store which burned only in recent years. On the east side of the road is the building which served as the ranch jail. The house has been gone since the 1930s.

COWBOY HILL CEMETERY is located just across the Salt Fork River bridge on the east side of the road. This plot was given to the Cherokee Strip Cowpunchers Association in 1930 by Zack Miller who is now buried here.

WHITE EAGLE MONUMENT is located 1.5 miles south in Noble County (named for John W. Noble, President Benjamin Harrison's secretary of the interior). The monument on the southeast side of the road was erected by the Miller brothers to the memory of a Ponca Indian chief White Eagle, who selected the area as a reservation for the tribe in 1879. The hill was once used as a signal station by the Indians. Buried at the base is **Bill Pickett**, the black cowboy who invented the rodeo event of bulldogging while a 101 Ranch cowboy. Although there are several other graves in this area, Pickett's is the only one marked. Many people think the monument to White Eagle marks his grave but he is buried in the Ponca Indian Cemetery.

SH 156 rejoins US 77 eight miles west of Marland (pop. 280), a town originally named **Bliss** but renamed in 1922 to honor the oilman. It is 16 miles south on US 77 from here to **Perry**, seat of **Noble County**.

PERRY

The town name of PERRY (pop. 4,978) honors **J. A. Perry**, member of the Cherokee Strip Commission during the administration of Grover Cleveland and is one of the towns born with the opening of the Outlet.

At sundown on the day of the run there were 25,000 people in Perry but as in other Oklahoma towns settled by land run, within a few days most of these had drifted on to other places. Just east of the present town square an area known as "Hell's Half Acre" sprang up. It is said that for a time over 100 gambling houses and saloons were operating in this area.

Deputy U.S. Marshals Heck Thomas and Bill Tilghman were sent in to help establish law and order but apparently they didn't completely rid the area of all bad influences. **Nathaniel E. "Wild Charlie" Wyatt** and other outlaws held up a Santa Fe train at Perry on May 9, 1894. Wyatt killed the station agent

Chief White Eagle, a friend of the Miller family connected with the 101 Ranch Wild West Show, is honored by this monument erected in his memory north of Marland.

when he tried to telegraph for help during the robbery.

COURTHOUSE SQUARE, in the center of the downtown business district, was known as Government Park and was the site of the wooden land office and government buildings when the Outlet was opened for settlement. Today the tree-shaded square contains the county courthouse (NRHP), begun in 1915; a post office building, and a **Carnegie Library**, built in 1909 and still in use.

FIRST NATIONAL BANK BUILDING (NRHP), 300 W. 6th, is Perry's contribution to the list of Oklahoma properties designed by Belgian architect **Joseph P. Foucart**. Foucart, once the private architect of the king of Belgium, came to the **Guthrie** area soon after the Run of '89 and by 1903 had designed a number of buildings and homes in the territory. Many unfortunately, are now gone. The distinctive horseshoe-shaped white stone frame around the window of this one is a Foucart trademark.

CRUSADER STATUE is located across the street on the north side of the square. This sculpture of the son of Neptune was created by **Sascha S. Schnittmann** for the 1939 American Cancer Crusade. It is now owned by Triton Insurance Group which has its home office in Perry.

CHEROKEE STRIP MUSEUM is located on Fir Street near I-35 on the west side of town. Set in a grove of native trees, the museum has both inside and outside exhibits. Inside are artifacts of pioneer and early day settlers of the Outlet. Outside are the restored Rose Hill School, Kaw City jail (Section 9), farm machinery, and an authentic Otoe Tipi. It is open from 9 a.m. to 5 p.m. Tuesday through Friday; from 2 to 5 p.m. weekends. Admission is free.

If taking the following optional side trip leave Perry to the south on SH 86. Otherwise follow US 77 west and then south through **Orlando** and **Mulhall** to Guthrie.

A SIDE TRIP

This 100-mile tour begins 12 miles south of Perry at the intersection of SH 86/51. Thirteen miles east is **Stillwater**, county seat of **Payne County** (named for Boomer leader David L. Payne).

STILLWATER

"Where Oklahoma Began" is the slogan STILLWATER (pop. 36,676) has chosen for itself. Although it was one of the towns formed during the Land Run of 1889, Stillwater actually traces its beginnings to four years earlier. In December, 1884, 200 settlers came from Kansas to establish a town on the banks of **Stillwater Creek**. They were part of Payne's **Oklahoma Colony**, formed in 1879 to force the opening of the Unassigned Lands in Indian Territory to non-Indian settlement. Led by Payne's number one assistant, **William L. Couch**, this group of colonists called their town Stillwater before they were escorted back to Kansas by federal troops. Many returned to this area when the land was officially opened. Largest employer in Stillwater is **Oklahoma State University**, a land grant school established in 1890 as Oklahoma A & M College. The main campus covers 425 acres and most of the buildings are modified-Georgian in architecture.

OLD CENTRAL MUSEUM OF HIGHER EDUCATION (NRHP and OHS) is located at University and Knoblock. This was the first building on the campus, dedicated June 15, 1894. It is the oldest collegiate building in the state devoted exclusively to higher education and still in its original configuration. The exhibits include restored original classrooms and offices, photographs, textbooks, and articles about OSU as well as higher education in the Twin Territories and the state. It is open from 9 a.m. to 5 p.m. Tuesday through Friday; from 2 to 5 p.m. weekends. Admission is free.

SHEERAR CULTURAL AND HERITAGE MUSEUM is located at 7th and Duncan. The exhibits include a 4,000 specimen button collection early-day American glass and china, and historic photos. It is open from 1:30 to 4 p.m. Monday through Saturday. Admission is free.

NATIONAL WRESTLING HALL OF FAME/MUSEUM is located on the north side of the campus on Hall of Fame Blvd. It is the nation's only museum dedicated to the sport of amateur wrestling. Displays trace the history of wrestling from ancient times to modern. It is open from 9:30 a.m. to 4:30 p.m. weekdays and by appointment on weekends. An admission is charged.

PFEIFFER FARM COLLECTION is on permanent display at the Payne County Fairgrounds east of Stillwater on SH 51. Featured is a collection of antique farm machinery and equipment. It is open by appointment, 405/ 377-1275.

East on SH 51, 9.5 miles from downtown Stillwater, is the turnoff, south, to **Ingalls**.

INGALLS

Now almost a ghost town, INGALLS was founded a few weeks after the opening of the Unassigned Lands and was

This historical marker has been moved to Ingalls and tells the story of the battle between law enforcement officers and the Dalton-Doolin gang in 1893. Three marshals and two residents were killed in the shootout.

named for **Sen. John J. Ingalls** of Kansas.

A noted gun battle between a gang of outlaws and U.S. marshals occurred in Ingalls on September 1, 1893.

Seven members of the **Dalton-Doolin** gang had come into town for some relaxation. One of the gang members, Roy Daugherty, alias Tom Jones, who was ill, retired to an upstairs room at the O.K. Hotel (still standing). The others, including Bill Dalton, Bill Doolin, Dan "Dynamite Dick" Clifton, William "Tulsa Jack" Blake, George "Bitter Creek" Newcomb, and George "Red Buck" Weightman, were relaxing at the Ransom and

Murray Saloon. Bill Dalton gained notoriety as an outlaw but was never a member of the Dalton gang involved in the Coffeyville, Kansas, raid of October 5, 1892, where his brothers, Bob and Grat Dalton were killed in the attempt to rob two banks simultanously and Emmett was seriously wounded and eventually sentenced to prison. Bill Doolin, on the other hand, had been a member of the Dalton gang and participated in several bank and train robberies but was spared when, for one reason or another, he did not take part in the Coffeyville massacre. The authorities were tipped off about the outlaw gathering in Ingalls and on the night of August 31, according to Stillwater author Glenn Shirley, "a white-topped wagon left Stillwater and another left Guthrie. Each boasted a single driver but carefully concealed beneath the flapping canvas were arms, ammunition and (between the two wagons) 13 U.S. deputy marshals.

The Stillwater wagon arrived at the rendezvous point southwest of Ingalls a little before midnight. It was expected marshals would surround the hotel around midnight, continues Shirley, but the Guthrie wagon was delayed and didn't show up until dawn. It was about mid-morning before they arrived in town. Before the marshals could secure positions they were spotted.

Lawman **Dick Speed** fired upon Newcomb, wounding him as he sat on his horse outside of the saloon. Daugherty witnessed the shooting, grabbed his rifle and fired, striking Speed in the shoulder. Speed turned and Daugherty fired a second shot killing the lawman instantly. In the meantime, Newcomb fled. The posse and outlaws exchanged gun fire and four citizens were wounded and 14-year old Dell Simmons was killed.

In the meantime Daughtery spotted lawman **Tom Houston** moving in on the gang still in the saloon. He fired two or more times to fatally wound Houston. The five remaining outlaws made a break for freedom and Doolin shot officer **Lafayette "Lafe" Shadley** three times fatally wounding him. Speed and Shadley were taken to Sillwater where they died the next day. The quintet rode safely out of town under a hail of gun fire. Daugherty was captured in the early afternoon. He was convicted of manslaughter and sentenced to a 50-year prison term. He was paroled in 1910 but by 1917 was back to robbing banks. In 1924, he was killed in Joplin, Missouri, while resisting arrest.

A monument to the three slain lawmen was erected at First and Ash by the townspeople in 1938.

Ten miles east on SH 51 is **Yale**, one of the towns which boomed along with the Cushing Oil Field. In Yale, as well as Oilton, Drumright, and Cushing, watch for the large and ornate (for the size of the towns) churches and public buildings constructed with oil wealth.

BATTLE OF ROUND MOUNTAINS. About four miles west of Yale note the two distinctive round mounds to the north of the highway. These will first be noted several miles away. Many historians now believe this was the site of the first Civil War battle fought in Indian Territory rather than the previously selected site some 20 miles northeast. This engagement began November 19, 1861, when Confederate **Col. D. H. Cooper's** white and Indian vanguard clashed with a band of warriors from Creek **Chief Opothleyahola's** Indian allies, a Union force. After suffering heavy losses Opothleyahola's men withdrew, fleeing north in an attempt to reach Kansas.

YALE

The name for YALE (pop. 1,392 and established 1895) was selected by the first post master for no other reason than there was a Yale lock on the post office door.

MEMORIAL OBELISKS are located at Main and Broadway. In 1921 four concrete obelisks were placed, one on each corner, as a memorial to those area men who lost their lives in World War I. An electric lamp at the apex of each cast a glow that caused the intersection to be known locally as "the great white way." They are still standing though all four are not completely intact.

JIM THORPE HOUSE/MUSEUM (NRHP and OHS) is located at 706 E. Boston. A direct descendant of the famous Chief Black Hawk, Thorpe was proclaimed the "World's Greatest Athlete" at the 1912 Olympic Games when he became the first person ever to win gold medals in the pentathlon and the decathlon in the same Olympic year. Thorpe, a Sauk and Fox, and his wife owned and lived in this house with their three children from 1917 to 1923. It has been restored to that period. It is open from 9 a.m. to 5 p.m. Tuesday through Friday and from 2 to 5 p.m. weekends. Admission is free.

In the municipal park on the east edge of town is a plaque marking one of the camps of Washington Irving's party during their tour of the prairies.

It is seven miles east to SH 99 and three miles south to **Oilton** (pop. 1,060), another Cushing field town, established in

This was the home of Jim Thorpe, called the "World's Greatest Athlete" at the 1912 Olympics, in Yale for six years, from 1917 to 1923. Today it is a museum.

1915. Six miles south, then west on SH 33 is Drumright at the west edge of **Creek County** (named for the Creek Nation).

DRUMRIGHT

First known as **Fulkerson** for the townsite landowner, the name was soon changed to DRUMRIGHT (pop. 2,799) to honor another local landowner. The town was established in 1912 and for three years, until a crusading town police chief restored law and order, Drumright was mostly tents, wood shacks, oil rigs, and a haven for those on the shady side of the law.

Roy Daugherty, alias Tom Jones, the outlaw captured in the Ingalls shootout in 1893, operated a restaurant in Drumright for two years after being paroled from prison in 1910.

SANTA FE DEPOT (NRHP) at Broadway and Harley was the first depot built in the Cushing Oil Field. It is now an oil field museum featuring early oil field equipment and tools. The local historical group recently placed large signs at each of the town's nine NRHP properties. It is open from 1:30 to 5 p.m. Sunday. Admission is free.

WASHINGTON SCHOOL (NRHP), 214 W. Federal, is the first permanent school in the area and one of the first permanent buildings in Drumright. It was built in 1915 of locally quarried native sandstone. It is located high on a hill and offers a good view of the surrounding countryside.

WAY PARK on the west edge of the downtown area contains two monuments. One honors the local lives lost during the two World Wars and the Korean Conflict. The other was put up in 1986 to commemorate local Boy Scout Troop 8 on its 50th anniversary.

WHEELER WELL NO. 1 (NRHP) was drilled in 1912 and is located one mile north of downtown and .3 mile west of North Smather Street. Drilled by "King of the Wildcatters," oilman **Tom B. Slick,** this well opened Cushing Oil Field.

TURKEY TRACK RANCH. About two miles north of the SH 33/99 junction was the headquarters for this large ranch which was used during Texas cattle drive days (1866-85) as a stop to fatten cattle on the way north to market. Roundups were held on the site of present-day **Cushing,** nine miles west of Drumright on SH 33.

CUSHING

In 1894, CUSHING (pop. 7,218) was founded on the old Turkey Track Ranch in the northern part of the Sauk and Fox Territory. It was named for Marshall Cushing, private secretary to the postmaster general. Until 1912 it remained the archtypical agricultural community. Then on April 11 in Drumright the Wheeler No. 1 "wildcat" blew in—one of the state's half-dozen or so true watershed discovery wells. Cushing was never the same. By 1915, there were 710 wells producing 72 million barrels of oil annually. At one time there were 23 refineries in the Cushing area and 17 percent of the U.S. and three percent of the world production of oil was here. To this day Cushing remains the crossroads terminal site for a sprawling network of oil, gas, and petroleum products pipelines that crisscross the nation from ocean to ocean and Canada to Mexico. At Oak and Cleveland there is a Historical Society monument to Cushing Field.

SHOTGUN HOUSES, in Cushing, especially on East Cherry and Maple and North and South Central, were the early boomtown houses that once dominated here. Usually one room wide and two to three rooms deep, they were named because supposedly one can fire a shotgun through the front door and the shot will pass through the house and out the back door without hitting anything.

C. R. ANTHONY STORE, 118 E. Broadway, is now a sporting goods store but this is the location of the first store (opened in 1922) by the department store founder. Some literature states there is a plaque on the front of the building noting this historic spot. Present occupants say the former owner of the building objected to the plaque and it was never put in place.

CIMARRON VALLEY RAILROAD MUSEUM, 1.3 miles south of SH 33 on Kings Highway, is housed in the old Santa Fe Depot from Yale. It is restored to 1930s condition and features a large collection of railroad items. It is open by appointment, 918/225-1657. Admission is free.

Fifteen miles west on SH 33 is Perkins.

PERKINS

One of the towns settled in the Run of '89 was PERKINS (pop. 1,925), named for U.S. Senator **B. W. Perkins** of Kansas. One of the homesteaders was **Frank "Pistol Pete" Eaton** who had been a deputy U.S. Marshal for the court of hanging judge **Isaac Parker** in Fort Smith, Arkansas. Eaton was a resident of the Perkins area until his death at 97 in 1958. He was the model for the OSU school mascot, "Pistol Pete."

DAVE SASSER MEMORIAL MUSEUM, 202 E. Thomas, is housed in the former Methodist Episcopal Church, the oldest original building in Perkins and one of the oldest buildings in Payne County. The exhibits are dedicated to pioneer life in the Cimarron valley and include antique guns, furnishings, and native American artifacts. It is open from 1 to 4 p.m. weekends and by appointment, 405/547-2131. Admission is free.

Four miles west on SH 33 is a small schoolhouse and a stone marker topped by a metal cutout of a horse. The marker was placed there by school children to commemorate **Washington Irving's** visit to the area during his **"A Tour on the Prairies"** in 1832. Irving's group camped about 1.5 miles northwest of this spot along **Wild Horse Creek**. The creek was named after the author's designation of this camp as "Wild Horse Camp" because a colt from a wild herd of horses was captured near here.

Nine miles west is **Coyle** in **Logan County,** named for **Senator John C. Logan** of Illinois. (Logan is credited with the founding of Memorial Day.)

COYLE

Originally named **Iowa City,** this Cimarron River town's name was changed a year later (1900) to COYLE (pop. 289) to honor **William Coyle** of Guthrie. The town site was originally two miles northwest but was moved when the Santa Fe railroad built through the present location.

GERALD JOHNSON'S MUSEUM, located on the main street in what was a saloon during territorial days, seems to catch the attention of all those who travel through town. The business is listed as being open weekdays but the hours vary. When the owner is in, the visitor can see turn-of-the-century typewriters, tools, Indian artifacts and antique office equipment. Admission is free.

About a mile west is one of the several all-black communities established in Oklahoma.

LANGSTON

Founded in 1890, LANGSTON (pop. 1,471) was named for **John M. Langston,** a black educator and congressman from Virginia. Town founder was **E. P. McCabe,** an early Guthrie real estate broker and county treasurer. McCabe, along with many other blacks in Kansas saw the opening of Oklahoma Territory as an opportunity to create all-black communities. It was even hoped by some members of the group to form an all-black state. In 1897 the territorial legislature authorized the establishment of **Langston University.** Although originally only for black students, enrollment is now open to all.

This historical marker briefly describes Zack Mulhall and the town named for him.

INDIAN MERIDIAN MARKER, in the intersection of Logan and Washington Streets on the east side of town. This tall concrete monument was put up in 1967 to commemorate the surveying of the meridian in 1870. All farms, town lots, and oil wells in Oklahoma east of the Panhandle are designated from the Indian Meridian and base line located near **Davis**.

It is 10 miles west to the junction of SH 33 and I-35. **Guthrie**, on US 77, is a mile further west or go north on the interstate for 13 miles to the Mulhall Road exit, then west about three miles to rejoin US 77 at **Mulhall.**

MULHALL

Another Run of '89 town, MULHALL (pop. 199) was originally named **Alfred.** In November, 1889, the name was changed to Mulhall. One of the first-day settlers was **Zack Mulhall,** an assistant livestock agent for the Santa Fe. Mulhall was a rancher who later became a showman, organizing one of the three "Wild West" shows headquartered in Oklahoma.

Mulhall's "Congress of Rough Riders and Ropers" produced two important figures in the entertainment world, three counting Tom Mix, who performed as a roper for a time. Will Rogers was the best known but also a star was Zack's daughter Lucille who was the first woman to be called a "cowgirl." Lucille lived at the ranch, just across the tracks from the downtown area of Mulhall, until her death in an automobile accident in December, 1940. Two structures in town listed on the NRHP are the **United Methodist Church,** Bryant and Craig, and the **Oklahoma State Bank,** Baty and Main.

Nathaniel E. "Wild Charlie" Wyatt, a notorious robber and killer, sometimes known as Dick Yeager, appeared in Mulhall on June 3, 1891 and decided to shoot up the town. The townspeople opened fire on Wyatt as he galloped down the street. He wounded two of them before riding out of town.

Fourteen miles south is Guthrie.

GUTHRIE

Today, GUTHRIE (pop. 10,518) is the seat of Logan County; but until statehood in 1907, it was the capital of Oklahoma Territory and until 1910, the capital of the state. On the day of the Run of '89, a prime destination was the land near the post office designated as Guthrie (for **John Guthrie,** a Topeka, Kansas, jurist). By nightfall 15,000 people were there. In recent years the town has been undergoing a historical revival. Fourteen hundred acres, virtually the entire town, has been placed on the NRHP as a historic district. Many of the 60 downtown buildings surviving from territorial days have heen restored to the 1910 period.

Among the well-known who have lived here are entertainers **Lon Chaney, Tom Mix,** and **Will Rogers;** Indian fighter **Chris Madsen,** Dodge City marshal **Bill Tilghman,** territorial governor **Cassius M. Barnes,** and temperance leader **Carry Nation.** Also **Fred G. Bonfils,** later publisher of the *Denver Post,* and **William Wrigley,** who made his first package of chewing

Early day Guthrie was the capital of the Oklahoma Territory and briefly served as state capital. The photo at the top was taken on June 8, 1889. The photo below show wagonloads of cottton bales being delivered in Guthrie during Territorial days. The large building in the background is the Victor Building which has been restored and is listed on the NRHP.

gum at 113 Division.

STATE CAPITAL PUBLISHING MUSEUM (NRHP and OHS) is located at 301 W. Harrison. One of the men who arrived in Guthrie on the first day was **Frank Hilton Greer** who came with little education, some printing experience, and $29. He built one of the largest printing operations in the southwest and published three of the most widely circulated newspapers in Oklahoma. The building has been restored and contains a large display of working, turn-of-the-century printing equipment. It is open from 9 a.m. to 5 p.m. Tuesday through Friday; from 10 a.m. to 4 p.m. Saturday and from 1 to 4 p.m. Sunday. Admission is free.

A free WALKING TOUR is conducted every Sunday afternoon of the downtown area. It leaves from the Publishing Museum. Visitors also can take their own tours through the area as each block contains green Historical Society markers telling about the buildings or sites.

TERRITORIAL MUSEUM/CARNEGIE LIBRARY (NRHP and OHS), 406 E. Oklahoma, features displays of all phases of life in Oklahoma between 1889-1907. The library was built in 1902-03. This is believed to be the only Carnegie library to have a dome and it should be noted Mr. Carnegie didn't approve of this feature being added to one of his buildings. On the steps both the last territorial and the first state governors took their oaths of office. Tom Mix ran a gymnasium in the basement of the library before he left for Hollywood and fame. It is open from 9 a.m. to 5 p.m. Tuesday through Friday and from 2 to 5 p.m. weekends. Admission is free.

SCOTTISH RITE MASONIC TEMPLE (NRHP), Capitol and Oklahoma Sts., is located on the site designated in 1890 for the Oklahoma state capitol building. The farthest east part was used as part of the capitol complex until 1910. The temple is one of the largest Masonic buildings in the world. The rooms are furnished with authentic decorations, furniture, and artifacts of ancient civilizations and cultures. It is open from 9 a.m. to 5 p.m. weekdays. An admission is charged.

COURTHOUSE (NRHP), 301 Harrison, was built in 1907. After completion county officials leased it to the state for the capitol offices. When Oklahoma City (Section 2) became the state capital in 1910 the county regained the ornate building for its own use.

SUMMIT VIEW CEMETERY. There are a number of his-

This stone marks the site of the Land Office in Guthrie where claims were filed after the Run of 1889. The other two such offices were located in Kingfisher and Oklahoma City.

torically interesting people buried here including outlaws **Charley Pierce** and **Bill Doolin**, both killed in the Payne County area. The most interesting story, however, has to do with **Elmer McCurdy** who died at the hands of an Osage County posse in 1911 but wasn't actually buried until 1977.

Apparently his body was taken to a Pawhuska funeral home, embalmed and left for relatives to claim. Here the story gets rather sketchy but eventually McCurdy entered "show business" as a wax-covered dummy in carnival side-shows and on Hollywood movie lots. When it was accidentally discovered in 1977 that this was no wax figure but the remains of a human, a group of Guthrie historians, led by artist/sculptor **Fred Olds** traveled to California, claimed the body and brought it to Guthrie for a proper burial. In keeping with the time in which he lived and died, McCurdy's body was taken to the cemetery in a glass-sided hearse pulled by six black horses and accompanied by a mounted posse.

Going south on Division Street (US 77) to I-35 note the restored green and white wooden pavilion in Mineral Wells Park, only one of its kind in the state. It originally was built in 1894 for band concerts and outdoor plays.

Take I-35 south past the Edmond exit (Section 5) and Oklahoma City (Section 2) to Exit 113 (US 77) between **Moore** and **Norman.**

NORMAN

Seat of **Cleveland County** (named for the president) is NORMAN (pop. 80,071). The town, settled during the Run of '89, was named for **Abner Norman**, a Santa Fe railroad surveyor who pitched camp on this site in 1886. **Camp Norman** was construction headquarters when the track was laid in 1887. Norman is home of the **University of Oklahoma**, opened September 15, 1892, the town's second seat of higher learning. September 18, 1890, **High Gate Female College** was established by the Indian Mission Conference of the Southern Methodist Church. The school closed a year after the opening of OU. It was located at the present site of Central State Griffin Memorial Hospital, a state mental health facility.

Actor **James Garner** was born in Norman. Actors who attended OU, as did Garner, were **Jack Ging, Alice Ghostley, Van Heflin,** and **Dennis Weaver.** Others who have called Norman home are ballerina **Yvonne Chouteau,** opera star **Thomas Carey,** and authors **Jack Bickham** and **C.J. Cherryh.**

This historical marker describes the work of Abner Norman as supervisor of the U.S. Survey of western Indian Territory. The town of Norman was named for this early pioneer.

HISTORIC DISTRICT includes the 100 block of W. Main and 100 to 232 E. Main.

OKLAHOMA MUSEUM OF NATURAL HISTORY, 1335 Asp on OU campus, houses a natural history collection as well as natural science, archaeological and ethnographic material. In 1991, an expert on sauropods, a family of dinosaurs that includes the brontosaurus, examined the collection of brontosaurus bones stored here but found in 1936 in the Oklahoma Panhandle near **Kenton** (Section 12). The researcher believes the Norman museum may have in its storage room, carefully wrapped in 55-year-old newsaper, the largest brontosaurus specimen in existence. It is not known yet if there are enough bones to make a mounted exhibit. The museum is open from 10 a.m. to 4 p.m. Tuesday through Friday and from 2 to 5 p.m. weekends. Admission is free.

OLD PRESIDENTS HOUSE, 401 W. Boyd, is now the official OU Visitor's Information Center. For more than 50 years this was the home of the presidents of the university. Built in 1902 as a private residence by **Dr. David Ross Boyd**, first OU president, the property was purchased by the state in 1914. A later president, **George L. Cross**, always liked to point out he would prefer the designation be the "Presidents Old House" rather than the "Old" President's House.

It is four miles south to **Noble**.

NOBLE

Named for **John W. Noble**, Benjamin Harrison's Secretary of the Interior, NOBLE (pop. 4,710) was settled April 22, 1889. It is in this region that Oklahoma's state rock, the barite rose rock, is found. The reddish-brown rocks are named for their resemblance to roses in full bloom. Indian legend says the rocks represent the blood of the braves and the tears of the maidens who made the "Trail of Tears" journeys to Indian Territory in the early 1800s.

ROSE ROCK GALLERY/MUSEUM, 419 S. US 77, has a diorama featuring the rare rock clusters in a natural setting. There also are educational and historical exhibits. It is open from 10 a.m. to 6 p.m. Monday through Saturday. Admission is free.

Lexington is 10 miles south.

LEXINGTON

Named for the town in Kentucky, the post office was established early in 1890. Northwest, along the **South Canadian River**, was **Camp Holmes**. In 1835 a large council of some 5,000 members of the Five Civilized Tribes and several Plains Indian tribes met here to agree to peace terms that lasted until the Civil War. A granite marker has been placed in a small roadside park north of **Lexington** (pop. 1,776) by the Colonial Dames of America to commemorate the treaty. Nearby is a historical sign noting the south boundary of the Unassigned Lands opened during the Run of '89.

Just across the river from Lexington is **Purcell**. For many years after the opening of the Unassigned Lands a sand bar saloon on stilts was located in the river bed as close as was

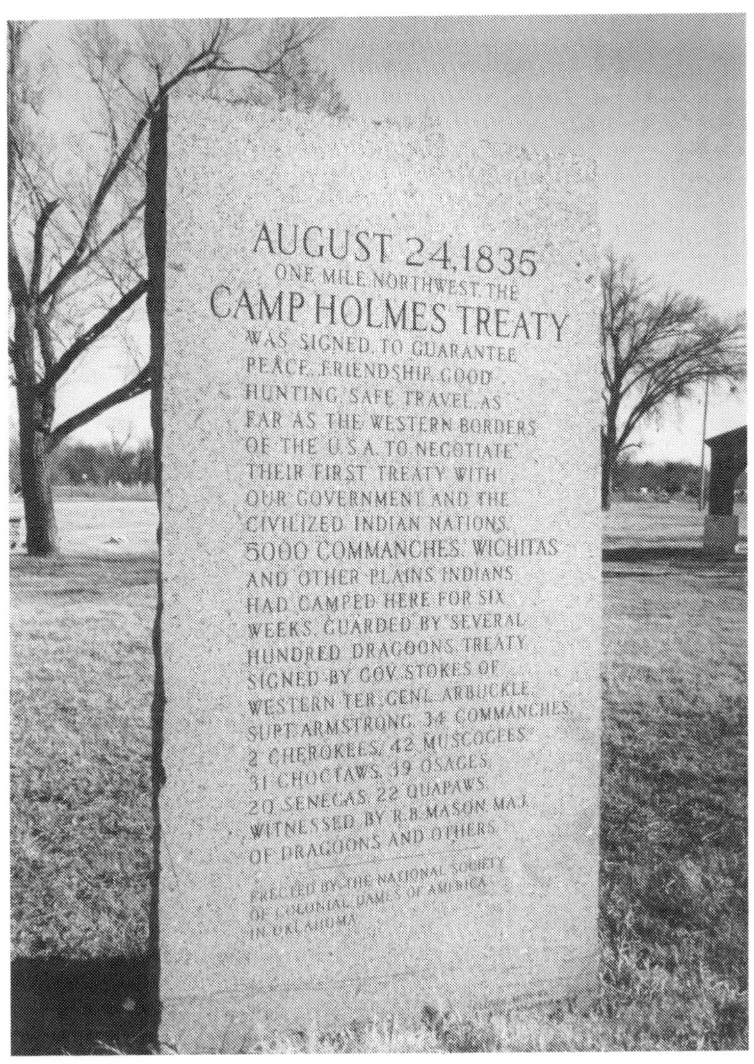

This marker commemorates the 1835 Camp Holmes Treaty which was signed near Lexington. The treaty, to protect Indians and whites alike, was witnessed by some 5,000 Indians. Both Plains Tribes and Five Civilized Tribes were represented. The Indians camped here for six weeks, guarded by several hundred dragoons.

possible to Purcell, in "dry" Indian Territory, by enterprising businessmen in "wet" Oklahoma Territory. Though the saloon washed away frequently it was always hastily rebuilt and back in business.

PURCELL

Established in 1887 in the old **Chickasaw Nation**, along the railroad, PURCELL (pop. 4,784) was named for a Santa Fe director, **E. B. Purcell,** and is the seat of **McClain County**. The name comes from Charles M. McClain, member of the Oklahoma Constitutional Convention. The Santa Fe Railroad building south from Kansas and north from Texas met here in 1887, opening a new rail link across Indian Territory.

In the early days a branch of the **California Trail** crossed the river north of the present town as did a branch of the **Chisholm Cattle Trail.**

MCCLAIN COUNTY MUSEUM, 203 Washington, features 11 different theme rooms pertaining to county history. It is open from 2 to 4 p.m. Wednesday and Sunday. Admission is free.

It is 20 miles to **Pauls Valley,** seat of **Garvin County** (named for prominent citizen of the Chickasaw Nation, **Samuel Garvin**).

PAULS VALLEY

Settlement began in this **Washita River** valley when **Smith Paul,** a white man who came west with the Chickasaws settled here. Though there was a post office as early as 1871, the town (pop. 6,150) did not incorporate until 1897. Then, logically enough, it was named for its location in "Smith Paul's valley."

HISTORIC DISTRICT is roughly bounded by the railroad tracks, Grant Ave., Joy, and Cedar.

WASHITA VALLEY MUSEUM, 1100 N. Ash, features items pertaining to the early pioneer life of the people of Garvin County as well as artifacts of the Washita River Indian culture. It is open from 12:30 to 4:30 p.m. Wednesday through Sunday. Admission is free.

OLD CEMETERY, three blocks west of S. Chickasaw (US 77) on Rush, contains graves of Indians and non-Indians, lawmen and outlaws, Confederate and Union veterans. Among the notable: **Jessie Paul,** scout for General Custer; **Smith Paul,** the town founder; and **F. T. Watie,** speaker of the house in the Chickasaw legislature. The last burial was in 1901.

WALKING/DRIVING TOURS of the area have been mapped out by the Pauls Valley Historical Society showing the historic points of interest in the town and the county. Copies are available at the museum.

Wynnewood is nine miles south.

WYNNEWOOD

Like a number of Santa Fe Railroad towns in south central Oklahoma, WYNNEWOOD (pop. 2,451) is named for a town in Pennsylvania. It was established in 1887 when **John Walner** moved his home and store from **Cherokee Town**, four miles north, to a loading station on the railroad.

ESKRIDGE HOTEL MUSEUM (NRHP) remains almost unchanged in architecture since it was built in 1907. On exhibit are many original furnishings. It is open from 1 to 5 p.m. Thursday through Sunday, May through August, and weekends the rest of the year. An admission is charged.

MOORE-SETTLE (MCCREA) HOUSE, (NRHP), 508 E. Cherokee. This house was built in 1899 but many of the furnishings the present owners have placed in the house date back to the early 1800s. It is open from 9 a.m. to 5 p.m. weekdays and by appointment on weekends, 405/665-2421. An admission is charged.

Ten miles south is **Davis** in **Murray County**, one of two counties in the state honoring former governor **William H. "Alfalfa Bill" Murray**. The other is **Alfalfa County**.

DAVIS

Although Chickasaws began moving into this area in the 1830s, DAVIS (pop. 2,543) wasn't born until 1887. **Samuel H. Davis** was a prominent settler.

Seven miles west of town on SH 7 is the site of **Fort Arbuckle** established in 1851 to protect simultaneously the Chickasaws and the California-bound immigrants from the less peace-minded Plains Indians. For many years the last remaining relic of the once important outpost was an impressive stone chimney. Recently a bolt of lightning reduced it to rubble and today only a historical marker remains to tell the story.

One mile south of the fort, on private land, is the spot from which all post-Civil War surveys of Oklahoma have been made except for the three Panhandle counties. The N-S line is the Indian Meridian and the E-W line is the base line. Both sites are listed on the NRHP.

ARBUCKLE HISTORICAL MUSEUM is located in the old Santa Fe Depot. Featured are Indian, Fort Arbuckle, and railroad artifacts. It is open from 9:30 a.m. to 5 p.m. Wednesday

through Friday; and from 1:30 to 4 p.m. weekends. Admission
is free.

<h2 style="text-align:center">A SIDE TRIP</h2>

Nine miles east of Davis on SH 7 is **Sulphur**, seat of Murray
County.

<h2 style="text-align:center">SULPHUR</h2>

Long before SULPHUR (pop. 4,824) became a health resort
built around medicinal springs, Indians knew of and patronized
these "healing waters." The town originally began around the
Pavilion Springs but was moved in 1902 and again in 1904
when the Chickasaws deeded land, including 30 springs, to the
federal government. For many years this government land was
known as **Platt National Park**, the smallest national park in
the system. In 1976 it became part of the new **Chickasaw
National Recreation Area.** Many people still come to the
springs to fill their water jugs with one of the many varieties of
mineral waters. The first fire bell used in Sulphur is now
displayed in front of the fire station on SH 7, across from the
historical marker telling about the area.

ADMINISTRATION BUILDING, built in 1894, is the site of
a marker honoring the work done by the Civilian Conservation
Corps in the park during the 1930s.

Return to Davis and US 77. It is about 20 miles to **Ardmore**
on the hilly, winding road through the **Arbuckle Mountains**.
Students come from all over the United States to study the rock
formations in this ancient range.

LOOKOUT POINT overlooks Turner Falls and the park,
oldest park in Oklahoma. The falls was a popular recreation spot
as early as 1868. There are three stone markers in this vicinity.
One notes the road was built with prison labor in 1925-26 and a
second honors **George A. Ramsey** who initiated construction of
the road. The third marker tells of the development of the
reflection seismic technique of oil exploration in Oklahoma. The
Arbuckle region was used for the pilot survey of the technique.

<h2 style="text-align:center">ARDMORE</h2>

When the Santa Fe laid track into the Chickasaw Nation the
railroad crew set up a camp exactly 100 miles from both Fort
Worth and Oklahoma Station (now Oklahoma City) and a tent
city began. The stop, ARDMORE (pop. 23,079), was named for a
town in Pennsylvania as were several other towns along the line.
When the railroad crew arrived the only structure was the old
700 Ranch House, built in the early 1880s. Ardmore is the seat

One of the springs in Chickasaw National Recreation Area near Sulphur. Indians used these medicinal springs in the 1800s. The park was once the smallest National Park in the United States.

This is one of the markers at an overlook of Turner Falls.

of **Carter County,** named for **Ben Carter,** an early settler.

HISTORIC DISTRICT includes the commercial area along Main St. and Hinkle Ave. and is listed on the NRHP.

RINGLING RAILROAD DEPOT (NRHP) is located at N. Washington and NE 3. In 1912 a railroad began building west from Ardmore and with typical hope it was christened the **Oklahoma, New Mexico, and Pacific.** Not surprisingly, construction ended 25 miles away at the town of **Ringling** (Section 10). The railroad soon became known unofficially as the Ringling Railroad because the principal owner was circus man

John Ringling. The line's depot can still be seen, the date 1915 and name Ringling still displayed though the railroad no longer is in existence. The building is now the home of American Legion Post 65.

COUNTY COURTHOUSE (NRHP) was completed in 1910, one of the 17 courthouses in the state designed by the firm of **Solomon Layton**.

ELIZA CRUCE DOLL MUSEUM, Grand at E St. NW, is housed in the Ardmore Public Library. The exhibit includes 300 of the world's finest dolls. It is open from 10 a.m. to 8:30 p.m. Monday through Thursday and from 10 a.m. to 4 p.m. Friday and Saturday. Admission is free.

CARTER COUNTY HISTORICAL MUSEUM, 35 Sunset Dr., includes a museum and genealogical library that are housed in the 40,000 square foot armory built as a WPA project in 1935-36. Exhibits reflect the social, cultural, home, and work life of the period between Indian Territory days and the 1930s. In the great hall is a recreated village. The Military Annex honors veterans of all branches of the Armed Forces. It is open from 10 a.m. to 5 p.m. Wednesday through Saturday and from 1 to 5 p.m. Sunday. Admission is free.

South of Ardmore on US 77 five miles is the entrance road to **Lake Murray** (1930s), Oklahoma's first lake built strictly for recreational purposes. It is two miles east to SH 77S which goes south around the end of the lake to **Tucker Tower**.

TUCKER TOWER

High on a bluff, 65 feet above and overlooking the lake, is this handsome structure made of native stone quarried nearby. Work began on it in 1934 with WPA labor. Original plans called for it to be a summer retreat for Oklahoma's governors. Completed were the basement, three rooms on the first floor, including a kitchen, and two rooms on the second floor. The building was to have had three bedrooms in the tower and a large reception hall on the south side of the first floor but this work was never finished. At one time the unfinished structure was considered as a federal ranger headquarters. In 1950 it became a geological museum and also displayed are western and Indian artifacts. It is open from 9 a.m. to 5 p.m. Monday through Saturday; and from 1 to 5 p.m. Sunday. Admission is free.

Near the entrance road to Tucker Tower, SH 77S branches south and goes into **Marietta**, seat of **Love County**, named for a Chickasaw family.

The Love County courthouse in Marietta.

MARIETTA

This town of 2,306 takes its name from the wife of one of the area's ranchers in early days. Brothers **Jerry** and **Bill Washington** owned or leased two of the biggest ranches in the Chickasaw Nation. Jerry's wife was named Marietta. Brother Bill ran his empire from an imposing Victorian-style mansion, built in 1888, southwest of town. The home, privately owned, is listed on the NRHP. Many scenes in the 1989 five-part educational television production "Oklahoma Passage" were filmed there.

Bill ("Uncle Billy") Washington ran thousands of head of cattle over what is now Love County, a privilege he received when he married a Chickasaw woman. He also grew cotton and to help him with his enterprise, had over 100 hands, enough to warrant maintaining a commissary and several stores and for shopping in them, he issued his own script which also was accepted at local banks. When he had this $50,000 mansion built "Uncle Billy" took certain precautions against unfriendly neighbors. The basement is equipped with gun slits and the walls, up to the height of at least six feet, are filled with bullet resistant gravel.

COURTHOUSE (NRHP) was begun in 1910. Among the features that make this building special are the dome with its clock and the flying wings on either side of the building's center.

LOVE COUNTY PIONEER MUSEUM, 101 SW Front, is housed in the Santa Fe Depot, built in 1913. Displayed are

The Love County Historical Society Museum is housed in the Old Santa Fe depot in Marietta. The railroad depot was built in 1913.

artifacts from early Love County history, Civil War artillery, barber equipment, and genealogy research center. It is open from 8 a.m. to 5 p.m. Monday through Saturday in summer and from 1:30 to 4:30 p.m. Monday, Wednesday, and Friday in winter. Admission is free.

POST OFFICE MURAL was done by artist Solomon McCombs and is entitled "Chickasaw Family Making Pah Sho Fah." It is painted on the west wall of the post office. Born near **Eufaula**, McCombs attended **Bacone College** where one of his teachers was famed Indian artist **Acee Blue Eagle**. This was one of the last murals to be commissioned by the Section of Fine Arts of the WPA and was completed in early spring of 1942. A shortage of canvas forced McCombs to paint on the plaster walls.

SECTION 7
US 69

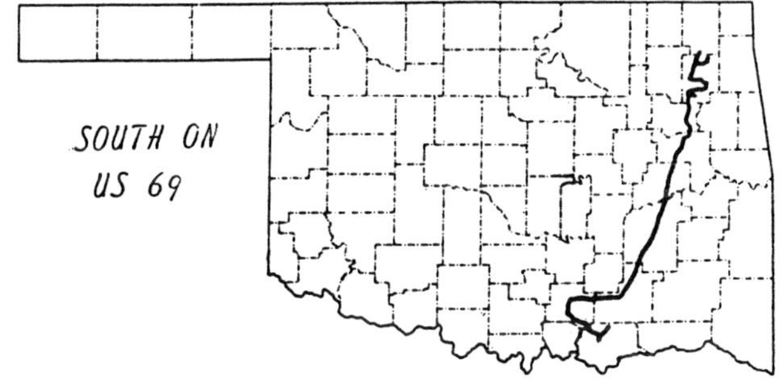

The Battle at Middle (or Muddy) Boggy at the crossing on the Boggy Depot Road took place on February 13, 1864, and this monument memorializes the 47 Confederates who died here. The Southerners were camped here when they were attacked by three companies of the 14th Kansas Cavalry. After a hard fought 30 minute battle the Union forces retreated to Fort Gibson.

SECTION 7
US 69

Basically US 69 was, and remains today, a well-trafficked passageway defined by the footprints of man to begin with, then by a progression of his vehicles. As the Osage Trace it stretched from Kansas to the Three Forks area of the Arkansas River. In subsequent years the route was retraced and extended to the Red River and Texas as the Texas Road. Over it flowed US Army supply trains and the lumbering wagon caravans of southwestern homeseekers. With time came the iron wheel of the pioneering MK&T Railway, Oklahoma's first, in 1872; then the rubber tires of today's ubiquitous cars and trucks. Today this prototype history route across the eastern third of Oklahoma is marked by a modest forest of signs, markers, and memorials calling attention to the significant points of interest, the "firsts" in military outposts and missions, in Civil War battle claims and frontier cultural institutions, the steady procession of explorers, adventurers, military expeditions, goldseekers, and missionaries on their way to play their role in the development of the American west. To pause and note these markers—and follow up even a handful of the modest detours they suggest—will give the motorist a surprisingly full-blown picture of the Sooner State past and present.

SOUTH ON US 69

This tour down the old Texas Road will begin at **Big Cabin**, just south of the Will Rogers Turnpike near Vinita (Section 5) and will end at Durant. The road from Big Cabin to **Atoka** is 173 miles but a few extra will be added with several short side trips and one short loop to the east of US 69. At Atoka a 64-mile alternate route loop will be outlined to the west of US 69, ending at Durant.

BIG CABIN

Located in southeastern **Craig County** (named for prominent Cherokee **Granville Craig**) is BIG CABIN (pop. 271). The post office was established August 21, 1871, and named for nearby **Big Cabin Creek**. The creek was named for the large cabin which had been built here along the Texas Road. The cabin was called the "Planche" Cabin because it was built of planking instead of logs, the more common building material.

Four miles south of Big Cabin in **Mayes County** (named for

Samuel H. Mayes, Cherokee chief) is a historical marker for the **Cabin Creek Battlefield**. The site (NRHP), eight miles east, is where two Civil War skirmishes took place, one July 1 and 2, 1863; the second, September 18, 1864.

A SIDE TRIP

At **Adair**, four miles south of the marker, turn east on SH 26. It is eight miles to **Pensacola**, a town built on the site of **Hopefield Mission and School** for Osage Indians moved here from **Union Mission** in 1828. At Pensacola (pop. 69) go 2.5 miles north, then a little east and back north.

CIVIL WAR MONUMENT, a stone memorial, marks the location of the Second Cabin Creek engagement. During the skirmish Confederate **Gen. Stand Watie**, a Cherokee, captured 120 wagons of a Union supply train enroute to **Fort Gibson** from Fort Scott, Kansas. This was the last major Civil War engagement in Indian Territory. The same maneuver had been tried the year before (First Battle of Cabin Creek) with much less success. That time Federal troops forced Confederate withdrawal. This memorial plot has been conveyed to the Oklahoma Historical Society by the Vinita Chapter of the United Daughters of the Confederacy and contains many unmarked graves of those killed here in 1864. It is open year-round. Admission is free.

Return to Adair and US 69.

ADAIR

A prominent Cherokee family was honored when a name was selected for ADAIR (pop. 685).

The **Dalton gang**, led by Bob Dalton, robbed the evening train in Adair on July 15, 1892. The seven outlaws drove a wagon up to the depot and after commandeering the engine, backed their wagon up to the express car door. They looted a $17,000 shipment of currency on the Missouri, Kansas and Texas train. Word leaked out about the planned holdup and a posse of deputy marshals was on the train when it arrived at the station. A fierce gunfight ensued and three guards and a civilian were wounded and a bystander killed by a stray bullet. The Daltons escaped with the money. It is believed the loot is still buried in a cave near **Sand Springs** (Section 9).

It is nine miles to the county seat town of **Pryor**.

PRYOR

First designation for PRYOR (pop. 8,327) was **Coo-y-yah**. The post office was established in January, 1882, and in 1887 the name was changed to **Pryor Creek** (Creek was dropped in 1909).

The nearby creek was named for **Nathaniel Pryor**, scout for the Lewis and Clark expedition, Osage Indian trader and, later, Indian agent who settled here sometime after 1820.

COO-Y-YAH COUNTY MUSEUM, US 69 at 9th St., features historic items relating to Mayes County and artifacts of the Cherokee, Creek, and Osage Indian tribes. It is open from 1 to 4 p.m. Wednesday through Friday and Sunday. Admission is free.

PRYOR'S GRAVE is located in a cemetery 1.5 miles east of town on SH 20 and is marked with a Mayes County historical marker at the gravesite of Nathaniel Pryor. A War of 1812 veteran, Pryor, who died in 1830, is one of the first veterans of a U.S. war to be interred in Oklahoma. His grave has been moved from its original location near his home south of town on Pryor Creek.

A SIDE TRIP

Continue east on SH 20 for 8.5 miles to **Salina**.

SALINA

The first permanent white settlement in Oklahoma was at SALINA (pop. 1,153). This area was first visited in 1796 by a group of French traders and trappers led by **Major Jean Pierre Chouteau** of Missouri. Chouteau and his brother had long held a license to trade with the Osage Indians who lived in Missouri. They came southwest into this area in search of new business opportunities. Chouteau liked this spot on the wide, navigable river (called **Grand** in Oklahoma, Neosho in Kansas) and by 1802 established a trading post here.

Chouteau's son, **August Pierre**, took over the business in 1817 and in 1832 a guest in his large, two-story log home was **Washington Irving**, who was in Indian Territory to take "A Tour on the Prairies." Paradise trees on the south side of US 20 and on the east bank of the Grand River mark the homesite.

After the younger Chouteau's death in 1838, the settlement became known as the **Grand Saline** for the extensive salt works nearby (Salina is a variation). Cherokee chief **John Ross** and his brother, **Lewis**, acquired many of the Chouteau holdings. The Rosses built a large brick home in what is now a school yard along the highway and a historical marker is located here. The home was later used as the **Cherokee Orphan Asylum.** A stone blockhouse (NRHP) built by Ross encloses a spring used by the Chouteaus in the early days.

CHOUTEAU MEMORIAL (OHS), on E. Main, houses family artifacts. One of the Chouteau descendants is **Yvonne**

Chouteau Terekhov, Oklahoma City, one of Oklahoma's five internationally acclaimed Indian ballerinas. It is open from 9 a.m. to 5 p.m. Wednesday through Saturday and from 1 to 5 p.m. Sunday from November through April. It is also open Tuesdays, May through October. Admission is free.

Seven miles south of Salina, on SH 82, is **Locust Grove**.

LOCUST GROVE

This old Cherokee Nation settlement was established in 1872 and took its name from a nearby grove of trees. LOCUST GROVE (pop. 1,326) was the home of famed Native American artisan and sculptor **Willard Stone**.

STONE MUSEUM, one mile east of town on US 412, is maintained by the family and features the works of Willard Stone as well as those of his three sons, also sculptors, and of other family members. Oldest son, **Jason Stone**, is a Master Artist of the Five Civilized Tribes as was his late father.

BATTLE OF LOCUST GROVE is identified by a historical marker in a bank driveway on US 412. This July 3, 1862, skirmish took place on a ridge near the south edge of town when a detachment of 300 Union soldiers surprised a Confederate camp. After a day of fighting, Confederate **Col. J. J. Clarkson** surrendered along with the members of his force still in the area. In addition to the 110 Confederates, the Yankees also captured 60 wagons of ammunition and salt, 64 mule teams, and other provisions.

Leave Locust Grove going west on US 412 for 11 miles to Chouteau and US 69.

CHOUTEAU

The town of CHOUTEAU (pop. 1,771) was established October 18, 1871, and named for the Chouteau family. The settlement began when the MK&T railroad was built through the area.

Southeast of town is the site of **Union Mission**, first mission and school established in Indian Territory. A historical marker for the mission is located two miles south of the US 69/412 junction south of Chouteau, near the turnoff to the east on a black top road to the site.

A SIDE TRIP

UNION MISSION (NRHP) was established November, 1820. Follow the road almost three miles to a dirt road turnoff to the southeast. The mission was at an almost right angle curve in the road a scant mile. A stone marker on a small hill on the east side

This marker at Chouteau commemorates Union Mission, founded in 1820 by the Rev. Epaphras Chapman to become the first mission in Oklahoma. The first press was established here and the first book printed in 1835 by the Rev. Samuel A. Worcester.

of the road marks the spot. The mission buildings were grouped around the spring 300 yards southeast of the marker where several foundation stones can be found. Nearby is a marker put up by the Oklahoma Library Association honoring Union Mission as the site of the state's first printing press. It was installed in the vacant mission buildings (the mission had been relocated to Hopefield) in 1835 by **Rev. Samuel Austin Worcester** who moved his printing operation to Park Hill (Section 8) in 1837.

CHAPMAN GRAVE. Located across the road from the mission site, under a shelter erected by the OHS, is the grave of **Rev. Epaphras Chapman**, the Presbyterian minister who established the mission. Chapman, 35, died of typhus, June 7, 1825, and his is one of the oldest marked burial sites in Oklahoma.

Back on US 69, it is 12 miles to **Wagoner** in **Wagoner County**. Both are believed to have been named for a popular Parsons, Kansas, MK&T railroad dispatcher known as **"Big Foot" Wagoner**.

WAGONER

The town of WAGONER (pop. 6,894) was settled in 1886 at the place the **Kansas and Arkansas Valley Railway** (later the **Iron Mountain**, now the **Union Pacific**) met the MK&T in 1890. The town still has many well-kept, territorial era homes and business buildings and many of these are marked by plaques near the street.

COURTHOUSE construction began in 1940 and was completed using a federal relief work force funded through the Works Progress Administration.

OKLAHOMA HISTORICAL FASHIONS INC., 810 N. State, is one of two fashion museums in Wagoner. It features "fabulous fashions from the past." It is open from 10 a.m. to 4 p.m. Monday through Saturday and from 1 to 4 p.m. Sundays. An admission is charged.

ORIGINAL HISTORICAL FASHION HOUSE MUSEUM, 804 E. Cherokee, is also a textile research center. The museum features original clothing from the early 1800s to the present. The museum is in the 1902 home built by a school teacher from Ohio, **George Strawn**. The ornate carved woodwork, furnishings, and hangings are original. It is open from 10 a.m. to 3 p.m. Wednesday through Saturday and from 2 to 4 p.m. Sundays. An admission is charged.

ALTERNATE ROUTE

Leave Wagoner going south on SH 16 which is the old US 69.

The present US 69 is a four-lane road a few miles west. It is 10 miles to **Okay**.

OKAY

One of the older settlements in the state is OKAY (pop. 528) which might also hold the record as the town having the most names. A trading post was established about half a mile south, near the Okay end of the bridge over the **Verdigris River,** early in the 1800s. The post was sold to Col. A. P. Chouteau (see Salina) in 1810. This was a busy spot because it was near the place where the Verdigris, Arkansas, and Grand Rivers converge. Through the years the settlement was known by many names: **Falls City, Verdigris Falls, Verdigris Landing, Creek Agency, Sleepyville,** and **Three Forks**, the latter a name by which this entire area was known. During the Civil War the settlement was devastated by the guerilla fighting between the northern and southern factions that divided the Creeks and Cherokees. The town was rebuilt at its present site and more names followed including **Coretta Switch, North Muskogee, Rex,** and finally, **Okay**.

THREE FORKS MARKER, at the east end of the river bridge, commemorates the Texas Road, old trading post, Three Forks Landing, Osage and Creek Agencies, Washington Irving's visit, and Wigwam Neosho. The marker was erected by the Daughters of the American Revolution.

WIGWAM NEOSHO. Between this spot and **Fort Gibson**, a few miles southeast on the Grand River, stood the trading post established in 1829 by ex-Tennessee governor **Sam Houston**. Houston and his Cherokee wife, **Diana Rogers**, entertained many famous guests during the four years he was here including Washington Irving. By a special act of the Cherokee Council in 1829, Houston, called **Colonah** (The Raven) by his friends, was formally adopted into the tribe. He left here in 1832 and went to Texas. Diana remained behind.

In 1904 the remains of a woman thought to be Houston's wife were taken to Fort Gibson National Cemetery (Section 8) for reburial beneath a stone reading "Talihina R. — wife of Gen. Sam Houston." In recent years historians have begun to doubt this is her grave. They think it may be the grave of one of two other Cherokee women, all three of whom have been called by variations of a name such as Tiana, Tyania, Tyhana, and Talihina. All three woman also had a connection with one of the five men named John Rogers connected with the Cherokee tribe at that time. Diana Rogers, who died in November of 1838, was the daughter of one. Perhaps at some future date this historic mystery will be solved.

CHIEF PUSHMATAHA. Also east of this spot is the site where a hunting party of Choctaws, led by **Chief Pushmataha**, attacked the camp of Indian trader **Joseph Bogy**. Bogy later tried, unsuccessfully, to sue the tribe for the $9,000 in lost goods. Pushmataha is buried in the Congressional Cemetery in Washington, D.C.

SH 16 goes into the north part of Muskogee and US 69 is three miles west of the SH 16/US 62 junction in **Muskogee County**.

A short distance east of this junction is **Bacone College**.

BACONE COLLEGE. In the early 1880s, **Rev. A. C. Bacone** received permission from the Creek Council to move Indian University from Tahlequah to Muskogee. The name of the school was later changed to honor Bacone. Originally a seat of higher education just for Indians, enrollment is now open to all. Many of Oklahoma's best-known Indian artists received their schooling here. A leisurely drive or stroll through the small campus is recommended as there are many signs and monuments of interest to be seen and read.

MUSKOGEE

Established in 1872 with the arrival of the MK&T railroad, MUSKOGEE (pop. 37,708) and the county were named for the Muskogee (Creek) Indians whose forced emigration to this area from Alabama began in 1829. The original Creek Agency was established near here. When the government located the **Union Agency** of the Five Civilized Tribes (Choctaw, Chickasaw, Cherokee, Creek, and Seminole) in the city (1874) its future was assured. More than a score of NRHP properties attest to Muskogee's pre-statehood importance.

The visitor is well advised to make a leisurely loop of two main thoroughfares, **Broadway** and **Okmulgee Streets**, to get a feel for the old city as the parallel streets take in both the pre-statehood commercial district and some of the older, tree-shaded residential areas. There is a pamphlet prepared by the Historical Preservation Committee listing some of these historic homes with a map showing locations. Though most are private homes and can only be viewed from the street, they are still of interest to visitors. The Chamber of Commerce, 425 Boston, is a good place to stop for area information.

The Thomas-Foreman home, built by a judge appointed to the Indian Territory in 1897, is shown above. The old Union Agency building (below) today houses the Five Civilized Tribes Museum in Muskogee. The two story building was completed in 1876.

THOMAS-FOREMAN HOME (NRHP and OHS), 1419 W. Okmulgee, is one historic home open for visitors. In this house lived two of Oklahoma's most respected historians, **Grant and Carolyn Foreman.** The house was built by Mrs. Foreman's father, **Judge John Robert Thomas**, a congressman from Illinois who was appointed Judge-at-Large for Indian Territory in 1897. It is open only during the Azalea Festival, first three weeks in April, from 10 a.m. to 4 p.m. Admission is free.

WAR MEMORIAL PARK, Port of Muskogee, north of US 62 on the east side of town. Located here is the *USS Batfish*, a 312-foot World War II submarine which holds the record for sinking the most enemy subs in a single patrol--three in 72 hours. Adjacent is a military museum with artifacts from World War II through Vietnam. It is open from 9 a.m. to 5 p.m. Monday through Saturday; and from 1 to 5 p.m. Sundays from March 15 to October 15. An admission is charged.

FIVE CIVILIZED TRIBES MUSEUM (NRHP), Honor Heights Drive on Agency Hill, is housed in the old **Union Agency** building, a two-story sandstone structure completed in 1876 when the five civilized tribes consolidated their agencies. The museum includes art and artifacts from each of the tribes. It is open from 10 a.m. to 5 p.m. Monday through Saturday and from 1 to 5 p.m. Sunday. An admission is charged.

NOTABLES: Among the well-known who have lived in Muskogee are jazz guitarist **Barney Kessel**, Indian artists **Jerome** and **Johnny Tiger**, and the only woman sent to the U.S. Congress from Oklahoma (1920) **Alice Mary Robertson.**

It is 11 miles south on US 69 to the Oktaha-Rentiesville exit. Historian **John Hope Franklin** was born in Rentiesville. Between these two settlements, east of the highway, was fought what historians consider to be the largest and most important of the 89 combat actions in Indian Territory during the Civil War.

BATTLE OF HONEY SPRINGS (site NRHP and OHS), occurred July 17, 1863. Union **Gen. J. G. Blunt**, with 3,000 men, attacked a Confederate force of 6,000 led by **Gen. D. H. Cooper** encamped on **Elk Creek**. The Confederates, sustaining heavy losses, withdrew. In recent years the OHS has staged two re-enactments of this battle and because of its popularity plans to continue this every two or three years. The pavilion is open year-round and contains several markers honoring Union, Confederate, Black, and Indian soldiers who participated in the battle.

Back on US 69 it is five miles to Checotah.

This monument in Oktaha Cemetery near Muskogee honors the Confederate soldiers of the Honey Springs Battle fought July 17, 1863. In this engagement the Confederates suffered heavy casualties and were forced to withdraw.

A trooper particpating at a re-enactment of the Battle of Honey Springs. The Oklahoma Historical Society stages these popular re-enactments. Several markers here honor Confederate, Union, Black and Indian troops taking part in the battle.

CHECOTAH

A post office was established here in 1886, named for the last fullblood chief of the Creek Nation, **Samuel Checote**. CHECOTAH (pop. 3,290) tried for the county seat of **McIntosh County** (named for a well-known Creek family) twice after statehood. At one point a group of citizens even traveled to Eufaula by train to "steal" the government but were stopped by the forewarned folks of Eufaula.

HISTORIC DISTRICT (NRHP). This area is on Gentry Ave. between West 1st and West Main and on Broadway between Lafayette and Spaulding.

KATY DEPOT CENTER, north of I-40 at the US 69/266 junction, includes the museum housed in the MK&T Depot built in 1890 and recently relocated here. Exhibits include railroad memorabilia. Outside is a Union Pacific caboose. It is open from 1 to 5 p.m. Sunday or by appointment, 918/473-6377. Admission is free.

South of Checotah where US 69 crosses Lake Eufaula, there is a granite Oklahoma Historical Society marker for the **Green Corn Dance**, one of the most colorful Indian events held in Oklahoma. This dance ushers in the new year and was one of the major annual events of the Creek Nation. Symbolic bundles of sticks were sent to tribal members by the chief to invite them to attend. Fines were levied on those who failed to respond to the call. Dances, ball games, songs, and religious rites were all part of the celebration.

Fourteen miles south is the county seat town of **Eufaula**.

EUFAULA

The name for EUFAULA (pop. 2,652) was taken from an old Creek town in Alabama. Settlement in this area began shortly after the Creeks began moving in from the east in 1836. **North Fork Town** was the name of the population center established two miles east of present Eufaula near the juncture of the **North and South Canadian Rivers**. The Texas Road and a branch of the **California Road** crossed here adding importance to the town. **Asbury Methodist Mission School** was located two miles north. These sites are now covered by the water of **Lake Eufaula** but a historic marker on US 69 Business Route on the north side of town commemorates them. When the MK&T arrived in 1872 the residents and businesses at the Creek settlement moved west to the present location to meet the railroad.

ALEXANDER POSEY, the famous Creek poet, was born a few miles southwest of the city park in 1873. A marker in the park, half a mile east of the US 69/SH 9 junction, commemorates his achievements. Besides being a man of letters, Posey took an active part in tribal government. He died in a flood on the North Canadian River near Eufaula in 1908. Posey was for a time editor of the *Indian Journal*, founded at Muskogee in 1876 as a tribal newspaper. Still being published in Eufaula, it is the state's oldest newspaper.

JEROME TIGER, Creek and Seminole Indian, was born in 1941 and reared on the campgrounds surrounding his grandfather's Indian Baptist Church near Eufaula. A high school dropout, street and ring fighter, and a laborer he was nonetheless one of the most talented of Indian artists. Although he had little formal training he could draw virtually anything and between 1962 and 1967 he produced hundreds of paintings. He died in 1967 at the age of 26 of a gunshot wound.

COURTHOUSE (NRHP), constructed in 1927, replaced an earlier structure destroyed by fire. Two county seat elections were held, in 1908 and 1909, to establish a winner in the rivalry between Eufaula, Checotah, and **Stidham**. Although Checotah received the most votes each time, it did not get a majority so Eufaula retained the seat of government.

HISTORIC DISTRICT (NRHP), Main St. between Pine and Grand Sts., was placed on the register in 1988. In 1987 Eufaula became an official Main Street City.

BELLE STARR, the notorious outlaw queen, lived in this area. The rugged countryside in this area with trees, caves, and river valleys provided a perfect setting for those on the fly from the law. Belle Starr's friends included the **Jameses**, the **Youngers**, the **Reeds,** and the **Daltons**. Belle lived east of Eufaula (where she often shopped) near **Porum** in the **Younger's Bend** area. Born Myra Belle Shirley in Carthage, Missouri, in 1848, she had an illegitimate child by the outlaw Cole Younger and then married Jim Reed, a horse thief. Upon his death, she moved to Indian Territory and became involved in all kinds of illegal enterprises. Here she met and married Cherokee outlaw Sam Starr. After his untimely death in 1886, Belle married Jim July, a Creek Indian. She was ambushed by an unidentified assailant on a lonely road not far from her hideout at Younger's Bend on February 3, 1889. Her grave is located here in a difficult to locate spot on backroads.

It is 28 miles to McAlester.

A few miles north of this seat of **Pittsburg County** (named for the town in Pennsylvania but not spelled the same) was the settlement of **Bugtussle**. Also known as **Flowery-Mound**, this was the boyhood home of the **Hon. Carl Albert**, now of McAlester, Speaker of the U.S. House of Representatives from 1971 to 1977. A granite OHS marker is located two blocks north of the corner of Electric Ave. and A St. in **McAlester**, the birthplace of Albert.

This is the grave east of Eufaula of the "Outlaw Queen" Belle Starr. She was killed in an ambush in February, 1889. Her grave is not easy to find.

McALESTER

The crossing of the Texas Road and the California Road made a perfect spot for **James J. McAlester** to establish his store (in a tent) in 1870. As he was married to a Chickasaw, McAlester was automatically a citizen of the Choctaw Nation (as the tribes owned land in common, members of each tribe enjoyed the benefits of citizenship in both). As a citizen McAlester was able to mine the coal from a lease he bought near here and he is credited with being the one to discover coal in this county. A year or two after McAlester opened his store, the MK&T built through, the first railroad in Indian Territory. When the **Choctaw Coal and Railway Company** made its junction with the MK&T two miles farther south in 1889, the original settlement became known as **North McAlester** and the railroad junction became McAlester (pop. 16,370).

McALESTER CONSISTORY (NRHP) is the headquarters for the International Order of Rainbow for Girls, started in McAlester in 1922. It is housed in the Scottish Rite Masonry and Rainbow Temple, Adams and 2nd. A 170-foot copper sphere crowns the block-long structure.

McALESTER HOUSE (NRHP), 14 E. Smith, is the recently restored mansion of James J. McAlester who served as lieutenant governor of the state 1911-1915.

TOBUCKSY COUNTY COURTHOUSE, N. Main and Park, was constructed in 1876 and served as the courthouse for Tobucksy County of the Choctaw Nation until statehood.

PITTSBURG COUNTY COURTHOUSE (NRHP), Washington Ave., was begun in 1926. Most unique feature is the U-shaped, recessed front entrance.

McALESTER BUILDING FOUNDATION, 220 E. Adams, features exhibits reflecting life in the late 19th and early 20th century. Included is a mining section. It is open from 9 a.m. to noon Monday through Friday. Admission is free.

PITTSBURG COUNTY GENEALOGICAL/HISTORICAL SOCIETY, 113 E. Carl Albert Pkwy, displays mining tools and an old walk-in vault. Also on site is a genealogy library. It is open from 9 a.m. to 3 p.m. Monday through Friday. Admission is free.

Three miles south of the city limits on US 69 is a historical marker for Perryville, a trading post established by **James Perry** in 1849. During the Civil War a Confederate military post and supply depot was located here. After the Battle of Honey Springs, Maj. Gen. James G. Blunt and his federal force attacked here

August 25, 1863. The Confederates withdrew and the Union troops destroyed the supplies.

It is 40 miles to **Atoka**, seat of **Atoka County**, both named for **Captain Atoka**, a Choctaw sub-chief. Enroute, nine miles south of Kiowa, is the settlement of **Limestone Gap** named for a break in the limestone ridge. Choctaw Lighthorseman **Captain Charles LeFlore** lived here and operated a ferry across **Buck Creek**. A portion of the L-shaped house (NRHP) he built is still standing. Two miles south is the village of **Chockie**, originally named **Chickiechockie** for LeFlore's daughters who had been named for the nationalities of their parents (Chickasaw and Choctaw). Chickie married **Lee Cruce**, who was the second governor of Oklahoma.

Born in Chockie was singer **Reba McEntire.**

ATOKA

In 1867, **Rev. J. S. Murrow**, Baptist missionary, established a settlement here and then **Atoka Baptist Academy.** Oklahoma's first Catholic Church was built in ATOKA (pop.

West of Atoka, in the Clarita area, is Oklahoma's Amish Country. This is a contemporary photograph taken in this rural area.

147

3,298) in 1872. First resident priest was **Fr. Isidore Robot** who founded Sacred Heart Mission (Section 13). A historical marker is located in front of the Catholic Church on US 69 near the south edge of town.

MIDDLE BOGGY RIVER BATTLE SITE (NRHP), north side of Atoka on US 69 (usually known as **Muddy Boggy River**), is the site of a Civil War battle. An engagement was fought here February 13, 1864, when Union **Major Charles Willette** and three companies of the 14th Kansas Cavalry came upon a poorly-armed Confederate encampment along Old Boggy Depot Road. In an hour of fighting, 47 Confederates were killed and many others wounded. A Confederate cemetery is located at this site.

CONFEDERATE MEMORIAL MUSEUM, near the cemetery, features memorabilia from the battle. It is open from 10 a.m. to 3 p.m. Monday through Saturday. Admission is free.

Clyde Barrow, Raymond Hamilton and another gangster friend stopped at a barn dance in Stringtown, north of Atoka, on August 5, 1932. Ray Hamilton wanted to stop off and dance for awhile. As the three men were sitting and drinking in their car outside the dance hall the county sheriff and a deputy approached. The gangster opened fire wounding the sheriff and killing Deputy Gene Moore. Clyde and his friends easily escaped in the confusion that followed. Although some accounts of this incident claim Bonnie Parker was also present, reliable sources stated she was in Dallas at the time.

ALTERNATE ROUTE

Leave Atoka going west on SH 7 south of town. Ten miles west, just across **Clear Boggy Creek** is the turn, south, to **Boggy Depot State Park**. The park is on the site of the old town of Boggy Depot (NRHP). New Boggy Depot is two miles farther south.

OLD BOGGY DEPOT

This settlement began in 1837 when **Cyrus Harris**, future Chickasaw Nation governor, built a log cabin on the divide between Clear Boggy and **Sandy Creek**. It was first designated "the depot on the Boggy," where the Indians came to collect their government annuities. For over three decades it was one of the most important settlements in Indian Territory.

A church was built in 1840 by **Rev. Cyrus Kingsbury**, called the Father of the Choctaw Missions. In 1859 the church served for a time as the Choctaw Capitol. An early Masonic

This monument marks the site of the Boggy Depot on the Butterfield Overland Mail route.

Lodge in the state was chartered here in 1869 and a granite monument in the park marks the location and lists names of original members.

Boggy Depot received a post office with rural mail routes in 1848 and in 1858 it became a stop on the Butterfield Overland mail route (Section 11) from St. Louis to San Francisco.

Several fine, two-story homes were built here. That of Choctaw Chief **Allen Wright** stood until 1952. Wright is the man who suggested the name "Oklahoma" for a proposed Indian

Territory. When the federal government decided to join Oklahoma and Indian Territories into one state in 1907, the name was selected for the state. Still to be seen in this camping and recreation spot are traces of old streets, several signs marking important sites, and the cemetery. Among those buried here are Wright and Kingsbury, a Presbyterian missionary.

Back on SH 7, west seven miles, is the town of **Wapanucka** (pop. 402) in **Johnston County** (named for **Douglas A. Johnston**, governor of the Chickasaw Nation). **Wapanucka Female Manual Labor School** (site NRHP) was established in 1852 a few miles northwest on **Delaware Creek**. It was one of the first schools in the Chickasaw Nation. Wapanucka is a Delaware Indian word meaning "eastern people." A group of Delawares lived in the Choctaw Nation.

It is 13 miles to the junction with US 377. Nine miles south is **Tishomingo**.

TISHOMINGO

Seat of Johnston County is TISHOMINGO (pop. 3,116), named for a Chickasaw chief. Settlement began in 1850 at a

The Johnston County Courthouse in Tishomingo once served as the Chickasaw National Capitol.

campsite called **Good Springs.** Soon **Jackson Frazier** built a home here, then a store or two appeared. In 1851 the **Chickasaw Manual Labor School** opened a few miles southeast. When the Chickasaws won the right to a separate government from the Choctaws in 1855, they established their capital in the new settlement.

The first capitol was a log building, the second a brick structure that burned. The ornate structure still standing was constructed for the tribe in 1898. After statehood, when the frame Johnston County Courthouse burned, the Chickasaw National Capitol Building was purchased and is still used for county government. In the yard is a marker honoring the first Corn Club of 50 boys in Oklahoma, established here in 1909. In 1910 the Tomato Canning Club for girls was organized. The Corn Club and Tomato Canning Club were forerunners of the 4-H Club.

CHICKASAW NATIONAL CAPITOLS (NRHP), on Capitol Ave. Both the log structure and the third building are located here. The log building is inside a museum on the east side of the square. Other exhibits highlight the culture of the Chickasaws from 1540 to the present. The museum is open from 9 a.m. to 5 p.m. Tuesday through Friday and from 2 to 5 p.m. weekends. Admission is free.

CHICKASAW BANK MUSEUM, 413 W. Main, is open from 9 a.m. to 3 p.m. weekdays. Admission is free. The interior has been restored on this banking facility used by the Chickasaws from 1901 to 1907.

TISHOMINGO CEMETERY, 600 S. Murray, is one of the older cemeteries in the state. Many well-known Oklahomans are buried here including William H. "Alfalfa Bill" Murray, a governor of the state (1931-1935). Murray, who was married to a niece of Douglas Johnston, also presided over the Constitutional Convention of 1906-07. Two counties, Murray and Alfalfa, are named for him. His son, **Johnston Murray**, also was a state governor (1951-55). **Murray State College**, located in Tishomingo, was not named for Bill Murray but for his brother, **Shade.**

Leave town on SH 78 east, three miles to the junction with SH 22. Thirteen miles southeast is **Fort Washita** (NRHP).

FORT WASHITA HISTORIC SITE

In the summer of 1841 **Gen. Zachary Taylor** was sent out to find a site for a new military outpost to protect the Choctaws and Chickasaws from the raiding Plains tribes. This isolated post, 80 miles west of the nearest fort, was occupied in April, 1842, and closed in 1861. It was named for the river. Among the well-known who served here were **Gen. Taylor, Captains Randolph B. Marcy** and **George B. McClellan, Gen. William G. Belknap,** and **Col. Braxton Bragg.**

The visitor can see ruins, including cobbled roads, of the old fort and some reconstruction. On display is the **Cooper Cabin** belonging to **Brig. Gen. Douglas Cooper.** The cabin was built by Cooper when he served as Indian agent for the Choctaws and Chickasaws in the 1850s, at the time it was located about three fourths of a mile away at Government Springs. After the Civil War, in 1867, Cooper had the cabin moved up the hill to its present location and lived here until he died in 1879. Although the fort had ceased to function as any kind of military installation by 1865, it was still listed by the Army as an active post until 1870.

According to a spokesman at the interpretive center at the fort, the Cooper Cabin was occupied continuously by various families until 1962 when the fort site was purchased by the Oklahoma Historical Society.

"In fact," he added, "if I could gather everyone up who has told me over the years they have lived in that cabin or was born in that cabin, I would have quite a group here."

Signs are placed at most spots of interest, and the visitor center has a map of the area with more detailed information. It is open from 9 a.m. to 5 p.m. weekdays and from 2 to 5 p.m. weekends. Admission is free.

Durant and US 69 are 12 miles east, via SH 78 and 48. North on US 69 ten miles is **Caddo** (pop. 918), a Choctaw court town. In 1890 the largest cotton market in Indian Territory was located here.

CADDO INDIAN TERRITORY MUSEUM/LIBRARY, 110 Buffalo, houses pioneer items, Indian artifacts, and a library. It is open from 8 a.m. to noon and from 1 to 3 p.m. Monday through Saturday; until 4 p.m. during the month of July. Admission is free.

For more historic sites to visit in the Durant area see Section 15.

SECTION 8
US 62

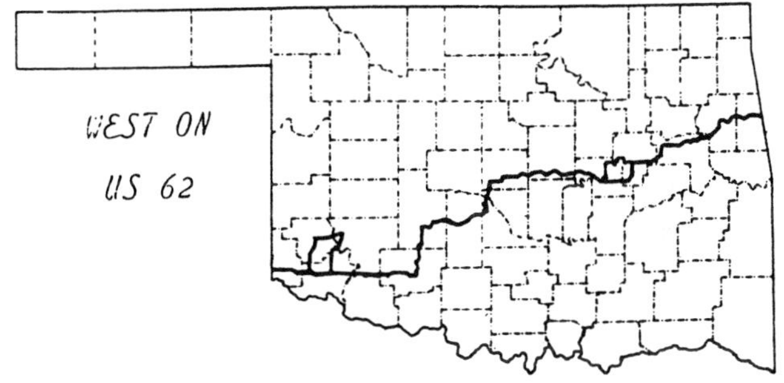

The only National Cemetery in Oklahoma is located at Fort Gibson. Flags are flown at half staff 30 minutes before and after a burial in all National Cemeteries.

US 62

If one were to select an official "Indian Highway" for Oklahoma, it would have to be US 62. Along the 412 miles of the road, which runs from Arkansas to the Texas Panhandle, lie the one-time homelands of three of the Five Civilized Tribes and eight other Indian tribes.

The highway passes through the one-time capitals of the Cherokee and Creek Nations. In Muskogee and Anadarko it serves the two cities from which area administrators of the Bureau of Indian Affairs oversee the lives of the 175,000 members of the state's 35 resident tribes.

Still, US 62 is ecumenical. In the Okmulgee area the route passes through a number of small, nearly all-black towns and scattered communities. They were settled by slaves freed by the Creeks in a curious aftermath of the Civil War when, as citizens of the Creek Nation, they were given allotments along with the Indians. Subsequently, their numbers were swelled by blacks brought from the South by developers, often working with railroads anxious to exploit the rich agricultural potential.

Also on the route is "Old Oklahoma"—officially the Unassigned Lands in the central part of the state—an area not given to any Indian nation or tribe and opened to all comers, April 22, 1889. The area was originally given to the Creeks and Seminoles but taken back after the Civil War.

Today, it boasts the state's capital city as well as a clutch of smaller communities, several of which still reflect the German, Bohemian, and other ethnic backgrounds of their first settlers.

WEST ON US 62

This trip begins at the Oklahoma-Arkansas state line in Adair County and ends in the southwestern corner of the state west of Hollis. Included are one short alternate route and one long alternate route trip in southwestern Oklahoma for those interested in learning more about history of this area.

WESTVILLE

WESTVILLE (pop. 1,374) lies two miles inside the Oklahoma-Arkansas boundary, on the edge of the heavily wooded **Cherokee Hills**. It has been an important lumbering town since its establishment in 1895 with construction of the Kansas City, Pittsburg, and Gulf Railroad (name changed to Kansas City

Southern in 1900). The name honors **Samuel D. West,** a local resident. At statehood the town was made the seat of Adair County (for a prominent Cherokee family). It lost that status three years later to **Stilwell.** On the west side of town along the highway is the ornate **Westville School,** a WPA project featuring stone and three kinds of brick.

At the west edge of town US 62 crosses US 59 and here is a historical marker noting the establishment, in 1839 by **Rev. Jesse Bushyhead**, of a Baptist Mission. **Bacone College** (Section 7) is an outgrowth of this mission school. Bushyhead is buried near the original site of the Baptist Mission Church, about three miles north on SH 59. He was the first Supreme Court Judge of the Cherokee Nation West, before his death in 1844.

Thirteen miles beyond Westville is the community of **Proctor.**

PROCTOR

PROCTOR'S sole claim to fame is the man for whom it was named, Ezekiel Proctor, and the bloody episode in history in which he starred. The so-called **Goingsnake Massacre** erupted in May, 1872. It was the wildest shoot-out in the history of law enforcement in pre-statehood Oklahoma. Proctor was being tried in tribal court for the murder of **Polly Chesterton** at **Hildebrand's Mill** near Flint (Section 11).

The trial, at Goingsnake Schoolhouse just south of Proctor, was underway when federal officials from Fort Smith arrived in response to a complaint from the victim's husband that the Cherokee judicial system was moving too slowly. With both sides tense, wary, and heavily armed, action picked up considerably. When the shooting died down, seven officers were dead, along with the court clerk. Wounded were the judge and Proctor. Curiously enough, all indictments and charges were eventually dropped. With time, Proctor's law-abiding life led to his becoming Flint District sheriff and member of the Cherokee National Council.

West of Proctor, which is on the **Cherokee County** line (named for the Indian tribe), US 62 ducks and bobs its way for 12 miles through the pleasantly wooded Cherokee Hills. The route offers a soaring vista of the **Baron Fork River** and then, topping one last crest drops down into the **Illinois River Valley.** The Illinois is protected as one of Oklahoma's Scenic Rivers. US 62 intersects SH 10 three miles east of **Tahlequah.** The section of SH 10 between this junction and the town of **Kansas,** 26 miles north, has been designated the **Illinois River Scenic Drive.**

TAHLEQUAH

Mecca to the more than 50,000 Cherokees living in north-eastern Oklahoma is TAHLEQUAH (pop. 10,398). It became the capital of the Cherokee Nation in 1839. With statehood in 1907 its political status was reduced to that of Cherokee County seat but its handsome **Cherokee Capitol** (OHS), built in 1870, continued to serve as county courthouse until the 1980s. Tribal affairs are now conducted at the Cherokee Nation Tribal Complex south of town.

In the heart of Tahlequah and feature of its Main Street project, Cherokee Square now surrounds the restored capitol building, which houses the Tahlequah Chamber of Commerce

The Cherokee National Supreme Court was built in 1844 at Tahlequah.

These columns at Park Hill, near Tahlequah, are all that's left of the first Cherokee National Female Seminary. The seminary burned in 1887. In the background is the Cherokee Museum Complex (Tsa La Gi).

Visitor Center. On the lawn are several monuments. One honors one of the state's oldest newspapers, *The Cherokee Advocate* begun in 1848, and one, the installation of the state's first telephone connected for service in September of 1888. It also was the first telephone in the Mississippi Valley west of St. Louis. The massive drinking water fountain was put in place in 1913 as

Plans call for rebuilding the Bacone College chapel (shown above), destroyed by fire during the winter of 1991.

a memorial to "Our Confederate Dead" by the local chapter of the Daughters of the Confederacy. Nearby is a memorial to "Veterans of All Wars," a 1950 Boy Scouts of America Miss Liberty, and a sign telling of the establishment of a Masonic Lodge in 1848. Large granite markers on the grounds honor **John Ross**, principal chief of the Cherokees from 1828 to 1866, and Confederate brigadier general **Stand Watie**, who was a Cherokee.

Other downtown Cherokee Nation buildings, both on the NRHP as is the capitol, are the old **Supreme Court Building** (dating from 1844), Keetoowah and Water Ave., and the onetime **Cherokee National Prison** (1874), Choctaw and Water. Also of special interest in the downtown area are the windows and street signs which use the Cherokee written language.

Just north of the business district is **Northeastern Oklahoma State University** and yet another reminder of the city's rich Cherokee heritage. When the **Cherokee National Female Seminary** (established in 1851) burned in 1887 at nearby **Park Hill**, the Nation decided to rebuild in Tahlequah. **Seminary Hall** (NRHP) was constructed in 1888. The state took over the seminary in 1909, making it first a normal school, then a college, and finally NEOSU. Through all the changes Seminary Hall has served as an administration building.

There are two other NRHP properties in Tahlequah. At 121 E. Smith is the **Dr. Irwin D. Loeser Log Cabin**, one of the City's oldest structures, listed on the Historic American Buildings Survey. At 320 Academy is the two-story residence in which **Indian University** was established in 1879. Moved to MUSKOGEE (see Section 7) in 1885, the school still plays a strong role in Indian education and culture as **Bacone College**. The building was deeded to NEOSU in 1988 for use, after restoration, by the Native American Student Association.

Twelve miles southeast of Tahlequah is the Rabbit Trapp community where Ned Christie, a Cherokee, had his log fortification built to protect himself and his family. For five years lawmen tried to capture or kill Christie for a crime recent research indicates he never committed. For almost 100 years Christie, a blacksmith, gunsmith, and member of the Executive Committee of the Cherokee National Council, has been labeled a vicious, cold-blooded killer, a horse thief, a bootlegger, train robber and outlaw. Many of the activities he was accused of were proven to be done by other people. Many others occurred only in the fertile minds of "dime" novel and Western adventure magazine authors and movie and television script writers. A carefully researched biography of Christie published in 1990 seems to offer the proof needed to clear his reputation of almost all charges.

A little over one mile south of Tahlequah on US 62 is a historical marker calling attention to Riley's Chapel, built in 1843 by **Rev. Thomas Bertholf** to replace an earlier structure built in 1833 to honor Bertholf's mother-in-law's family. The first annual meeting of the Indian Mission Conference of the Methodist Church was held here on October 23, 1844.

Also in this vicinity stood the **Cherokee Male Seminary** which burned in 1910.

A mile farther is the road (east, then south) to **Tsa-La-Gi** Cherokee Heritage Center, a tribally operated complex in a natural woods setting

TSA-LA-GI ANCIENT VILLAGE is a meticulously authentic re-creation of a 17th century Cherokee settlement. A living museum, Cherokee guides help visitors turn back the calendar three centuries as other Cherokees, young and old, go through their daily activities, creating baskets and pots, crafting weapons, preparing food, and playing games. It is open from 10 a.m. to 6 p.m. Monday through Saturday; from 1 to 6 p.m. Sundays, from mid-May through August. An admission is charged.

CHEROKEE NATIONAL MUSEUM/ADAMS CORNER utilizes the most modern techniques and technology to present the Cherokee story from man's arrival on the North American continent to the present. Exhibits include Indian artifacts, Native American art, and audio-visual presentations. The entrance to the museum is dramatized by three tall red brick columns, all that remains of the original Cherokee National Female Seminary located here. Adjacent to the museum is Adams Corner, a reconstruction of a small crossroads community typical of the Cherokee Nation in the 1875-1890 prestatehood era. It is open from 10 a.m. to 5 p.m. Monday through Saturday; from 1 to 5 p.m. Sundays during the winter months. During the summer it is open from 10 a.m. to 8 p.m. Monday through Saturday; from 1 to 6 p.m. Sundays. An admission is charged.

TSA-LA-GI THEATRE is an innovative outdoor amphitheater (with air-conditioning) completed in 1969. Nightly, except Sunday, from early June to late August, the colorful musical drama "Trail of Tears" tells the tragic story of the Cherokees' trek from the Southeast United States to present Oklahoma (1838-39) and their struggles to rebuild their lives and institutions in a new and unfamiliar wilderness setting. An admission is charged.

Back on US 62, veer to the left at the junction of US 62/SH 82 for a short detour back into the earliest recorded Oklahoma history. A few hundred yards south of the junction and on the left is Murrell Road. Follow it one mile to the **Murrell Home** in old Park Hill.

PARK HILL

Now a ghost town, PARK HILL was once the center of life in this part of the Cherokee Nation. **Rev. Samuel Austin Worcester** established his Park Hill Mission here along the Illinois River in 1836. **Park Hill Press** (historical marker at US 62/SH 82 junction) was founded in 1837, also by Rev. Worcester, and, in 1851, the Cherokee Female Seminary. Many important Cherokee families built fine homes in the area as did intermarried merchants like **George M. Murrell**. Murrell married a niece of **Chief John Ross** and for her, in 1844, he built the gracious two-story "Hunter's Home."

MURRELL HOME (NRHP, OHS, and National Historic Landmark) has been restored and authentically furnished to the period as a tribute to the gracious, genteel life that existed in Park Hill in its heyday.

Materials for this home were brought by river boat from New Orleans. The two-story house with its wine cellar and servants quarters certainly qualified as a mansion in the Indian Territory of 1845. This home was the scene of many socials which attracted the young officers at nearby Fort Gibson, eager to meet the belles of Tahlequah and Park Hill. Although this house managed to survive the turbulent Civil War years, almost all the surrounding houses, many as large and beautiful as this one, were destroyed.

The house is open from 9 a.m. to 5 p.m. Tuesday through Saturday; from 1 to 5 p.m. Sundays, May through October. It is closed on Tuesdays the rest of the year. Admission is free.

Also of interest in the vicinity are the **Worcester Cemetery** and the **Ross Cemetery**, both filled with ornate old monuments that represent a virtual "Who's Who" in the Cherokee Nation. Ask for directions at the Murrell Home.

Back on US 62 head west into Muskogee County (named for the Creek Indians, sometimes Muskogee for the Muskogean

162

These monuments honor Indian servicemen on the campus of Bacone College. The campus chapel appears in the background.

The Murrell Home Museum is located in Park Hill near Tahlequah. George Murrell called this house "Hunter's Home."

language they spoke). The route plunges directly into the so-called Cradle of Oklahoma History—the historic **Three Forks** area where the **Neosho** (Grand) and Verdigris Rivers join the **Arkansas. Fort Gibson** was established here in 1823, the first military post in Indian Territory, and for the next half-century most people or events affecting Oklahoma history had some tie with the fort. On the east side of the town are two cemeteries of importance and interest.

CHEROKEE NATIONAL CEMETERY (NRHP) was set aside by the Cherokee Nation in 1857. On a gentle, wooded hill overlooking the Arkansas River valley, its stones yield such well-known Cherokee names as **Ross**, **Rogers**, **Adair**, and **Bushyhead**. With the Nation dissolved in 1907 with statehood, the cemetery became the Fort Gibson town cemetery as well.

FORT GIBSON NATIONAL CEMETERY is located one mile north of US 62 and is the state's only national cemetery. To it in the 19th century were transferred the graves from other state military posts as they were abandoned. Among those

The Ross family plot is in the Cherokee National Cemetery at Fort Gibson. The Rosses were an important Cherokee family.

buried here are **Capt. Billy Bowlegs** of the Seminoles who fought on the Union side in the Civil War; Medal of Honor recipient **Pvt. John N. Reese**; **John Decatur**, brother of naval hero Stephen Decatur, and Indian artist **Acee Blue Eagle**.

Many legends are told about people buried here. One concerns **Mary Eliza Mix** who died in 1844 at the age of 51. She was supposed to have been a spy but for what war? She was born after the Revolution and died before the Civil War. She was 19 at the time of the War of 1812 but no documentation can be found to link her to that conflict. There are many versions of the story of **Vivia** (died 1870), the young woman who masqueraded as a man and joined the Army to be near her sweetheart. Finding her unfaithful lover with another she shot and killed him, or so one version of the story goes. For many years it was thought **Sam Houston's** Cherokee wife was buried here but is almost certain the woman buried by the stone reading "Talihina R—wife of Gen. Sam Houston" isn't **Diana Rogers**. The grounds are open daily

Elias Boudinot, a leader in the Cherokee Nation, is buried in Poulson Cemetery near Jay. This memorial stands in the Worcester Cemetery south of Tahlequah.

from 8 a.m. to 4:30 p.m. Admission is free.

FORT GIBSON

The town of FORT GIBSON (pop. 3,359), with its cluster of stone business buildings, began as a service town for Oklahoma's first and most important military post. Today it continues to serve the post as guardian of its historic relics.

FORT GIBSON MILITARY PARK includes a reconstruction of the original fort, a traditional four-sided affair protected by a high log stockade. The reconstruction was done in the 1930s by the National Fort Stockade Commission. There is much to be seen here in the various exhibits and displays. It is operated by the Oklahoma Historical Society. It is open from 9 a.m. to 6 p.m. weekdays, from 10 a.m. to 5 p.m. Saturdays, and from 1 to 5 p.m. Sundays. Admission is free.

This replica, built on the original site, stands on a bench overlooking the Grand (or Neosho) River to the west. The original fort was erected only 150 feet from the river, a swampy, disease-breeding location that prompted the move to the hills above when more permanent stone buildings replaced the rot-

This church bell from the Fort Gibson chapel, dating back to 1833, is displayed on the porch of this reconstructed building at the old fort.

ting log structures.

Throughout the town and fort area bright blue signs mark a historical tour. Along the way sites of the first hotel and theatre are noted along with the many relics of the fort including the two-story reconstructed barracks, post bakers, well, and adjutant's office.

Among the well-known who sheltered at Fort Gibson were

three future presidents, **Lt. Jefferson Davis** (Confederacy), **Gen. Zachary Taylor** (United States) and **Sam Houston** (Republic of Texas). **Capt. Nathan Boone**, son of the famous frontiersman, Daniel Boone, also was stationed at the fort and between 1867 and 1873 several companies of the famed **Buffalo Soldiers** of the 10th Cavalry were here. The fort and its buildings are now registered as a National Historic Landmark and as individual properties on the NRHP.

Three miles southwest of Fort Gibson, US 62 crosses the McClellan-Kerr Arkansas River Navigation System completed in 1971 which connects the Port of Catoosa near Tulsa with the seaports of the world. To the right is the Port of Muskogee (Section 7)and just beyond the city of Muskogee. Eight miles west of Muskogee on US 62 a road strikes north one mile to a deadend at **Taft**.

TAFT

A predominantly black community, TAFT (pop. 400) dates back only to 1902 but its reason for being is rooted in the Civil War after which many one-time slaves of the Creeks were granted allotments in this area.

The town was originally called **Twine**, for the black leader, **W. H. Twine**. Two years later the name was changed to honor President William Howard Taft. The town has long hosted various state educational and correctional institutions. In 1974, **Lelia Foley** became the first black woman to be elected to the office of mayor in the U.S. and as mayor of Taft, was honored as one of the year's 10 Outstanding Young Women in America.

At Elm and Seminole is the **Taft City Hall**, listed on the NRHP as part of the Historic Government Buildings in Oklahoma All-Black Towns grouping. The other three historic all-Black towns are **Langston** (Section 6), **Boley**, and **Tatums.**

US 62 cuts west and south from Taft across the one-time Creek Nation for another 32 miles before reaching **Okmulgee**, seat of **Okmulgee County**. The town (and later the county) were named for the Creek town in Alabama. Okmulgee is the Creek word "oki mulgi" which means "boiling water."

OKMULGEE

Serving the Creek Nation as its capital from 1868 until it was dissolved in 1907 was OKMULGEE (pop. 13,441). Like Muskogee, Okmulgee owes much of its early-day size and importance to its service as an Indian administrative center.

Following the Civil War the Creeks moved their capital here

The Creek Council House in downtown Okmulgee houses a museum today concentrating on Creek Indian artifacts. It was built in 1876, replacing the original log building. The Creek Indians, one of the Five Civilized Tribes, were driven from Alabama in the early 1830s and settled on reservation lands in Indian Territory, later to become Oklahoma.

from **High Springs,** some 20 miles to the southeast. Although the tribal government was dissolved at statehood, the tribe still conducts its affairs from the **Creek Tribal Center** off US 75 on the north edge of town. Although many of the downtown business buildings have been lost to fire in recent years enough remains to give the commercial district the appearance of a vintage movie set. This is an image Main Street Project planners are emphasizing as they strive to revitalize the downtown.

CREEK COUNCIL HOUSE MUSEUM (NRHP and National Historic Landmark) is located on the downtown square. A handsomely plain two-story-with-cupola sandstone building, it was built in 1876 to replace the original log capitol. After statehood and until 1916 it served as the Okmulgee County

Courthouse. Exhibits include Creek Indian artifacts, art, and archaeology. It is open from 9 a.m. to 5 p.m. Tuesday through Saturday. Admission is free.

On the grounds outside the building are two historical markers. One tells about the Creek capitol, the other about noted Creek leader **Samuel Checote** whose grave is located about two miles northwest.

From Okmulgee US 62 drops south 11 miles to **Henryetta**, then joins I-40 for the 19 mile trip west to **Okemah**. A scenic route between Okmulgee and Okemah lies along SH 56 and this alternate route will be listed after Henryetta for those who would prefer it.

HENRYETTA

This town of 5,872 dates from 1900 with the arrival of the Frisco Railroad. **Henry Beard** and his wife **Etta,** or perhaps a man named **Hugh Henry,** supplied the name. For years the town was one of the state's important smelting centers. This activity has been in decline in recent years.

Henryetta is the hometown of rodeo star **Jim Shoulders**, winner of five World Championship titles.

The Henryetta Historical Society has funded the construction of a gazebo in Territorial Park. Topping the structure is the 1917 dome and spiral from the old city hall.

HISTORICAL MUSEUM, 406 Moore, is housed in the town's first school building. It features mementos and relics of the early Henryetta area. It is open from 9 a.m. to noon on Saturdays and by appointment, 918/652-3331. Admission is free.

ALTERNATE ROUTE

SH 56 strikes west from downtown Okmulgee. At 12 miles is the marker for Presbyterian founded **Nuyaka Mission.**

NUYAKA MISSION (NRHP and OHS) site is two miles north. Nuyaka (Creek approximation of "New Yorker") was a Creek school started here in 1882 following the loss of **Tullahassee Mission** near Fort Gibson to fire. When the Creek Council voted to establish this new mission and boarding school the daughter of the Tullahassee superintendent, **Alice M. Robertson**, was largely responsible for raising the money for Nuyaka. Miss Robertson is the only woman ever sent to the U.S. Congress from Oklahoma (1920). Her sister, Augusta, was superintendent of Nuyaka (which closed in 1921) for 10 years.

Still at the site are the old laundry buildings, original well, cistern, storm cellar, and the building which served as the superintendent's home and boy's dormitory. The latter has been a private residence but the present owners have donated (1990) the property to the Oklahoma Historical Society, though they retain a life estate. The historical society will soon have a full-time staff person at the site to welcome visitors.

West of the sign SH 56 turns south toward Okemah. Along the way it enters Okfuskee County (named for an old Creek town in Alabama) and passes through several dwindling black communities. A number of these were colonized by the Fort Smith & Western railroad (FS&W or sometimes, Foot Sore & Weary) anxious to capitalize on the rich, surrounding farmlands. Cotton soon became the dominant crop in this area augmenting the rich annual harvest of native pecans.

OKEMAH

The birthplace of composer, singer, and folk hero **Woody Guthrie** (1912-1967) has only recently begun to take grudging pride in the fact (note the freshly-painted name on the town's water tower). OKEMAH (pop. 3,085) was established in 1902 by the FS&W. It is Creek for "big chief."

OKFUSKEE COUNTY HISTORICAL MUSEUM, 121 S. Pine, features exhibits including tools, clothing, and utensils depicting the history of the county. It is open from 2 to 5 p.m. Thursdays and by appointment, 918/623-2027. Admission is free.

TERRITORY TOWN MUSEUM, five miles west on I-40, features exhibits that include Civil War relics, Wells Fargo items, and pre-statehood artifacts. It is open from 9 a.m. to 8 p.m. daily from March through September. An admission is charged.

Eleven miles west of Okemah on US 62 is Boley.

BOLEY

Yet another all-black colony owing its birth to the FS&W, BOLEY (pop. 908) owes its early prosperity to cotton. The town once boasted 27 gins. Today it supports, and in turn is supported by, several correctional institutions. The town was named for FS&W roadmaster **W. H. Boley**.

It is 13 miles to **Prague**.

PRAGUE

PRAGUE (pop. 2,308) was started in the early 20th century by Bohemian farmers who named it to honor the capital of Czechoslovakia. A strong Bohemian aura which clings to the town throughout the year heightens each May when the community holds its colorful Kolache Festival.

Center of life in Prague, and of interest to the visitor, is the **St. Wenceslaus Church** and its shrine. On the NRHP is the ZCBJ Lodge No. 46 on S. Barta Ave.

NATIONAL SHRINE OF INFANT JESUS OF PRAGUE, SH 99 South, dates back 300 years. It was established here when Czechoslovakia became one of the Iron Curtain countries. It is open from 7 a.m. to 7 p.m. daily. Admission is free.

As US 62 approaches Oklahoma City from the east it becomes something of a Memory Lane for longtime baseball fans. Twelve miles west of Prague is **Meeker**.

MEEKER

Hometown of former New York Giants' southpaw pitching ace **Carl Hubbell** is MEEKER (pop. 1,003). The town was established in 1892 as **Clifton** but the name was changed to honor Julian L. Meeker in 1903.

CARL HUBBELL MUSEUM, 510 W. Main, houses the memorabilia of the baseball star. It is open from 8 a.m. to 5 p.m. weekdays. Admission is free.

Seventeen miles west is **Harrah.**

HARRAH

Baseball brothers **Paul and Lloyd Waner** were born at HARRAH (pop. 4,206). Paul ("Big Poison") and Lloyd ("Little Poison") received their nicknames as Pittsburgh Pirate stars because their heavy hitting was "poison" to opposing pitchers. A resident of Harrah for many years was cowboy movie star **Tim Holt.**

Harrah was established first as **Pennington**, then **Sweeney** in 1894 and named, finally, for local civic leader and merchant **Frank Harrah.**

Six miles west is **Choctaw** in **Oklahoma County.**

CHOCTAW

Established in 1890 as **Choctaw City**, CHOCTAW (pop. 8,545) took its name from the Choctaw Coal & Railway Company, later the Rock Island. The "city" was dropped in 1896. Novelist **Louis L'Amour** was reared at Choctaw and began his writing career in Oklahoma. L'Amour was the first novelist to receive the Congressional Gold Medal. President Ronald Reagan presented it to him in 1983 in recognition of his novels, known for their historical accuracy.

CABOOSE MUSEUM, 1701 N. Triple X Rd., features exhibits including miscellaneous railroad items, historical photos, and small historic relics. It is open from 10 a.m. to 4 p.m. Saturday and from 2 to 5 p.m. Sunday from Memorial Day through Labor Day. Admission is free.

US 62 becomes NE 23rd Street in Oklahoma City (Section 2). When reaching I-35, go south for two miles, then on I-40 west to the I-44 south junction. Follow I-44 (H. E. Bailey Turnpike) for about 35 miles to the **Chickasha** exit.

CHICKASHA

Seat of Grady County (named for Henry W. Grady, a well-known editor of the *Atlanta Constitution*), is CHICKASHA (pop. 14,988). The town of Chickasha was born in 1892 with the arrival of the Rock Island railroad though a post office, called **Waco**, then **Pensee**, was established here in 1890. It has long prospered on the manufacturing and processing of products in the agriculture and petroleum fields.

The spelling of the town name is the correct spelling of the name of the Chickasaw Indian tribe. Outsiders often try to pronounce the town the same as the tribe (as well as a number of other ways). Chickasha, however, is one of the state's better-known shibboleths (a peculiarity of pronunciation) and only a native would call it, correctly, CHICK-a-shay.

Actor **Clevon Little** was born in Chickasha.

In 1908, **Oklahoma College for Women** was founded here by an act of the state legislature, one of the few state-supported women's colleges in the United States. Today, the now co-educational school is the **University of Science and Arts of Oklahoma**.

COURTHOUSE, an ornate, highly decorated art deco building complete with floral and geometric patterns and cast aluminum lamp posts at the main entrance, was completed in 1934. The first courthouse in Chickasha served as the federal court building of Recording District 19 of the Chickasaw Nation.

ANTIQUE AUTOMOBILE MUSEUM OF TRANSPORTA-TION, 18th and Chickasha Ave., presents transportation-related memorabilia in addition to automobiles. Plans call for the relocation of the museum to the nearby Rock Island Depot (NRHP) currently undergoing restoration. It is open the third weekend of each month excluding holiday weekends. Admission is free.

GRADY COUNTY HISTORICAL MUSEUM, 628 S. 6th, contains articles relating to the history of the county. It is open from 2 to 4:30 p.m. the third Sunday of each month. Admission is free.

OKLAHOMA FILM REPOSITORY, 17th and Grand on USAO campus, contains rare film footage of Oklahoma available on videotape that may be of interest to some history buffs. It is open from 8 a.m. to 10 p.m. weekdays; from 8 a.m. to 5 p.m. Saturday, and from 3 to 10 p.m. Sunday. Admission is free.

Nine miles west is **Verden.**

VERDEN

This town of 546 (named for 1899 townsite developer A. N. Verden) is best known as the site of the massive convocation in May, 1865, of Indians determined to present a united front to the white man. The site of Camp Napoleon, as the gathering was called, covered almost the entire area of the present town. It was finally agreed among the tribes represented that if they were to survive "an Indian shall not spill an Indian's blood." A giant boulder on the school grounds along the highway commemorates the meeting.

As US 62 winds west from Chickasha to **Anadarko** 16 miles away the traveler moves into the heart of the Plains Indian country.

ANADARKO

The seat of **Caddo County** (for the Caddoan group of Indians) is ANADARKO (pop. 6,586). The name of the town is a corruption of a Caddo word "Na-da-ko" which is one of the Caddoan tribes.

Anadarko has long been an "agency town" where Indians can be seen on the streets moving in and out of the turn-of-the-century brick business buildings and the federal, state, county, and tribal agencies. Anadarko is one of the state's Main Street cities with restoration underway in the downtown area.

Anadarko was one of the three townsites authorized with the opening of the Comanche, Kiowa, Apache, Wichita, and Caddo reservations to non-Indian settlement in 1901 (Hobart and Lawton were the other two, Section 4). However, as early as 1878 the Kiowa, Apache, and Comanche agencies were consolidated here with the Wichita office. The post office dates back to this period.

Among the well-known from Anadarko are Indian scout **Black Beaver,** author **Russell Bates,** and poet **John Berryman.**

NATIONAL HALL OF FAME FOR FAMOUS AMERICAN INDIANS, on US 62 East, features bronze portrait busts of famous American Indians in an outdoor display. An information center also is located here. It is open from 9 a.m. to 5 p.m. Monday through Saturday, and from 2 to 5 p.m. Sunday. Admission is free.

DELAWARE TRIBAL MUSEUM, two miles north on US 281, reflects the history of the Delaware tribe through artifacts, artwork, and resource materials. It is open from 8 a.m. to 5 p.m. weekdays. Admission is free.

PHILOMATHIC MUSEUM, 311 E. Main, was established in 1936 and is now located in the old Rock Island railroad depot. Preserved here are antiques pertaining to the region and Indian artifacts, railroad memorabilia, and military equipment and uniforms. It is open from 1 to 5 p.m. daily, closed Sundays in December, January, and February. Admission is free.

SOUTHERN PLAINS INDIAN MUSEUM/CRAFTS CENTER, east of town on US 62, features permanent exhibits including historic arts and crafts of the Plains tribes. Of special interest is the display of traditional costumes of the Southern Plains men, women, and children. During the summer months, full-scale tipis are displayed on the museum grounds. The museum is open from 9 a.m. to 5 p.m. Monday through Saturday, and from 1 to 5 p.m. Sunday, June through September. It is closed on Tuesday the remainder of the year. Admission is free.

INDIAN CITY USA, two miles southeast of town on SH 8, is a large outdoor museum featuring authentic villages depicting the daily lives, religions, and cultures of seven American Plains Indian tribes. The villages were planned by and constructed under the supervision of the Department of Anthropology of the University of Oklahoma. In addition to guided tours, there is an indoor museum. The American Indian Exposition is held annually in August. It is open from 9 a.m. to 6 p.m. daily in the summer. It closes at 5 p.m. during the winter months. An admission is charged.

HISTORIC DISTRICT (NRHP), downtown, includes 86 buildings and only received listing in 1991. The area is bounded by the Chicago Rock Island and Pacific railroad right-of-way, East Second, West Third, and the alley between Broadway and Oklahoma streets. Also recently added to the NRHP was the municipal swimming pool in Randlett Park. This above-ground, oval pool was built in 1926 of poured concrete and dark brick. Nothing quite like it appears anywhere else in the state. Most unique are the decorative collonades on the lower level entrance.

The pool was used until 1985 and is slated for restoration.

RIVERSIDE INDIAN SCHOOL, one mile north of town on US 281, is the oldest operating Indian boarding school in the U.S. A historical marker near the entrance to the school provides some background. The school was established in 1871 by Quaker agents at the old Wichita Agency on the Washita River. Eight students were in the first class. In 1872 a new building was constructed and the school became a boarding school for Caddo and Wichita children. The institution is operated by the U.S. Department of the Interior through the Bureau of Indian Affairs for Wichitas, Caddos, and affiliated tribes.

WPA MURALS, in the Anadarko Post Office, were painted in 1937 by three of the famous "Kiowa Five" Indian artists. Heading up the Anadarko project was **Stephen Mopope**, assisted by **James Auchiah** and **Spencer Asah**. The 16 panels were painted in oil directly on plaster walls. The other two members of the "Kiowa Five" were **Monroe Tsatoke** and **Jack Hokeah**. The term "Kiowa Five" is actually a misnomer as there were six young Indian artists included in this program for promising art students begun at the University of Oklahoma in the 1920s. All were accepted in the art school as special students because of their talent and the promise they showed. **Lois Smokey** was among the first five selected. When she married and didn't have the time she needed to paint she dropped out and Auchiah joined the group. When the Federal Projects of Art were phased out these Indian artists and others such as **Woody Crumbo**, **Dick West**, and **Solomon McCombs** (all Oklahomans) had completed over 50 murals in the state. Many can still be seen today.

Twenty miles south of Anadarko is **Apache**.

APACHE

Named for the Indian tribe, APACHE (pop. 1,591) dates back to 1901. Almost as old is the Apache State Bank, a two story, rock structure that serves as a museum today.

APACHE HISTORICAL MUSEUM (NRHP), Evans and Coblake, features exhibits that include antique furniture and a memorial roll of pioneer Apache citizens. It is open from 9 a.m. to 5 p.m. weekdays and from 9 a.m. to noon on Saturday during the summer. In the winter it is open by appointment, 405/588-3392. Admission is free.

US 62 enters Lawton (Section 4), about 15 miles south of Apache, at the northeast corner of town, then swings west into

The Apache Historical Museum is housed in an old bank building listed on the National Register of Historic Places.

the southwestern part of the state.

Sixteen miles west of **Lawton**, seat of **Comanche County**, is **Cache**, just south of present US 62.

CACHE

The name for CACHE (pop. 2,251) is a French word for "something buried underground" and hints at the colorful rumors of rich buried treasures that have long given the shadowy Wichita Mountains an aura of excitement and drama. The region indeed had its brief moment of gold rush glory (Section 14) but perhaps its real treasure has been in the role in helping the American bison avoid extinction.

In 1907, a handful of animals were brought here from eastern zoos. These have developed into herds and each year are studied, evaluated, then thinned, with the surplus animals auctioned off to ranchers around the country.

Quanah Parker, son of Cynthia Ann Parker and great Comanche leader, had a 12 room home near Cache. The residence, with 14 stars on the roof, symbols of authority, was locally

177

referred to as the Comanche White House (Section 4).

Cache was established in 1901 and in 1924 the late **Frank Rush Sr.** and his wife established **Craterville Park** in a natural amphitheater in the hills three miles north. The American Indian Exposition was held here in 1924 and then annually until 1935 when it was moved to Anadarko. For several years this small amusement park was a popular spot for southwestern Oklahoma families, school, and church groups. **Eagle Park**, another entertainment center, can still be found north of town (Section 4).

Also south of US 62 is **Indiahoma**, six miles west.

INDIAHOMA

INDIAHOMA (pop. 337) was established in 1902. The name was coined by joining parts of two words–Indian and Oklahoma.

Until the ground was claimed by Fort Sill, the **Post Oak Mission** stood five miles northeast of town. It was established by the Mennonites in 1894, the first group of missionaries allowed to work with the Comanches by **Chief Quanah Parker**. Until 1957 the chief and his white mother, **Cynthia Ann Parker**, were buried in the mission cemetery. Their graves are now in the Chiefs Knoll section of the post cemetery at Fort Sill.

Twelve miles west but this time north of the highway is **Snyder**.

SNYDER

SNYDER (pop. 1,619) was established in 1902 with the arrival of the Frisco railroad (now the Burlington Northern). The town was named for railroad official **Bryan Snyder**.

The town is perhaps best known historically for the 1905 tornado that killed 105 and destroyed half the new town. It is widely recognized, too, as center of Oklahoma's granite industry. Snyder granite possesses a distinctive, light rose-reddish hue.

For a time Snyder residents thought their town was going to be county seat of **Swanson County**. Before the state Supreme Court (in 1911) killed the governor's executive order (1910) creating the county from parts of Kiowa and Comanche counties, maps were published with the county drawn in. Occasionally, one of these maps turns up leaving people, today, who have never heard of Swanson County, wondering how the mapmakers could have made such a gigantic error. One of these maps, framed, hangs in a drugstore in **Hinton** (Section 5).

West of Snyder, about eight miles, US 62 crosses the North Fork of the Red River to enter Jackson County (for two famous

Jacksons, Stonewall and Andrew). Before 1907, however, the entry would have been to Greer County, Oklahoma Territory, and before 1896, it would have been Greer County, Texas. Not until that year did the U.S. Supreme Court finally determine the Prairie Dog, not the North, was the principal fork of the Red River and hence the boundary line between Oklahoma and Texas east of the 100th Meridian.

Texas ranchers first began moving their herds onto "Old Greer's" lush, short grass rangelands in the 1880s and the area, now divided into the Oklahoma counties of Jackson, Harmon, Greer, and part of Beckham, maintains a strong aura of West Texas in speech, dress, and social mannerisms.

Fourteen miles inside the Jackson County line is the county seat of **Altus**.

ALTUS

The town of ALTUS (pop. 21,910) was established in 1890. In July 1901, the town's name was changed to **Leger**, then back to Altus in 1904. It began when an earlier settlement (two miles west) called **Frazer** was flooded out in the fall of 1890.

It has often been told that the entire town of Frazer moved to the new location, calling it Altus, the Latin word for "high," for the higher ground. Apparently someone stayed at the old Frazer site as there was a post office listed for the town until 1895. Frazer has an interesting history. Because of its location about halfway between the **Doan's Crossing** of the Red River (southeast of Altus) and **Mangum**, it was a popular stopping place for travelers through the area including trail drivers, ranchers, settlers, and Indians. The cowboys gave it the nickname of **"Butter Milk Station"** as that was the principal beverage served there.

COURTHOUSE (NRHP), Main and Broadway, was finished in 1910 complete with a large dome that, because of its weight, was removed in the 1920s. A worker doing maintenance above the third floor ceiling of the courthouse in 1991 discovered a surprise. The dropped ceiling was concealing an ornate, leaded glass dome, about 12 feet in diameter. This dome presently is covered with silver paint and concealed from view on the roof by a wooden covering. It apparently was part of the original large metal dome. Plans are underway to restore this unique feature of the building.

The imposing courthouse, in the neo-classical style, has smooth stone on the exterior except on the ground floor which is

Doan's Crossing, south of Altus, was an important crossing on the Red River bringing in cattle herds and settlers from Texas.

of rusticated stone. A granite monument on the lawn of the courthouse square marks the spot where the town pump once stood.

MUSEUM OF THE WESTERN PRAIRIE (OHS), 1100 N. Hightower, emphasizes the history of the 10 southwestern Oklahoma counties, plus seven adjacent Texas counties. This museum building is a modern adaptation of the pioneer half dugout home, common building form in this area of the state. Featured are exhibits explaining the development of life on the prairie from prehistoric time to the present. It is open from 9 a.m. to 5 p.m. Tuesday through Friday, and from 2 to 5 p.m. weekends. Admission is free.

US 62 continues 40 miles west to the Texas Panhandle. For those interested in seeing more of "Old Greer" County the following alternate route is suggested.

ALTERNATE ROUTE

Leave Altus traveling north on US 283, continuing north on SH 44 when US 283 veers west.

QUARTZ MOUNTAIN STATE PARK is 20 miles north of Altus on the shores of man-made Lake Altus. The small and large hills of granite blocks (Quartz Mountains) in which the park is set represent the farthest western extension of the intermittent mountain ranges stretching across southern Oklahoma from Arkansas. In this park is one of only two known burials in Oklahoma State parks.

CHIEF BUGLERS GRAVE, reached by following a paved walkway from the back of the lodge northeast toward the lake, is final resting place of **William Gruber,** chief bugler of the 19th Kansas Cavalry. Gruber was killed in a hunting accident in 1865 while his regiment was in bivouac with a supply train near here. His original burial site was slated to be covered by water when Lake Altus, originally dammed at a lower elevation in 1926, was enlarged in the 1940s. So the grave of this 20 year old from Topeka, Kansas, was moved to this location on the lake shore. The other state park burial was that of **Carl Weaver,** politician and publisher, in **Robbers Cave State Park** near **Wilburton** (Section 13). Six miles north of the park on SH 44, then west eight miles on SH 8 is **Granite,** in Greer County.

GRANITE

The town of GRANITE (pop. 1,844, established in 1889) owes its name, history, fame, and fortune to the mass of red boulders that surround it. Residential and business houses are constructed of locally quarried granite as is the crenelated castle on the edge of town built to house the state's minor criminals. On the north edge of town, at the base of **Headquarters Mountain**, is a quarry which has been active since 1910.

GIANTS OF THE GREAT PLAINS, feature a granite mosaic portrait, said to be the world's largest, of **Will Rogers**. The 30 by

Chief Bugler William Gruber, 20, 19th Kansas Cavalry, was accidently killed near here in 1869 and was reburied in the 1940s on the shore of newly enlarged Lake Altus.

26-foot portrait is made of native red granite. Other famous Oklahomans to be portrayed here are **Jim Thorpe** and **Sequoyah.** When completed the Giants will stand 116 feet tall on the mountain at the head of Main Street.

FORD'S MUSEUM, Main St., houses displays which include early-day pioneer items, old cars, and an exhibit of Aladdin lamps. It is open by appointment, 405/535-4710. Admission is free.

Leave Granite on SH 9 going seven miles west, then six miles south on SH 34 to **Mangum.**

MANGUM

The seat of Old Greer County, when it was still a part of Texas, and present seat of **Greer County**, Oklahoma, is MANGUM (pop. 3,344). The county was named for **John A. Greer,** a lieutenant governor of Texas. In 1881 money-shy Texas rewarded its Confederate veterans with free land. **Capt. A. S. Mangum** located here on the old **Mobeetie (or Texas) Trail.** In 1883 **Henry Sweet** platted the Mangum townsite on part of Mangum's land. The post office was established in 1886.

When Mr. Sweet came to survey the area for Colonel Mangum he located his house near a spring called Draw Spring.

These memorials to early pioneers are displayed just outside the Old Greer County Museum in Mangum.

A mail line and many travelers passed this way and Sweet decided to build a small store to sell grocery supplies. He went to Wichita Falls, Texas, and bought 1 x 12s to build the small store but forgot to get 1 x 4s to strip the building. He used tin cans for this instead and for many years "Tin Can City" was what the cowboys in the area called this future town of Mangum.

COURTHOUSE (NRHP), on Courthouse Square, was built in 1906. This building, like the one in Jackson County, was originally constructed with a dome. The only major alteration to this impressive three-story structure has been the removal of the striking copper dome and replacement of the roof.

OLD GREER COUNTY MUSEUM, 224 W. Jefferson, contains "theme" rooms displaying Indian and pioneer artifacts. On the grounds are an authentic half-dugout, early-day windmill, and outhouse.

HALL OF FAME, on museum grounds, features granite monoliths bearing etched faces and biographies of pioneers who settled in Old Greer County. Included are only pioneers who lived in the Old Greer prior to statehood in 1907. Space remains for many more of the impressive monuments which are made at nearby Granite.

SHELTER BELT, north of Mangum on SH 34, was near a sign commemorating the first tree planted in the first shelterbelt in the United States on March 18, 1935. The Prairie States Forestry Project planted the tree on the **Horace Curtis** farm. The program was one instituted by President Franklin D. Roosevelt to help control soil erosion by wind. During its eight year history the forestry project planted 20 million trees in 2,679 miles of shelterbelts on 5,000 farms in Oklahoma.

Leave Mangum going south on SH 34 which intersects with US 62 just east of **Duke**.

HARMON COUNTY

From here it is 20 miles on US 62 to **Hollis**, seat of **Harmon County**. Just another five miles west is the Oklahoma-Texas state line. Still to be found along this border are the tall, cone-shaped concrete markers set following the 1927-29 survey by an astronomical and geodetic engineer named **Gannet**. He was successful in pinning down, once and for all, the correct location of Oklahoma's wandering western boundary. These markers were placed .66 of a mile apart.

The first "false 100th Meridian" was placed a little east of Fort Sill in 1818 by a mapmaker and this was the boundary referred to as separating the United States and Spanish territory in an 1819 treaty with Spain. The U.S. government was not satisfied with this placement so in 1853, **Capt. George B. McClelland** was sent out to correct the error. Using imperfect instruments, and one of them broken, he did succeed in moving the boundary west but only about 30 miles. He placed it about six miles east of the spot where the Red River and its North Fork come together, another "false meridian." The government decided to try again and ordered another survey in 1859. This time the line selected was 4,000 feet west of what is the true meridian in this latitude. Other surveys were completed in 1892 and 1902, both unsatisfactory, especially to those who lived within the disputed area. A writer collecting information for an article on the boundaries of Oklahoma in the early 1940s interviewed a woman who resided west of Hollis.

"During the 45 or more years she has lived there her home has not moved a foot, yet she has lived in one territory, two states, and three counties," he wrote.

Actually this has little to do with the boundary survey for the 100th meridian. Anyone living in Harmon or Jackson Counties and in only one house over the same period (1895-1910) could say the same thing because of the awarding of Old Greer County to Oklahoma and then statehood.

The real problem with the boundary came in the 1927-29 survey when everyone thought the issue of the 100th meridian (and the Oklahoma-Texas state line) was settled once and for all.

Several farm families discovered their homes and barns were in Oklahoma while their farmland was located in Texas. However, today this is believed to be one of the most accurately located boundaries in the nation.

HOLLIS

Ranchers began settling in this corner of Old Greer County as early as 1889 but HOLLIS (pop. 2,584), named for townsite owner **George W. Hollis,** was not established until 1901. Harmon County (named for **Judson C. Harmon,** a governor of Ohio) was not formed until 1909, making it the 76th county. Cotton County was the 77th and last. The land for Harmon County was taken from part of Greer County.

Hollis is the hometown for now retired University of Texas football coach **Darrel Royal.**

COURTHOUSE (NRHP), W. Hollis St., was completed in 1926. This three-story brick building is typical of public structures during that era. (Note the dominant belt courses, contrast in building materials, and large pilasters.)

HARMON COUNTY HISTORICAL MUSEUM, 102 W. Broadway, an old hotel, exhibits Harmon County history from the earliest settlers to the present day. It is open from 1 to 5 p.m. Tuesday and Thursday, and from 1 to 4 p.m. Saturday. Admission is free.

This historical marker entitled "Peace on the Plains" at the junction of US 283 and SH 44 describes the 1834 meeting at the Wichita village in Devil's Canyon, just five miles southeast, between the Plains Indians and the military. The dragoons were commanded by Col. Henry Dodge.

SECTION 9
US 64

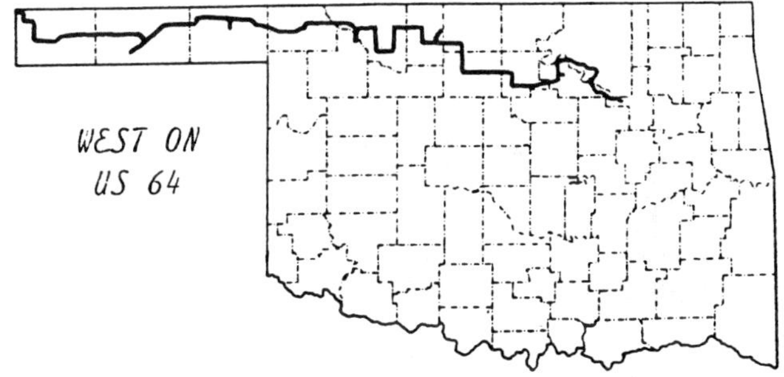

Petroglyphs have been found near Kenton in Cimarron County.

SECTION 9
US 64

One of the more interesting federal routes in Oklahoma–and clearly the longest–is also one of the more difficult to characterize. To put it in contemporary jargon, it is a route still trying to find itself.

US 64 enters Oklahoma from Arkansas at Fort Smith, ascends the Arkansas River northwest to Tulsa, then parallels (in the loosest possible way) the Cimarron River west across the Panhandle to New Mexico. First official attempt to give this 600-mile meander a proper identity came in 1953 when the state legislature dubbed it the **Kit Carson Highway**. The name was hardly adequate. The colorful frontiersman was indeed responsible for the short-lived Camp Nichols but his name and influence hardly extended beyond the Panhandle where it was located. The legislature's second attempt, in 1987, was no more adequate although **Cimarron Highway** did carry at least limited geographical justification.

Fittingly named or not, US 64 has never been far removed from the heartbeat of the figures and events shaping Oklahoma history over the years. From Coronado and Custer to Judge Isaac C. Parker, from giant oil pools to Plains Indian encounters, US 64 has them all. For an admittedly secondary route it offers the historically inclined motorist a surprisingly complete sampler of the people and events making up Oklahoma's history.

WEST ON US 64

This tour of US 64 will begin west of Tulsa at **Sand Springs** and end 450 miles west at the tip of the Oklahoma Panhandle at **Kenton**, two miles from the New Mexico state line.

In several places the tour will be along alternate routes off of US 64 because of the number of historical spots near but not actually along the primary road. These will be marked "Side-Trip" for those which leave and return to the same point on US 64. The others will be marked "Alternate Route" so travelers wishing to omit these sights will know they can continue on US 64.

SAND SPRINGS

Although SAND SPRINGS (pop. 15,346) was not platted until 1911, the area made an appearance in the history of Oklahoma long before.

Just a few miles west of town is the spot where the **Cimarron and Arkansas Rivers** meet, though this juncture is now covered by the waters of **Keystone Lake**. In 1832, while on his "A Tour on the Prairies," **Washington Irving** first caught sight of the Cimarron (which he called the Red Fork of the Arkansas) from a bluff just north of present Sand Springs. The following year a **Creek** settlement, named Adams Springs, was established in the area of the present Sand Springs business district.

This Victorian-style house built by Frederick Drummond in 1905 in Hominy today serves as a museum.

In July, 1892, there supposedly occurred an event which still draws the attention of treasure seekers. The **Dalton gang** took $17,000 in a railroad robbery at the MK&T railroad station at **Adair** and were said to have buried the loot in a cave near here.

In 1908, oil man **Charles Page** established the **Sand Springs Home** for widows and parentless children (he disliked the term orphan) on land he bought, then began to lay out the town around it. The name for Sand Springs was taken from the "sandy springs" located in the **Osage Hills** along the north bank of the Arkansas. It is 28 miles to **Cleveland** located in **Pawnee County,** (named for the Indian tribe).

CLEVELAND

At one time the only bridge across the Arkansas River between Tulsa and the Kansas state line was located at CLEVELAND (pop. 3,156). This earned the town the nickname "Gateway City."

First name for Cleveland, established in 1893 at the opening of the **Cherokee Outlet,** was **Herbert** for the townsite developer. The name was changed to honor **President Cleveland** a few months later. In 1904 oil was discovered in the area and the town quickly grew from a population under 1,000 to over 7,000. Today, Cleveland is experiencing another type of boom—of weekend tourists enjoying Keystone Lake which surrounds the town on three sides. In the downtown area note the brick streets and the building restoration efforts underway.

TRIANGLE OIL/HISTORICAL MUSEUM, west of town on US 64, offers displays of early day Cleveland and the vicinity as well as the importance of oil to this region. It is open from 1 to 4 p.m. Friday, Saturday, and Sunday, June through August. Admission is free.

ALTERNATE ROUTE

Leave Cleveland on SH 99 north. It is nine miles to **Hominy** in **Osage County** (named for the Indian tribe).

HOMINY

There is some speculation as to the origin of the name of HOMINY (pop. 2,342) even though all agree it was not named for the Indian corn. One source believes the name is a corruption of the Harmony Mission in Missouri. Others say it is named for **Ho-Moie** (He Who Walks in the Dark) an Osage leader. The town is one of three special Osage villages in the Osage Nation which served as a trading point or center for one of the three main Osage groups. Hominy was established as a subagency in 1874 for the "Dwellers in the Upland Forest" branch of the tribe.

Oil wealth was responsible for the many large, two-story homes which once lined the wide, tree-shaded streets of the town. Many of these homes are still standing. Other evidence of Osage tribal wealth can be found in the **Albert Joseph Powell Cemetery** (on SH 99), with its unusual number of large and elaborate monuments. Other NRHP properties in town are the **Bank of Hominy**, 102 W. Main, and the **Osage Round House** in the Indian Village section of town.

HOMINY SCHOOL (NRHP), just off SH 99 on S. Pettit, is the first permanent school building in Osage County, built in 1904. Completely restored, the stone structure is now the Hominy School Administration Building.

DRUMMOND HOME (NRHP and OHS), 305 N. Pine, is a Victorian-style home built in 1905 by **Frederick Drummond**, a Scotsman who was an Indian trader and a merchant. He gave his sons a start in cattle ranching and his descendants are still ranchers in this area. Fred Drummond died in 1913 at age 49. His wife lived in this house until her death in 1956 and her brother resided here until his death in 1978. The family then gave the house and almost all its contents to the Oklahoma Historical Society. The inventory done by the OHS of the things in the house (Mrs. Drummond was known to be a "saver of everything") was 2,000 pages long.

The period interpreted in this museum is the oil boom era, around 1915. It is open from 9 a.m. to 5 p.m. Tuesday through Friday and from 2 to 5 p.m. weekends. Admission is free.

Leave town to the west on SH 20. It is 20 miles to **Ralston** in northern **Pawnee County.**

RALSTON

Located on the southwest bank of the Arkansas River, RALSTON (pop. 405), established 1894, was originally named for its location, **Riverside**. The name Ralston honors the townsite developer.

In the early 1900s a small steamboat, said to be powered by a small threshing machine engine, made several trips on the Arkansas between Tulsa, to the southeast, and Ralston. During the same period residents of the **Kaw City** area, some 75 water miles upriver, enjoyed floating by boat downriver to Ralston. The boats would then be transported back to Kaw City, only 25 miles by wagon.

RALSTON OPERA HOUSE (NRHP), built in 1902, was

used until 1927 as an opera house as well as a community center. The native sandstone structure has been completely restored during the past five years and the owner plans to open the theater, offering programs reflective of the era in which it was built.

West, then south on SH 18 at 12 miles is the turn, to the east, to Skedee. The turn is one mile south of the junction with SH 15. The marked road is gravel but wide and hardpacked.

SKEDEE

The isolated community of SKEDEE (pop. 96) takes its name from the Skidi tribe of the Pawnee Confederacy. The Skidi was the largest of the four bands in the confederacy and the word comes from the Pawnee "tsikri" meaning "Wolf."

The town was home to **Col. E. E. Walters** (sometimes spelled Waters) an auctioneer during the million-dollar oil lease sales in Osage County. Walters usually conducted the lease auctions under the "million dollar elm" in Pawhuska (Section 12). On one June day in 1924, it is said he sold $10,888,000 worth of leases.

In the main intersection of the tiny, almost deserted business district, is a large concrete statue erected in 1926. Called "Bond of Friendship," it portrays Col. Walters shaking hands with Osage leader **Chief Bacon Rind**. Curiously enough the statue is said to bear little resemblance to Bacon Rind even though he was the most photographed Indian of his day. In spite of its location, away from any main road, the statue has been seen by thousands of people since 1926. It was seen from windows of passenger trains which passed through town a half block away, until passenger service came to an end on the line in 1956.

Back on SH 18 it is four miles to Pawnee and US 64.

PAWNEE

Seat of Pawnee County is PAWNEE (pop. 2,197), established in 1876 as a trading post to serve the nearby Pawnee Indian Agency. The word "Pawnee" was used by the French in the 18th century when referring to this group of people. It is uncertain what the original word was, it having been written a number of different ways: Pani, Pana, Panana, etc.

Pawnee is the hometown of **Chester Gould**, creator of the comic strip character "Dick Tracy." Gould had his studio in Woodstock, Illinois, and turned out his famous comic strip there from 1931 until 1977.

Frank M. Canton, who changed his name from Joe Horner,

This statue stands at the insection of the tiny village of Skedee and portrays Chief Bacon Rind and Col. E. E. Walters.

rode on both sides of the law for several years before he settled down to working as a lawman. He played a major role in Wyoming's notorious 1892 Johnson County War and in 1894 moved to Oklahoma Territory where he became a deputy U.S. marshal and under sheriff of Pawnee County. During the next three year period he helped to capture many Oklahoma outlaws. During his three years as under sheriff of Pawnee County, he was involved in three shootings in the county. In 1893, Canton wounded a hot tempered livery stable owner when he attempted to intervene in an arrest of a man charged with murder. In the winter of 1896, he was a member of a posse that recaptured two thieves who broke out of the Pawnee County jail, by burning them out of their hideout. On November 6, 1896, Canton shot and killed Bill Dunn, a fugitive, on the sidewalk near the courthouse. He was appointed adjutant general of the Oklahoma National Guard in 1907 and held the post for a decade. He died in Oklahoma in 1927.

Jennie "Little Breeches" Stevens and **"Cattle Annie" McDoulet** were teenage lookouts for the Dalton-Doolin gang among other pursuits including illegal whiskey traffic and stealing horses. From time to time they were caught but generally made bail or outran or escaped from the arresting officers. In his movie "The Passing of the Oklahoma Outlaws," Marshal **Bill Tilghman** took credit for finally capturing the two, but he was tampering with the truth in this case.

Actually the girls gave up to four other lawmen (one was Canton) after a brief fight during which several shots were fired. They were tried at Pawnee and Annie, at that time still underage, was sent to reform school and Jennie to prison, both in Massachusetts. Within a few months Annie was released and eventually went into settlement work in New York where she died of consumption two years later. Jennie returned to Oklahoma in 1896 and disappeared into a new life. It is said she married, lived in Tulsa, and "reared a fine family."

PAWNEE INDIAN AGENCY (NRHP) is three blocks east of the business district across **Black Bear Creek**. Several of the agency buildings are still standing. A pyramid-shaped marker on the grounds tells of some of the hardships this tribe has suffered.

COURTHOUSE (NRHP), on the downtown square, replaced an earlier courthouse built before the turn-of-the-century. This seat of government was built in 1932. This is one of two county courthouses in the state with Indian motifs in the frieze. The other is the **Adair County** courthouse at **Stilwell** (Section 11). On the west lawn is a "Doughboy" statue honoring veterans of World War I.

BLUE HAWK PEAK (NRHP and OHS), west of town on US 64, is the site selected by Pawnee Chief **Blue Hawk** for his lodge. Later it was the home and ranch of his friend, **Pawnee Bill**.

*The entrance to Blue Hawk Peak Ranch Museum (above)
and the Pawnee Bill Ranch House built by Gordon Lillie.*

Gordon W. Lillie (Pawnee Bill) was a frontiersman, scout,
Indian interpreter, teacher, and originator of Pawnee Bill's Wild
West Show, that made its debut in 1883. In 1908, the show was
merged with that of Lillie's friend **Buffalo Bill**. The complex at

Above is the old Pawnee Indian Agency and below is the Pawnee County Courthouse with its statue honoring World War I doughboys.

Blue Hawk Peak includes a museum building, ranch outbuildings, the original cabin Lillie and his wife, May, lived in before they completed their large home in 1908 (also on the tour). The three-story stone barn was built in 1926 especially for Lillie's Scottish shorthorn cattle. In the barn can be seen a 65 x 10 foot billboard announcing the opening of a Pawnee Bill Show October 27, 1900. It was found in 1982 when volunteer firemen in **Lamont** tore down an old drugstore to build a new fire station.

After the Wild West show closed in 1913, Pawnee Bill became involved in the preservation of buffalo and at one time had the world's largest private collection. Some can still be seen at the ranch. He was one of the people responsible for the establishment of a bison preserve near Lawton (Section 4), now the Wichita Mountains Wildlife Refuge.

Blue Hawk Peak is open year-round from 9 a.m. to 5 p.m. Wednesday through Saturday and from 1 to 5 p.m. Sunday and open additionally on Tuesday from May through October. Admission is free.

It is 27 miles to **Perry** (Section 6). US 64 combines with I-35 north from here for eight miles then exits west . About 14 miles west on both sides of the highway are wells and associated structures of the **Garber Oil Field** in **Garfield County** (named for President **James A. Garfield**). The field was opened in September of 1917 by the Sinclair Oil and Gas Company. It was one of the most spectacular discoveries of that decade with oil and gas production from 11 different horizons. One of the wells had the largest initial flow of any well up to that time—27,000 barrels daily from a depth of about 4,000 feet.

The town of **Garber** (pop. 959), seen three miles north of the highway, was the main supply center for the field. The post office was established as **McCardie** March 13, 1894, but the name changed to Garber a month later to honor local resident **Martin Garber**. Garber's homestead had been the original site of the town, about a mile southwest. When the Enid and Tonkawa Railway (now Rock Island) came through Garber, they bought the present townsite and moved the town to it. It is 14 miles from the Garber turnoff to Enid (Section 10).

Thirty-six miles north and west of Enid is the town of **Jet**, gateway to the **Great Salt Plains.**

JET

The town of JET (pop. 272) is in eastern Alfalfa County (named for **William H. "Alfalfa Bill" Murray**, chairman of the

Oklahoma Constitutional Convention in 1907 and ninth governor of the state). Jet was established in 1894 and named for **W. M. Jett**, a local miller and the first postmaster. The town dropped one if the "t's" in Jetts name.

GREAT SALT PLAINS STATE PARK/LAKE is north of Jet off SH 38. It is believed the first white men to see the area, long known to the Indians, were a group headed by **George C. Sibley**, Indian agent at Fort Osage, Missouri. Sibley had heard reports from Indians of peculiar saline deposits south of the Arkansas River and wanted to see for himself. He came to this section along the Salt Fork of the Arkansas in 1811 with two white companions and a band of Osage Indians on a summer buffalo hunt. Sibley found the site to be much more than he imagined and was fascinated with the dazzling white surface of salt which caused an optical illusion making things far away seem much closer.

CRYSTAL DIGGING is permitted in this State Park. In parts of the salt flat, gypsum and saline solutions in the soil are concentrated enough to promote growth of selenite crystals. Crystal digging is allowed weekends and holidays between April 1 and October 15.

Seventeen miles west of Jet, then north, on US 64, is **Cherokee** Seat of Alfalfa County.

CHEROKEE

CHEROKEE (pop. 1,787) takes its name from its location—the Cherokee Outlet (Section 6). An observation tower about four miles east of town gives a good view of the Great Salt Plains, called the Great Nescatunga (big salt water) by the Indians.

ALFALFA COUNTY HISTORICAL SOCIETY, 102 W. Main, is housed in the 51-room former Cherokee Hotel. Exhibits of early Alfalfa County life are displayed. It is open from 1 to 5 p.m. Tuesday through Friday from March through November. Admission is free.

STELLA FRIENDS ACADEMY, two miles north to the junction of US 64/SH 11, then east two miles, is described by a historical marker for the Quaker academy established near here in 1897. A group of Quakers (Friends) from Iowa settled in the area in 1893 seeking milder winter weather. Stella Academy took its name from the Stella Monthly Meeting. The name was selected in honor of **Stella Howard**, teacher of a small elementary school organized at the same time the meeting was established. Among Friends, a monthly meeting is not a church service but rather a meeting of the governing body of the group.

Sixteen miles west of the US 64/SH 11 junction is **Alva**, seat of **Woods County** (for Kansas politician **Sam Wood**). The addition of the "s" was an early clerical error.

ALVA

One of four designated land offices during the opening of the Cherokee Outlet in 1893 was ALVA (pop. 5,495). The town was named for **Alva B. Adams**, attorney for the Santa Fe Railroad who later became a governor of Colorado.

Alva is home of **Northwestern Oklahoma State University**, founded in 1897. Oldest building on campus is **Science Hall** (NRHP), constructed in 1906 and designed by **Solomon A. Layton** who designed many of Oklahoma's county courthouses.

CHEROKEE STRIP MUSEUM, 901 14th St., features 38 theme rooms in the main building that includes a chapel, kitchen, living room, military room, and clothes room. Other exhibits date from the mid-1800s to 1900s. Also displayed are an agricultural building and a one-room schoolhouse. The museum is open from 2 to 5 p.m. weekends. Admission is free.

NEOSU MUSEUM is located in Jesse Dunn Hall on the NEOSU campus. The museum features natural history, birds, mammals, fossils, and Indian relics. It is open weekdays by appointment, 405/327-1700, ext. 364. Admission is free.

ALTERNATE ROUTE

Leave Alva on US 281 south then west to **Waynoka**, 26 miles.

WAYNOKA

WAYNOKA (pop 947) began as the railroad siding Keystone when the Santa Fe built through the Cherokee Outlet in 1886. Three years later the name was changed to Waynoka for the Cheyenne word "winneoka" meaning good or sweet water.

By 1929, Waynoka had one of the two largest rail yards in Oklahoma and its **Railway Ice Company** was perhaps the largest in the world. It produced tons of ice to cool produce being shipped east from California.

Also in 1929, Waynoka became part of aviation history when one of the eight airports built across the country by **Transcontinental Air Transport** (later TWA) was located here, making it possible for a person to travel from coast to coast in 48 hours. Travelers from the east coast would arrive in Waynoka by air, eat at the Fred Harvey House, board a train here for an overnight trip to Clovis, New Mexico, and the next morning would board another plane for the western leg of their trip.

The Santa Fe depot and Harvey House in Waynoka were once part of the first coast-to-coast train / airplane trips begun in 1929.

Travelers from the west would arrive in Waynoka by overnight train, eat breakfast, then board a plane to fly east. These plane/ train trips only lasted about 18 months, until technology was developed that made night flying possible.

WAYNOKA HISTORICAL MUSEUM, W. Waynoka St., is located in the former Santa Fe Depot. It and nearby **Harvey House**, both built in 1910, are listed on the NRHP. The Harvey House served meals to train travelers until 1937 when the dining cars on trains made meal stops unnecessary. It is open from 2 to 4 p.m. weekends from Memorial Day through Labor Day and by appointment, 405/824-4741. Admission is free.

LITTLE SAHARA RECREATION AREA is four miles south of town on US 281. This area was known as the "walking hills" to early explorers, a reference to the shifting sand dunes.

Return to Waynoka and go north on SH 15 for 15 miles to US 64. Thirteen miles west is the junction with SH 50. Three miles south on SH 50 is the Cimarron River town of **Freedom**, gateway to **Alabaster Caverns State Park** (six miles farther south) where the largest gypsum cave in the United States open to the public is located.

FREEDOM

Originally established five miles north in 1901, FREEDOM (pop. 264) was moved to its present location in 1919 when the **Buffalo and Northwestern Railroad** (later part of the Santa Fe) built through a few miles south of the old town.

Freedom today reflects its western heritage. The downtown storefronts have been redesigned to resemble a town in the Old West. The red bluffs and sand hills near the town add to the illusion.

FREEDOM MUSEUM, Main Street, contains artifacts pertaining to the history of the area including furniture, quilts, instruments, documents, and early-day tools. There also is a barbed wire collection. It is open from 2 to 4 p.m. Tuesday through Sunday during the summer months. Admission is free.

CIMARRON COWBOY MONUMENT is a 15-foot red granite monument dedicated to the cowboys who settled the Cherokee Outlet. Included on the rock is a map showing the large ranches from 1883 to 1890 and it lists names of cowhands and brands of these old spreads. Now in the City Park, this stone was moved here from the original site six miles north.

Returning to US 64 it is 30 miles west on US 64 to **Buffalo**, seat of **Harper County** (named for **Oscar G. Harper**, clerk of the Oklahoma Constitutional Convention).

BUFFALO

First name for BUFFALO (pop. 1,312) was **Brule**. A post office was established June 15, 1899. The name came from the word "Brule," a sub tribe of the Sioux. The town name was changed in 1907 to honor nearby **Buffalo Creek**. In the early days the buildings in the business district were required to be fireproof so one early nickname for the town was "Stone City."

DOBY SPRINGS is nine miles west of Buffalo on US 64, then two miles north on a county road. The settlement was named for **Chris Doby** who staked the site with its artesian springs during the Cherokee Outlet Run. First name for the town, established in 1903, was **Ballaire** but was soon changed to honor Doby. At one time the town challenged Buffalo for county seat status.

The wooded area around the springs was a rendezvous spot for Indians and early-day drovers herding cattle on the **Great Western Cattle Trail**. Today the city of Buffalo maintains the site as a park.

Twenty-five miles west of Buffalo is the beginning of

Oklahoma's Panhandle, once known as **"No Man's Land."** This narrow strip, about 34 miles wide and 167 miles long, was unclaimed until the Organic Act was passed May 2, 1890, officially establishing the Territory of Oklahoma and declaring the public lands in the "No Man's Land" open to settlement.

In the Panhandle counties of **Beaver** and **Texas**, look for the wood frame elevators (NRHP listing as a group) built between 1900 and 1930 along the railroads.

A SIDE TRIP

Enroute, at the US 64/US 283 junction, drive seven miles south to Laverne.

LAVERNE

The post office for Laverne (pop. 1,269) was established March 30, 1898, and named for a local resident, **Laverne Smith**. Tree-shaded Laverne is something of a surprise in this relatively treeless plains country. This is the hometown of one of Oklahoma's "Miss America's" **Jane Jayroe** who was crowned in 1967. It is also the hometown of **Joe A. Dooley**, a noted wood sculptor.

LAVERNE MUSEUM is located in the old **Fox Hotel** (NRHP). The rooms of this hotel, started in 1912, are now "theme" rooms and among the displays are art, glass shoes, western and ranch memorabilia, and Indian artifacts. It is open from 2 to 5 p.m. weekends. Admission is free.

Other NRHP properties in the town are the **Clover Hotel**, Main and Oklahoma; **MK&T Depot**, Main Street; and the **Sharp Lumberyard**, 124 N. Broadway.

Return to US 64 and just inside the Beaver County line is **Gate**.

GATE

The name for GATE (pop. 159) was taken from its location—at the entrance or "gateway" to the old neutral strip. First called **Gate City** when the post office was established April 13, 1886, the "city" was dropped in 1894.

GATEWAY TO PANHANDLE MUSEUM, on US 64, is in the restored MK&T (Katy) railroad depot. Displays include farm and home items, Civil War memorabilia, prehistoric and more recent Indian artifacts. It is open from 9 a.m. to 6 p.m. Monday through Saturday. Admission is free.

It is 26 miles to the junction with US 270 and a side-trip.

A SIDE-TRIP

Turn south on US 270 to **Beaver City**, just called **Beaver** by the post office.

BEAVER

The county seat town of BEAVER (pop. 1,584) took its name, as did the county, from the **Beaver River** along which the town is located. The post office was established in 1883 and in 1887 Beaver City, as the only town in "No Man's Land," became the capital of **Cimarron Territory** that included the present Oklahoma Panhandle. This territory was never officially recognized by the federal government and with the Organic Act the territorial government was dissolved and the area became Beaver

This Presbyterian Church, still in use in Beaver, was built in 1887. It is listed on the NRHP.

County of Oklahoma Territory. It was divided into three counties at statehood in 1907. A plaque in the downtown area marks the site of the two-story capitol building.

PRESBYTERIAN CHURCH (NRHP), 3rd and Ave E., held its first service June 12, 1887, and services have been held continuously since. Animal bones, gathered on the prairie by local citizens, were hauled to Dodge City, Kansas, and exchanged for lumber and materials to construct the church.

LANE CABIN (NRHP), Main St. and Ave C., was built in 1880 by Jim Lane. The two-room sod house is now part of a larger stucco house. The combination home/store was on the **Jones-Plummer Cattle Trail** which ran from Tascosa, Texas, to Dodge City, Kansas.

JONES-PLUMMER TRAIL MUSEUM, on the county fairgrounds, displays antiques of "No Man's Land" including clothing, saddles, pictures, and medical supplies. It is open from 1 to 5:30 p.m. Wednesday through Friday, from 1 to 5 p.m. Saturday, and from 2:30 to 5 p.m. Sunday. Admission is free.

Return to US 64. It is 41 miles to **Hooker** (pop. 1,551 named for rancher **Joseph Hooker**), then 11 miles to **Optima** (pop. 92), both in **Texas County** (honoring the state). Between these two towns was a settlement called **Buffalo,** established March 8, 1888, an important social and business center for early settlers in "Cimarron Territory." Although the territory was not officially recognized it did send a delegate, **Owen G. Chase**, to the U.S. Congress. It is eight miles from Optima to **Guymon**.

GUYMON

An election in 1909 won county seat status for GUYMON (pop. 7,803) over two contenders, Optima and Hooker. The town was established in 1901 when the Rock Island railroad extended its line through the area from Liberal, Kansas. The townsite company was headed by Liberal resident, **E. T. Guymon**.

COUNTY COURTHOUSE (NRHP), with its ornate cut stone trim, was built in 1926. Texas County government rented space until 1918 when a hotel was purchased.

A SIDE-TRIP

Ten miles southwest on US 54 is Goodwell, home of **Panhandle State University**.

GOODWELL

Another Rock Island town is GOODWELL (pop. 1,065). The name comes from the "good well" drilled at the site for water.

When it came time to select a county seat for Texas County

the residents of Goodwell and Guymon reached a gentleman's agreement. Goodwell wouldn't bid for the county seat if Guymon would support Goodwell in its bid for a district agricultural school. Panhandle A&M was first established in 1909. It was a two-year school until 1925 when it became a four-year college.

NO MAN'S LAND HISTORICAL MUSEUM is located on the campus of PSU. Exhibits feature the history of "No Man's Land" and the Dust Bowl years suffered during the 1930s. There also is an archaeology collection. It is open from 9 a.m. to 5 p.m. Tuesday through Friday and from 2 to 5 p.m. weekends. Admission is free.

Return to Guymon and US 64. It is 64 miles to **Boise City**, seat of **Cimarron County** (named for the river). This is the only county in the U.S. that borders on four states in addition to its own (Kansas, Colorado, New Mexico, and Texas). The county seat is closer to the state capitals of two of these states (Colorado and New Mexico) than to its own state capital at Oklahoma City.

BOISE CITY

Established in 1907 as **Cimarron**, the name was changed a year later to BOISE CITY (pop. 1,509). The town may have been named for a Civil War hero (a Captain Boise) or for the Boice Cattle Company (with the spelling changed) or for Boise, Idaho. No one seems quite sure. If it was named for the town in Idaho, the pronunciation has been changed because in Boise City, Oklahoma, Boise is pronounced to rhyme with "voice."

During World War II, Boise City had the dubious distinction of being the only town in the Continental U.S. to be bombed. June 5, 1944, a plane from the Dalhart, Texas, Army Air Field took off on a night practice bombing mission. The plane was off course and the navigator mistook the lights around the courthouse square for the practice bombing range 45 miles away at Conlen, Texas, and dropped his six bombs. Fortunately the main damage was to the nerves of the sleeping townspeople although the bombs did leave craters, about 40 inches deep, and one small building, which was about to fall down anyway, was destroyed. The bombs weighed about 100 pounds each and were loaded with four pounds of powder and the rest sand. The next day six air force officers and an FBI agent arrived in town to try and explain things.

One of the bomb casings was found and was stored around town for years until it was dented and rusty. Recently it was taken to a local body shop to have the dents pounded out and

Ruts of the old Santa Fe Trail in Cimarron County are still plainly visible.

All that remains of old Camp Nichols in Cimarron County is this pile of rubble. Below is the rock where travelers on the Santa Fe Trail carved their names.

paint applied. It will probably be the only "guest of honor" at the 50th anniversary celebration the town is planning in June of 1993. Although the airplane's crew has already been sent invitations, none has accepted.

Actress **Vera Miles** was born near Boise City.

COURTHOUSE (NRHP), built in 1925, is visible for miles.

A monument on the north side of the square honors the **Mormon Battalion**, composed of several hundred Mormon recruits from Council Bluffs, Iowa, enroute to Santa Fe, New Mexico, and San Diego, California, in 1846 to fight in the Mexican War. Commanded by **Brig. Gen. Stephen Kearny**, many of these Mormon soldiers were on their way to Salt Lake City in their exodus from Nauvoo, Illinois, when they were recruited for military service against the Mexicans.

US 64 exits Boise City to the southwest into Texas. An alternate route is suggested.

ALTERNATE ROUTE

Leave Boise City traveling west then north on SH 325 to **Kenton**, the area where the Cimarron Cutoff of the Santa Fe Trail passed. A historical marker noting this is located 20 miles west of Boise City. Here can also be seen wagon ruts left by the many wagon trains that passed this way during the early days.

CAMP NICHOLS (NRHP) was established by **Col. Kit Carson** in 1865. About a mile farther than the historical marker commemorating the Cimarron Cutoff is another historical marker describing Camp Nichols. The fort was established to protect travelers from renegade Indian bands along the trail. Carson had been ordered to build the fort in New Mexico Territory and apparently thought he was there when he chose the site on a knoll overlooking **Carrizo Creek.** When the mistake was discovered, construction was halted, the site abandoned, and the army moved on. This site, about three miles west, is presently surrounded by private land and not accessible to the public. Stone footings and cobblestone pavement still remain, however.

KENTON

The only town in Oklahoma to observe Mountain Time is KENTON (pop. 40). This occasionally causes confusion in households with children as they attend school in Boise City on Central Time.

Kenton was first established in about 1886 a little west of the present town in New Mexico Territory. It was known as **Carrizo**, then in 1887 it was renamed **Florence**. During this time the village was a rambunctious, western town with several saloons and was known as **"The Cowboy Capital."**

In 1890 **Fairchild B. Drew**, a nephew of **P.T. Barnum** of circus fame, became postmaster of Florence. He changed the name of the settlement to Kenton (after his Civil War captain, whose last name was Kent) and moved the town four miles east, leaving the saloons behind. For a few months after statehood, Kenton was seat of Cimarron County.

DINOSAUR TRACKS are visible along Carrizo Creek. Go north on a road about .5 mile east of town and watch for a sign with a dinosaur, about four miles. Here, along the creek one can see the authenticated footprints of a prehistoric animal in the hardened, ancient mud of the stream bed.

ROBBERS ROOST. Enroute to the dinosaur tracks count the third cattle guard and off to the right, beyond the river, note the rocky hill with a rock rim around it. This was the area of Robbers Roost where **Capt. William Coe** and his outlaw band had their hideout in the 1860s. This was a perfect location to raid freight caravans on the Santa Fe Trail and the scattered ranches in Colorado and New Mexico Territory. The horses and mules at Forts Union and Lyons were fair game too. Coe was finally captured, taken to Pueblo, Colorado, and hanged.

THREE STATE MARKER, about four miles farther, is a concrete marker located just north of the road which sets, more or less accurately, the point where Oklahoma, Colorado, and New Mexico meet. An earlier marker lies about a quarter mile north. A few years ago yet another survey was taken which claimed the concrete marker is still a few yards off.

HIGHEST POINT, located atop Black Mesa, the long, dark mesa lying to the northwest of Kenton, is marked by an 11-foot tall obelisk of pink granite. This is the highest point above sea-level in Oklahoma, 4,972.97 feet. There is a footpath going up to the monument and many people make the long, steep climb.

SECTION 10
US 81

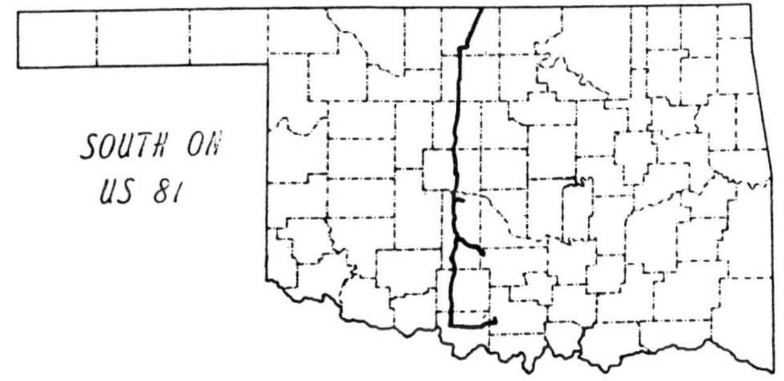

This is a bust of Jesse Chisholm for whom the Chisholm Cattle Trail was named. A trader, Chisholm's route follows the trail his supply wagons used in Indian Territory.

212

SECTION 10
US 81

US 81, it might be argued, dates from 1865. The Civil War had finally ended, leaving West Texas awash in unmarketable cattle and little else of value. But enterprising cattlemen were even then assembling the first herds of these half-wild longhorns with an eye to driving them north to Kansas railheads. Meanwhile, central and western Oklahoma was a vast rolling prairie covered for the most part by a variety of nutritional grasses. Although it belonged nominally to several tribes, few Indians lived this far west. The leisurely cattle drive, fattening the critters for market as they went along, in theory at least, was taking advantage of a golden opportunity. From central Oklahoma north to Kansas herds followed a trail cut by the supply wagons of Indian trader Jesse Chisholm, hence the name assumed in time by the entire trail. Few physical relics of the trail survive but the persistent motorist is seldom far from a strong visible reminder of it. The Chisholm mystique is everywhere, in commercial establishments, community celebrations, significant museums, and countless monuments and memorials that line the route. As for those scattered relics that can still be found, follow the suggestions listed below and with a bit of imagination the old Chisholm Trail can still appear surprisingly vital more than a hundred years after it ceased to exist.

SOUTH ON US 81

This tour of US 81 will begin at the Kansas State line in northern **Grant County** and end at Waurika, 205 miles south. The cattle, of course, traveled in the opposite direction. Three short side-trips are included.

GRANT COUNTY

The first few miles of US 81 in Oklahoma follows almost exactly the path of the old **Chisholm Cattle Trail**. This is in Grant County, established when the **Cherokee Outlet** was opened to non-Indian settlement, September 16, 1893 (Section 6). Although the county was eventually named for **President Ulysses S. Grant**, also considered for the county name was Simpson.

Six miles from the state line is **Renfrow** (named for fourth territorial governor **W. C. Renfrow**), located one mile west of the trail route. Ten miles farther is **Medford**.

MEDFORD

Second seat of Grant County was MEDFORD (pop. 1,172), selected in 1908 in an election between Medford, **Jefferson**, and territorial seat, **Pond Creek**. The town, established in 1893, was named for the town in Massachusetts. Two local brothers who received fame in the early days of aviation were **Apollo** and **Zeus Soucek**. In 1918, as schoolboys of 10 and 12, they constructed a homemade glider (launched into flight by mule power). The two became navy fliers and in 1930 Apollo established an altitude record (for that time) of 43,165 feet. Brother Zeus designed some of the flight equipment.

GRANT COUNTY MUSEUM, Cherokee and Main, features historic pictures, pioneer furniture, books, toys, and clothing. It is open from 2 to 4 p.m. Monday through Wednesday and Friday. Admission is free.

It is seven miles to **Jefferson**.

JEFFERSON/POND CREEK

Present-day JEFFERSON (pop. 36) is about a mile north of its original location where a post office named Pond was operated from November 13, 1879, to April 14, 1887. That was before the area was opened to homesteading in 1893 and it served the scattered ranchers, freighters, and trail drivers. Pond Creek was nearby, a stream named for a pond used as a water supply along the Chisholm Trail.

In 1889, the **Chicago, Rock Island**, and **Pacific**, building south across Indian Territory, located a depot and siding at this spot which it named **Pond Creek Station**.

Some four years later, before the land known as the Cherokee Outlet was opened to homesteading, the Department of the Interior mapped out the counties that would be set up and selected county seat sites. A few Cherokee Indians had taken up residence in the Outlet and they had prior right to select allotments of land for themselves before the race for homesteads. They thought it advantageous to select their land adjacent to towns that would later spring up.

County seat locations were to be secret until just before the opening but news leaked out and much of the land surrounding the proposed county seats was selected by Cherokees. To foil this maneuver the government moved the locations of most of the county seats. Pond Creek Station had been selected as a seat but the site was moved three miles south along the railroad and designated **Pond Creek**. This meant after the opening there were two towns, three miles apart with almost the same name.

The railroad owned the site at Pond Creek Station and refused to build a depot or stop trains at Pond Creek. The latter had the county seat and land office and its post office was established September 29, 1893, 11 days after the opening. The trains put the mail off at Pond Creek Station and it was taken by road to the post office in Pond Creek.

This situation turned into a war between the citizens of Pond Creek and the railroad (as it did down the line between Enid and the railroad). A train was wrecked in Pond Creek and men were arrested for tearing up the track. In the end a depot and siding were built at Pond Creek and trains stopped there. A post office was established at Pond Creek Station under the name of Jefferson on January 12, 1894. Shortly after, Jefferson moved a short way north to its present location.

SEWELL'S STOCKADE. On the south edge of Jefferson, east of the highway, is **Rock Island Park** with its tall cottonwoods and other trees. This was originally an 80-acre allotment taken by a Cherokee Indian when the Outlet was opened to settlement. The allotment was later turned over to a townsite company but a town never materialized. In the early 1870s, a

This monument near Jefferson in Grant County marks Sewell's Stockade that once offered protection against marauding Indians to drovers on the Chisholm Trail.

rancher named Sewell built a stockade here to offer drovers on the Chisholm Trail protection from Osage Indian mourning parties and other Indian war raiders. A large granite monument marks the spot.

COWBOY GRAVES MONUMENT, a few hundred yards south of stockade monument, reminds the passersby of one danger on the rough edge of the Indian/white man frontier. The east-west **Osage Black Dog Trail** crossed the Salt Fork a little to the south. It was an Osage custom then to bury tribesmen with a scalp from an enemy. As inter-tribal warfare drew to a close obtaining scalps was a problem so "mourning parties" were sent out to see what could be found. Isolated whites were often a target of these scalp searches and this monument honors two such unfortunates.

The stone tells the stories: "On this spot lie buried two cowboys who gave their lives in winning the frontier to civilization. Tom Best rode south from Kansas in 1872 to join the Texas cattle drives, but was killed by hostile Indians a short distance north of this point. Ed Chambers, in 1873, rode north with a herd from Texas and he, too, was killed by Indians about a mile southeast of here."

It is four miles to Pond Creek (pop. 982), former county seat, (see above). Enid is 21 miles south in **Garfield County**, named for the president. (Hancock and Berry also were considered as county names.)

ENID

Garfield County seat is ENID (pop. 45,309). There are at least two versions of the origin of the town name, well-known to crossword puzzle fans needing a "four letter town in Oklahoma." One story says Enid was selected by a Rock Island railroad official who liked Tennyson's "Idylls of the King" and chose the name of Geraint's wife for the new town. The second, and probably less-likely, version dates back to Chisholm Trail days when the cowboys stopped to camp at a spring (now located in **Government Springs Park**). This story says a cowboy turned around the sign on the cook tent reading "DINE," making it read ENID and the name stuck.

Enid is one of the state's "instant" cities, settled in one day when the Cherokee Outlet was opened for settlement. As at Pond Creek, the original townsite was planned three miles north (at **North Enid**) where the Rock Island had built its depot. When it was discovered enterprising Cherokee Indians had chosen

Entitled "Boomer," this statue in Enid honors Cherokee Strip pioneers who made that run.

allotments in the townsite area, the U.S. Secretary of the Interior ordered the official townsite be located three miles south and it was here the post office, territorial government building, and land office were located. Both settlements claimed to be the real Enid. When a railroad train was sabotaged, a presidential proclamation was needed to settle the feud with the southern settlement winning official designation.

NOTABLE: An early automobile, the Geronimo, was manufactured in Enid. It also is the hometown of astronaut **Owen K. Garriott**, opera star **Leona Mitchell** (both have streets named after them), and author **Marquis James**. An early day Enid automobile salesman was **Clyde Cessna** who designed and flew his own airplane in 1911 and went on to lead in the manufacture of corporate and private planes.

COUNTY COURTHOUSE (NRHP), Grand Ave., was built in 1934, Enid's third. Inside the building are six murals painted by **Ruth Monro Augur**, a Works Progress Administration artist, who worked on them between December, 1935, and June, 1937. The common theme is "Trails," including "The Hunting Trail," "The Explorers Trail," and "The Cattle Trail." Written descriptions of the murals are included. On the lawn is a bronze sculpture called the Tri-State Statue honoring the participants in the Tri-State Music Festival begun in 1932 in Enid and held each spring. Junior high and high school band, orchestra, and vocal music students from across the United States and from several foreign countries have participated.

ENID PUBLIC LIBRARY is one block south. A plaque marks this as the site of the first religious service held in Enid, September 17, 1893. Also in the area is a "Doughboy" statue honoring veterans of World War I. Across the street is the sculpture called "Boomer" honoring those who made the run into the Cherokee Strip.

CHEROKEE STRIP MUSEUM (OHS), 507 S. 4, presents artifacts and materials pertaining to the Cherokee Outlet. Farm exhibits are displayed in the barn. Latest exhibit showcasing Enid's important role in the oil patch is the first portable rotary drilling rig, patented by the **George E. Failing Company**, long one of the city's largest employers. It is open from 9 a.m. to 5 p.m. Tuesday through Friday and from 2 to 5 p.m. weekends. Admission is free.

MIDGLEY MUSEUM, 1003 Sequoyah Dr., is in a house built of petrified wood and stone. The museum features displays of rock, minerals, big game trophies, crystal, glassware, and antique furniture. It is open by appointment, 405/234-7265. Admission is free.

RAILROAD MUSEUM OF OKLAHOMA, 702 N. Washington, in the old Santa Fe freight depot, has railroad hardware, tools, signs, lanterns, dining car service, and telegraph equipment. Some rolling stock. It is open from 1 to 4 p.m. Tuesday through Friday and from 10 a.m. to 1 p.m. Saturday. Admission is free.

GOVERNMENT SPRINGS PARK, across the street and just east of the Cherokee Strip Museum, was a popular stop on the Chisholm Trail. Although the springs didn't produce enough water for the stock, there was an ample supply two miles east at Skeleton Creek. The cattle could graze between the springs and the creek while the trail drivers rested at the springs. The name Government Springs was used after government surveyors camped here while surveying the townsite and section lines before the Outlet was opened to settlement. A marker at the foot of a bluff in the park, near the Springs, notes this. A major restoration of the park's outstanding features and facilities is currently (1991) underway.

PHILLIPS UNIVERSITY, north of Garriott on University

Phillips University was chartered in 1906 and is named to honor a benefactor.

Blvd., is a private school chartered October 11, 1906, as Oklahoma Christian University. The name was changed seven years later to honor **T. W. Phillips** of Butler, Pennsylvania, whose generosity made the founding of the school possible.

From Enid south to Dover, US 81 follows almost exactly the

route of the Chisholm Trail.

Twenty miles south of Enid is **Hennessey** in **Kingfisher County** (named for **King Fisher**, early-day stage station operator). Before Hennessey, about 1.5 miles north of **Bison**, is a historical marker for **Buffalo Springs**, located .3 of a mile west. This was the last camp site of Pat Hennessey and his men before they were killed (see below). This was an important gathering place for those making the land rush of April 22, 1889, into the Unassigned Lands of central Indian Territory.

HENNESSEY

The post office for this town (pop. 1,902) was established July 10, 1889, just after the '89 land run. For three months, until it was corrected, the official post office spelling was Hennesy. The town was named for **Pat Hennessey**, a government freighter on the Chisholm Trail who was killed here July 4, 1874, along with three drivers. Although it was first believed the massacre was carried out by Indians, it was later thought the perpetrators may really have been outlaws masquerading as Indians.

The **Farmers and Merchants National Bank**, 107 Main, has NRHP recognition as one of the oldest commercial bank buildings remaining in what was Oklahoma Territory. Construction began in 1889.

HENNESSEY GRAVE, about two blocks west and one south of the downtown, is marked with a memorial in the form of a stone lighthouse. It marks the site where Hennessey and his men were slain. His grave also lies in this small park .

MEMORIAL PARK, north edge of town on US 81, is the location of a memorial to hometown boy **Roy V. Cashion**, first soldier from Oklahoma Territory to be killed in the Spanish-American War. Cashion rode horseback to Guthrie to enlist in the Rough Riders, May 5, 1898. He was a member of the First Oklahoma Volunteer Cavalry and served under **Col. Leonard Wood** and **Lt. Col. Theodore Roosevelt**. He died in a charge on San Juan Hill, July 1, 1898. Also in the park is a historical marker relating the story of the Pat Hennessey massacre and another for the first rural mail route in Oklahoma, established August 15, 1900, at Hennessey.

BULL FOOT STATION was a popular spot along the Chisholm Trail because of its water well. It is described on a historical marker at the south edge of town on US 81.

BAKER'S RANCH, four miles south of Hennessey, was a watering place on the trail, traces of which are visible in this

Pat Hennessey and three others were killed on this spot in 1874 at the hands of unknown, probably white bandits.

area. A historical marker on nearby US 81 describes the ranch.

It is five miles farther to **Dover** on the north bank of the **Cimarron River**.

DOVER
Original designation for DOVER (pop. 376) was **Red Fork**

Station, (the Cimarron was originally called the **Red Fork** of the **Arkansas**). It was a stop on the Chisholm Trail where teamsters could change horses at the stockade maintained here. When a post office was established in 1890 it was named for the town in England. On the north edge of Dover, at a roadside park, are historical markers for Red Fork Station and the Chisholm Trail.

April 3, 1895, five armed bandits held up a Rock Island train near Dover, stealing a box of gold, the payroll for Fort Sill. Treasure hunters believe the gold is still hidden in this area. This was the work of the Dalton-Doolin gang. A posse was quickly formed and soon caught up with the gang who had made camp on the Cimarron River. **William "Tulsa Jack" Blake**, left on guard, fired a shot at approaching deputy and a gunfight ensued. A bullet struck Blake's cartridge belt mortally wounding the robber. The rest of the gang, **George "Red Buck" Weightman**, **William "Little Bill" Raidler, George "Bitter Creek" Newcomb,** and **Charley Pierce**, made good their escape in a running gun battle. Arriving at a farm owned by an elderly preacher, the gang took his team and killed him when he objected.

In the foothills of the **Gloss Mountains** they broke up. Bitter Creek and Pierce remained together and were killed within a few days. Weightman headed for Cheyenne Country where he formed a new gang. He was killed in March, 1896, at a hideout on the South Canadian near **Taloga**.

In 1906, at the railroad crossing over the river, a Rock Island passenger train plunged through the bridge, weakened by a flood. Although two sleeping cars filled with passengers went in the river only four persons are believed to have died. The locomotive is still buried in the quicksand of the river bed.

From Dover to **Silver City**, about 45 miles south on the **Canadian River**, the Chisholm Trail split into two branches. The west leg continued along present US 81 through **Kingfisher**, nine miles south, and **Okarche**, then dropped southwest to Fort Reno before angling back southeast to Silver City. This was the freight and stage trail. The cattle trail moved southeast from Dover to just west of the present town of **Piedmont**, then headed south through Yukon and back to Silver City.

Two miles north of Kingfisher is a historical marker noting Rural Electrification in Oklahoma. The Cimarron Electric Co-Op energized Oklahoma's first co-op electric meter on Christmas

An appropriate landmark in the ghost town of Silver City is this cemetery.

Eve, 1937, at the nearby home of **Earl Harrison**.

KINGFISHER

Seat of Kingfisher County is KINGFISHER (pop. 4,095). The town, settled in the Run of '89, took its name from **Kingfisher Creek** which was named for stage operator and rancher King Fisher, owner of the townsite. Original name for the post office, established April 20, 1889, was **Lisbon**, changed two months later.

The Dalton family moved to a Kingfisher homestead by the time their sons had reached manhood. Frank, Grat, Bob, and Emmett served as deputy U.S. marshals for a period of time. Frank Dalton was killed in line of duty in 1887 but the other three brothers ran into trouble. Grat and Emmett were forced to resign and Bob was fired for accepting a bribe. The Dalton gang of outlaws, led by Bob Dalton, is credited with at least four train robberies in Oklahoma—at Wharton, Letitia, Red Rock, and Adair. They robbed a number of banks also before their ill-fated attempt of robbing two Coffeyville, Kansas, banks simultaneously.

The Oklahoma Historical Society was organized May 27, 1893, in Kingfisher; a historical marker is on the courthouse grounds. Another marker, Main and Roberts, is near the site (NRHP) of one of three U.S. Land Offices used for filing claims after the Run of '89. The other two were at **Guthrie** and **Oklahoma City**.

On the west edge of town on SH 33 is a historical marker for the Kingfisher Stage Station. The Chisholm Cattle Trail itself ran six miles east of the marker and in some places was 12 miles wide. About a mile east of town on SH 33 is a historical marker for **Kingfisher College** (NRHP) which was founded a mile north in 1890 and continued until 1922. The site contains only a few tumbled remains of this college.

Notable one-time residents of Kingfisher include the "vagabond" poet **Don Blanding** and **W. C. Coleman**, who started here with the improved gasoline lamp before moving to Wichita, Kansas, and starting the Coleman Company. **Sam Walton** (Wal-Mart) was born here.

CHISHOLM TRAIL MUSEUM (OHS), 605 Zellars Ave., traces the history of the trail. The complex includes a restored bank, school, church, and log cabins, one of which was the home of **Adeline Dalton**, mother of the notorious **Dalton Boys**. As a sign at the cabin notes, she was the mother of 15 children, several who were respectable, law-abiding citizens. Frank served as deputy U.S. Marshal and died in the line of duty while serving the court of Judge Isaac Charles Parker, the "Hanging Judge" in Fort Smith, Arkansas. It is open from 9 a.m. to 5 p.m. Wednesday through Saturday and from 1 to 5 p.m. Sunday, from November through April. It is also open on Tuesday, May through October. Admission is free.

SEAY MANSION (NRHP and OHS) next to the museum, was the home of local judge **Abraham J. Seay**. He built this home, called Horizon Hill, when he became territorial governor in 1892, speculating, wrongly, that Kingfisher might become the territorial capital (instead of Guthrie) with this house as the executive mansion. The home contains period furnishings. The hours are the same as those of the Chisholm Museum. Admission is free.

By April, 1906, Seay, a life-long bachelor, had gone to California and was staying in the upper floor of a San Francisco hotel. When the famous earthquake hit, he narrowly escaped injury. He was on crutches from a previous injury but put on his overcoat, picked up his lap robe and, on crutches, made his way to the elevator. He was carried to the street and put on a passing freight wagon. He rode to the nearest park, got off the wagon, and waited for order to be restored.

This mansion was built by Territorial Governor Abraham J. Seay who speculated that Kingfisher might become the territorial capital. Instead it went to Guthrie.

It is 10 miles to Okarche. Located on the **Canadian** and Kingfisher County line. The post office for OKARCHE (pop. 1,160) was established in June, 1890. The name was coined from the words OK(lahoma), AR(apaho), and CHE(yenne).

El Reno (Section 5) is 14 miles south. It is the seat of **Canadian County** (named for the river). About nine miles south of Okarche is the turnoff, west, to **Concho** and **Darlington**.

CONCHO/DARLINGTON

Now the Cheyenne/Arapaho Field Office, Concho was originally established in 1897 because the Cheyenne Indians no

This Moorish-style chapel is at the Cheyenne-Arapaho Agency at Darlington, north of El Reno.

longer desired to share the agency school with the Arapahos at Darlington (NRHP), two miles south. In 1909, the Darlington school was closed and consolidated with Concho, one of history's little ironies.

Darlington was originally established in 1870 to maintain the peace after **General Custer's** defeat of Cheyenne chief **Black Kettle** on the Washita near present-day **Cheyenne** (Section 5).

For a time Darlington was western Oklahoma's most important settlement. One of Indian Territory's first telephone lines linked the agency to Fort Reno, across the North Canadian River. Western Indian Territory's first newspaper, the *Cheyenne Transporter*, began publication here in 1879. Although none of the old buildings remain at the Concho site, Darlington, now part of the State Game Farm, can still boast a few. Here can be seen a Moorish-style chapel and large dormitory from the 1910-22 period when Oklahoma Masons operated Darlington as a boarding school for orphans and home for elderly lodge members. Also here are two homes from the 1870 period.

Back on US 81 it is 10 miles from El Reno to **Union City** (pop. 1,000) which is the popular name for this town. It was platted as **Sherman** in 1889 and is designated **Union** by the post office. It is about two miles to the **South Canadian River**, northern boundary of **Grady County**.

GRADY COUNTY

The northern edge of Grady County (named for *Atlanta Constitution* editor **Henry W. Grady**) is the beginning of the old **Chickasaw Nation**. Few tribal families lived so far west, however, and the region mainly was occupied by cattlemen. Many married Chickasaw wives and were adopted members of the tribe. The others operated their ranches illegally. It is about two miles to **Minco** (pop. 1,422) .

MINCO

Settlement began here in 1889 shortly before the railroad arrived in 1890. The name is an Indian word meaning "chief." The same year, the area's first school, which had been started at Silver City by Mrs. Meta Chesnut Sager, was moved here. Called first Minco Academy, the name later became **El Meta Bond College**.

A SIDE-TRIP

Go east on SH 37 eight miles to **Tuttle** (pop. 2,807).

Treasure hunters believe Jesse James and his gang once buried a cache of loot, which has never been found, east of this town. At the east edge of Tuttle stands a 12-ton boulder, marking the Chisholm Trail. Bronze tablets on the rock list the names of pioneer residents and tell of Silver City, two miles north.

SILVER CITY

Although now a ghost town, this was once a very important resting and trading stop on the Chisholm Trail. Just north was the always dangerous South Canadian River to be crossed and

This Chisholm Trail marker in Tuttle describes the site of the Silver City site, two miles north. Silver City is a ghost town.

trail drivers liked to rest themselves and graze their herds, stock up on supplies, and make repairs before attempting the mile-wide river crossing with its patches of quicksand. All that remains today of this once busy spot is the well-kept cemetery (NRHP).

Back on US 81, it is eight miles to **Pocasset**.

POCASSET

The name of this town, established December 13, 1902, was taken from an Indian village in Massachusetts. The word means "where the strait widens out." Pocasset is the site of a bungled train robbery attempted by **Al Jennings** who was, in his lifetime, a lawyer, train robber, convict, evangelist, author, and candidate for governor of Oklahoma. On this particular job, pulled in broad daylight while attempting to blow up a safe in the baggage/express car, Jennings and his gang managed to blow up the entire car. All they got away with was some jewelry and a little money taken from the passengers.

It is 10 miles to **Chickasha** (Section 8).

A SIDE-TRIP

South of Chickasha take SH 19 east to **Lindsay**, 22 miles. About one mile from the turnoff east is the site, long unmarked, of a stage station where the **Boggy Depot-Fort Sill** road crossed the trail. This trading point, established in the 1870s, was named **Fred** for **Col. Franklin L. Fred**, early-day Indian trader. A marker was recently dedicated to commemorate the historic post, just south of the US 81/SH 19 junction.

LINDSAY

Townsite owner **Lewis Lindsay** gave his name to LINDSAY (pop. 2,947), located in **Garvin County**. The county is named for **Samuel L. Garvin**, prominent early-day Chickasaw.

Two miles south of town on SH 76 is the community of **Erin Springs**, settled in 1875 on an old wagon trail between **Pauls Valley** and **Fort Cobb**. The stage stop of **Elm Springs** was located here.

MURRAY/LINDSAY MANSION (NRHP) was constructed in 1879-80 by Irish immigrant and rancher **Frank Murray** and his wife, **Alzira**, part Choctaw. After Murray's death in 1892 his wife had the large, square, stone house remodeled to its current look. The Murrays son-in-law was Lewis Lindsay who also lived in the house for a time. Restored in later years by the Oklahoma Historical Society, it is now maintained by a local group. It is open from 9 a.m. to 5 p.m. Tuesday through Friday and from 2 to 5 p.m. weekends. Admission is free.

Return to US 81 and it is 15 miles to **Rush Springs**.

RUSH SPRINGS

The post office established July 11, 1883, six miles east, was named **Parr**. The name was changed to RUSH SPRINGS (pop. 1,229) May 13, 1892, and the townsite moved to its present

The Murray-Lindsay House museum at Erin Springs is listed on the NRHP.

location on the Rock Island railroad in 1893. The name came from the springs on the Chisholm Trail at the headwaters of **Rush Creek**. One of the springs is in the municipal park.

One of the first Civilian Conservation Corps camps was located here in the 1930s.

On the north edge of town, on US 81 Business, a historical marker details the tragic 1858 attack by federal troops on a

Comanche band visiting the Wichita village here on Rush Creek. The Fort Belknap (Texas) troops were under the command of **Capt. Earl Van Dorn**. Seventy (one estimate says 90) Comanche warriors were killed in the attack which happened by mistake. The Comanches were on their way to **Fort Arbuckle** to discuss peace terms with the whites at the urging of the Wichitas. The remaining Comanches wrongly assumed they had been betrayed by the Wichitas and sought retribution and the frightened and innocent Wichitas sought refuge at Fort Arbuckle (Section 6). In the captain's defense, it should be said he had known nothing of the peace mission.

Marlow is nine miles south.

MARLOW

MARLOW (pop. 4,416) began as a tent city in 1892 along the Rock Island line. The history of this site in **Stephens County** (named for Texas Congressman **John A. Stephens**) goes back to trail days. It is believed the town took its name from **Dr. Williamson Marlow** who settled his wife, five sons, and one daughter in a cave on the east bank of **Wildhorse Creek** in present **Redbud Park.** The five Marlow boys are the source of controversy about the early days. Some say they were little more than outlaws, raiding herds moving along the trail, then returning the cattle for rewards. Others contend the Marlow boys worked their large cattle operations and in their spare time only rounded up strays left behind by the large cattle drives.

PEACE OFFICERS MONUMENT, southeast side of town at the SH 29 junction, is dedicated to All Oklahoma Peace Officers. The large pink granite monument was put up in 1930 near the spot where **Sheriff W. A. Williams** was killed.

It is 10 miles to **Duncan**, seat of Stephens County.

DUNCAN

Trader **William Duncan**, once a tailor at Fort Sill, settled near the site of present DUNCAN (pop. 21,732) in 1879 after marrying a citizen of the Chickasaw Nation. In 1889, Mrs. Duncan chose as her allotment a 500-acre tract in the area where the Rock Island was due to come through. She later sold lots, promising to give the buyers title when it was possible for her to legally do so. She kept her promise.

NOTABLE: **Earle P. Halliburton**, a local oilman, began offering to others in the business his now famous oil-well cementing service in 1924. **Mae Boren Axton** was a high school

This monument in Marlow honors Oklahoma peace officers and is dedicated to the memory of Sheriff W. A. (Wal) Williams killed in the line of duty on May 13, 1930.

English teacher in Duncan. In 1956 she wrote a song called "Heartbreak Hotel" for a young, unknown singer named **Elvis Presley**. Mrs. Axton has a son named **Hoyt** who became a singer, too. Born in Duncan was actor, later producer/director **Ron Howard** and former United Nations ambassador **Jeane Kirkpatrick**.

STEPHENS COUNTY HISTORICAL MUSEUM, US 81 and Beech, offers some unique displays and exhibits. The Boomer Room traces pioneer life from 1877 to 1920 including pioneer and Chisholm Trail displays. The Sooner Room shows life from 1920 to 1977 including the history of Halliburton Services. It is open from 1 to 5 p.m. Tuesday, Thursday, Saturday, and Sunday. Admission is free.

It is eight miles to **Comanche**. Five miles south of Duncan is the Sunray Refinery and less than a mile south of that is the spot where an old military road crossed this area. On this road passed the famous Dragoon Expedition of 1834 led by **Col. Henry Dodge**, on his way west to the Wichita village on the **North Fork** of the **Red River**. Near this spot, in 1852, **Capt. R. B. Marcy** of the Fifth Infantry, met his wagon train for an expedition west in search of the source of the Red River. Traces of the Chisholm Trail are visible about two miles east.

COMANCHE

Tucker was the first name selected for this post office in 1887. The name was changed to COMANCHE (pop. 1,695) in 1893 to honor the Indian tribe.

This is the hometown of **Clyde Burk**, five times World Champion Calf Roper and of baseball player **Alvin Dark**.

Oil drilling began in **Stephens County** as early as 1907 but first major production didn't come until 1912 when the Cruce Pool was opened. The **Comanche Pool** was found in 1918 when the **Comanche Petroleum Company** completed a 20 million-cubic-foot gas well here.

It is nine miles to **Addington** in **Jefferson County** (named for **President Thomas Jefferson**).

ADDINGTON

First postmaster, **James P. Addington**, gave his name to the post office at ADDINGTON (pop. 100) established January 8, 1896. In this area is the Price Ranch, established in 1886 by **J. C. Price** who drove herds of cattle through here before settling down to ranching. The Chisholm Trail ran right through the present ranch which has one of the principal landmarks on

Lookout Point monument on Monument Hill along the Chisholm Trail at Addington. Tom Lattamore, a black cowboy, is buried at this spot.

the trail, **Monument Hill**, also called Monument Peaks or Twin Peaks. Because of a natural spring nearby, this was a popular camping spot. Those who stopped would often add rocks to the hill and before long the monument had grown quite large.

Buried at this spot is the black cowboy Tom Lattamore. A large concrete shaft now marks this trail site.

It is six miles to **Waurika**, the county seat.

WAURIKA

Until 1912, **Ryan**, 10 miles south, was the designated seat of Jefferson County. A third challenge vote, held February 20, 1912, finally won county seat status for WAURIKA (pop. 2,088). The original name of the post office, established May 22, 1890, was **Peery**, changed to **Moneka** in 1895. In 1902 the town received its present name, an adaptation of an Indian word meaning "pure water." This area with its buffalo grass was a popular one during the Texas cattle drives northward. Herds were often held over here to fatten up. In 1892, the Rock Island arrived and for several years Waurika served as a crew-change point and busy rail center.

CHISHOLM TRAIL HISTORICAL MUSEUM (OHS), traces the 20-year history of the trail through its exhibits. It is open from 9 a.m. to 5 p.m. Tuesday through Friday and from 2 to 5 p.m. weekends. Admission is free.

ROCK ISLAND DEPOT (NRHP) was restored and opened in late 1990. The town library is housed in half of this building, constructed in 1912, and a Rock Island artifact room and civic center is in the other half.

South of Waurika, about 12 miles, near Ryan, is believed to be the site of early-day trading post San Bernardo on the Old Spanish Trail. The "Grand Chemin de Santa Fe" is thought to have run along and just north of the Red River. At this post were French and Spanish traders and many Indians. During it's height, 1750-1811, it had a population close to 3,000.

This is the end of the US 81 tour. For travelers seeking more information on the billion dollar **Healdton Oil Field** in this area a short side trip follows.

A SIDE-TRIP

Leave Waurika on US 70 going east to **Ringling**, 23 miles.

RINGLING

The post office for RINGLING (pop. 1,250) was established June 4, 1914, and named for circus entrepreneur **John Ringling**. Ringling was involved in oil exploration and business ventures in southern Oklahoma with Ardmore oilman **Jake L. Hamon.** Hamon talked Ringling into building 20 miles of railroad from Ardmore (Section 6) west to their oil leases. In 1914 it was extended 10 miles to Ringling. The first spike of the new railroad was driven August 4, 1913, in Ardmore. Coincidentally, that was the same day the **Franklin No. One** discovery well came in near Healdton, opening the rich Healdton field. Many of the wells in this field only had to be drilled to a shallow depth, less than 1,000 feet. This is one of the largest single fields ever found in Oklahoma.

The town of Healdton is seven miles east of Ringling on US 70, then five miles north on SH 76.

HEALDTON

Established in 1883, HEALDTON (pop. 2,872) was named for local merchant **Charles H. Heald.** The Healdton Field discovery well was drilled about two miles southeast of town.

As early as 1888 a petroleum prospector sank a well near Healdton using a foot-powered spring pole rig. The oil began to seep at 425 feet but he could not get a lease as this was Indian land. In 1904 **H. B. Goodrich** (Santa Fe Railroad) got title to land in this area and drilled several wells that produced both gas and oil while looking for a steady supply of fuel for his company. It was nine more years before the discovery well opening this field was drilled, however.

Actress **Rue McClanahan** ("The Golden Girls") was born in Healdton.

HEALDTON OIL MUSEUM (OHS), E. Main on SH 76, displays oil field equipment, photographs, and books relating to the oil industry. It is open from 9 a.m. to 5 p.m. Tuesday through Friday and from 2 to 5 p.m. weekends. Admission is free.

SECTION 11
US 59/259

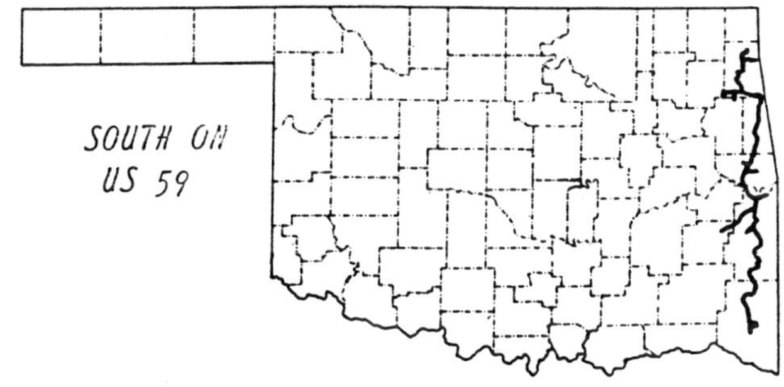

The prehistoric Indian Mortuary Figure Pipe is displayed in the museum at Spiro Mounds. The 12 remaining mounds built by a prehistoric civilization are among the most important archaeological remains in the United States.

SECTION 11
US 59/259

US 59/259 is Oklahoma's Lapland Cruise...a highly enjoyable meander through the state's seven most scenic counties. This is where the mountainous landscape and life styles of Missouri and Arkansas lap over into eastern Oklahoma, home of the Cherokees and Choctaws. Obviously, this easternmost tier of counties is not without its historical moments. Here was developed what may be the greatest prehistoric Indian ceremonial center yet uncovered by archaeologists. Here, too, are curious artifacts hinting at exploratory probes made into the heart of America centuries before the "discovery" of America. Also on the cultural front, deep in the woods of eastern Oklahoma, is the log cabin in which lived the inventor of the Cherokee alphabet, thereby making his tribe the first to boast a written language. Although not as profusely watered as Minnesota or forested as densely as Idaho or as mountainous as Colorado, Oklahoma can showcase creditable contenders in all three categories along this route. The motorist is well advised to drive at a leisurely pace so as to savor both scenery and history as he goes along. Relatively light traffic on the entire route makes it that much easier to enjoy.

SOUTH ON US 59/259

This trip will begin at **Grove** on the banks of **Grand Lake** in **Delaware County** (named for the Indian tribe) and continue to Idabel a few miles north of the Red River. Included are a number of short side trips which can be taken by those with the time and interest to visit the numerous historical spots along this route.

GROVE

Lying roughly at the northern edge of the old **Cherokee Indian Nation** is GROVE (pop. 4,020). The post office was established December 27, 1888, and the name comes from nearby **Round Grove**, a well-known landmark and a Civil War site.

Today, Grove is a resort area with many large and beautiful summer and retirement homes, restaurants, and boating, fishing, and camping areas. From statehood, in 1907, until 1912, Grove was the seat of **Delaware County**.

HAR-BER VILLAGE MUSEUM appears to be a log cabin village on the shore of Grand Lake, climbing from water's edge

Displays in the Har-Ber Village Museum complex encompasses 100 early American-style buildings. The museum complex contains a vast Americana collection amassed by a businessman and his wife.

up the side of a wooded hill. The village is actually Har-Ber Village Museum featuring household items and farm equipment from the late 1800s through the early 1900s. Each of the nearly 100 structures houses part of this Americana collection amassed over the years by Jones Truck Line owner **Harvey Jones** and his wife, **Bernice**, (thus the Har-Ber). A complete tour of this unique museum would take much more than a day but since the tour is self-guided, this allows the visitor to see as much or as little as time and inclination dictate. Signs point the way off of US 59 in Grove. It is open from 9 a.m. to 6 p.m. daily, May 1 to October 31. Admission is free.

CHEROKEE QUEEN is the name given to the two diesel-powered paddlewheel riverboats docked at water's edge on US 59 at the Honey Creek Bridge. A trip on one of these riverboats on the 26-mile cruise offered is an excellent way to see the Grand Lake area. The cruises are available from April through October. An admission is charged.

East of Grove on SH 25 go north three miles on SH 10, then east and south about 1.5 miles on county roads to the site of the near-ghost town of **Cayuga** and the **Splitlog Indian Mission Church.**

CAYUGA

When Mathias Splitlog, half French-half Cayugan, came to Indian Territory in the 1870s with his wife's people, the **Wyandots**, he chose to settle among the **Senecas** along **Cowskin Creek.** While living in Kansas, Splitlog became wealthy from flour milling and as a builder and real estate dealer, business ventures he continued in his new home. Soon he began the town of Cayuga Springs which had a post office from 1884 until 1912. Most of the town burned in 1913, long after Splitlog had been laid to rest in the burying ground by the church he built.

SPLITLOG CHURCH, the stone building not completely finished at the time of Splitlog's death in 1893, still stands. His funeral was the first service held in the structure. The building is listed on the National Register of Historic Places and is open on Sundays.

Returning to Grove, go south two miles on US 59 from the Honey Creek bridge, then about eight miles east on county roads to **Polson Cemetery**, about a mile west of the state line (two miles NW of Southwest City, Missouri). In this cemetery lie two Cherokee brothers, **Stand Watie** and **Elias Boudinot**, their cousin **John Ridge**, and Ridge's father, **Major Ridge.** These four

This monument in the Polson Cemetery honors Stand Watie, the only American Indian to attain the rank of brigadier general during the Civil War and the last Confederate general to surrender at the end of the war. He participated in the battles of Wilson Creek, Bird Creek, Pea Ridge, Honey Springs and Cabin Creek.

Mathias Splitlog, a mixed breed who married a Wyandot woman, was the first person buried from the Splitlog Church which he had built in the 1890s.

signed the 1835 Treaty of New Echota which led to the removal of the Cherokees from Georgia to Indian Territory. The four left Georgia voluntarily for the West in 1838. However, they were marked for assassination by the Cherokee faction opposed to the treaty who were later forcibly removed west. Because of advance warning Watie escaped the 1839 tragedy which claimed his uncle, cousin, and brother. Watie served the Confederacy as a

243

brigadier general during the Civil War. He died in 1871 and was buried in Polson Cemetery with the other three men.

It is 12 miles from Grove to **Jay**.

JAY

Present seat of Delaware County is JAY (pop. 2,220). The post office was established May 19, 1909. As is often the case when determining where a location got its name, history gets a little hazy and there are choices to be sorted through. One source says the town was named for Jay Washbourne, grandson of an early-day Cherokee missionary. This Washbourne, who is buried in Polson Cemetery, was actually named Claude L., the Jay being a childhood nickname. A second source says the town was named for Jay Washburn, nephew of Stand Watie.

Jay became the seat of Delaware County by a vote in December, 1908, though the move didn't occur until 1912. According to local legend, when the removal of the seat of government finally did take place there was a small war between two local Jay factions, each wanting the records stored in its own courthouse. After several days of wild firing between the two groups, the war was called off, the only casualty being a mule.

DELAWARE COUNTY HISTORICAL MUSEUM, located in Jay near the intersection of US 59 and SH 20, is housed in the community center. Featured are Indian artifacts and historical items collected from throughout the county. It is open on Thursdays and holidays. Admission is free.

Approximately 9.5 miles east of Jay on SH 20 is a historical marker for old **Fort Wayne**, a US Army post established in 1839 and named for Revolutionary War hero **Gen. "Mad" Anthony Wayne. Capt. Nathan Boone**, son of Daniel, conducted some early Indian Territory boundary surveys from this post. The fort was deactivated in 1842 and the site given to the Cherokee Nation. In July, 1861, Col. (later Gen.) Stand Watie established a Confederate Army post here and organized the Cherokee Mounted Rifles. Federal troops captured the post October 22, 1862. Today nothing remains of the fort.

Back on US 59, it is approximately 23 miles to the junction of US 59 and US 412 (formerly SH 33) and a side trip which includes two historic points of interest, the sites of **New Springplace Mission** and **Saline Courthouse**, a round trip of approximately 30 miles.

A SIDE TRIP

Turn right on US 412 to the town of **Twin Oaks** four miles

244

west. A historical marker is at the turnoff south (US 412C) to Oaks, where the original site of **New Springplace Mission** is west of town near a ford across **Spring Creek.**

NEW SPRINGPLACE MISSION was a Cherokee mission established in 1842 by the Moravian Church. At the site was a natural oil spring used by the Cherokees for medicinal purposes. Members of the mission included many prominent Cherokee families, among them the **Adairs**, **Ridges**, **Vanns**, and **Waties**. Near the log schoolhouse and church passed a branch of the old military road which ran from **Jefferson Barracks** in Missouri to **Fort Gibson.** All that remains today at this once busy site are the walled spring and a few graves.

Returning to US 412, continue west about 10 miles to the road marking the line between Delaware and **Mayes** Counties, (latter named for Cherokee Chief **Samuel H. Mayes**). About a mile south of this corner is the old frame Saline Courthouse.

SALINE COURTHOUSE (NRHP) is the only one of nine original Cherokee District Courthouses, all built in 1889, still standing. A small settlement soon grew up around this courthouse including a blacksmith shop, churches, school, doctor's office, and general store. The settlement was the site of one of the area's most brutal slayings in September, 1897, when the store owner was shot from ambush. A witness to this murder was in turn killed, and the sheriff investigating the two murders was himself killed. None of the murders was ever solved. A group of tombstones along the road in front of the courthouse testify to other tragedies which apparently happened in the vicinity during the 1890s. Today the tranquil setting around the old courthouse makes it difficult to imagine this had ever been anything but a quiet, peaceful spot.

Return to the junction of US 59/US 412 and continue east four miles to **Flint.**

FLINT

At various times known as Beckwith or Hilderbrand, FLINT (named for the Flint District of the Cherokee Nation) has been a settlement of some sort since the mid-1800s. Prior to the Civil War, a mill was established here along **Flint Creek**. For over a century grain was ground and lumber cut at **Hilderbrand's Mill** (NRHP). The present four-story mill, dilapidated but still standing, was built to replace the original which was washed away in a flood in 1892. Location is about a mile north of the highway. Along the way are a few shells of the old business

The Saline County Courthouse is the only one of several original Cherokee District Courthouses still standing.

district of Flint.

It is 24 miles on US 59 to **Westville** (pop. 1,374) (Section 8) in **Adair County** (named for a prominent Cherokee family). Thirteen miles south is **Stilwell.**

STILWELL

Seat of Adair County is STILWELL (pop. 2,663). The town was started in 1896 and named for **Arthur E. Stilwell,** the promoter of the Kansas City, Pittsburg & Gulf railroad (now Kansas City Southern). The county records and offices were moved here in 1910 from Westville. Until recent years a working water-powered grain mill was located nine miles northwest of town off of SH 51 along **Bidding Creek.**

BITTING SPRINGS MILL (different spelling) later was known as **Golda's Mill.** The scenic mill, tucked in the trees along the stream bank, was a popular visiting place for many Oklahomans who came to tour and buy ground meal at the scenic old mill before it burned only a few years ago.

Southwest of Stilwell about six miles along SH 100 and three miles by county road to Lyons, then 1.5 miles further southwest along Sallisaw Creek, stood **Fairfield Mission**, established in 1829. This particular school was not a boarding seminary but a "day school" open free to all who wished to attend. The mission cemetery contains some of the oldest graves in the state. The mission buildings, long since gone, stood in a grove of large trees east of the cemetery.

Twenty miles south of Stilwell on US 59 is **Brushy** and the turn-off to **Marble City**, about six miles west. It is located in **Sequoyah County** (named for the Sequoyah District of the Cherokee Nation which was, of course, named for the man who developed the Cherokee written language).

MARBLE CITY

The village of MARBLE CITY (pop. 232) dates back to 1835 when a post office called **Kidron** (for a Biblical stream) was established in the area. The settlement moved and became **Marble Salt Works** in 1858, then took back the name of Kidron until 1886 when it became **Kedron**; then **Marble** in 1895 and finally, in 1906, Marble City. Three miles southwest of town is **Dwight Mission**.

DWIGHT MISSION (NRHP) was established by the Presbyterians, first in Arkansas in 1821, then moved to Indian Territory in 1829. None of the original buildings of the co-educational school remain, but logs from one of the earliest buildings have been incorporated into a cabin that serves as a small museum on the grounds. Although the mission school was open for over a century (1830-1948), today the grounds are used by the Presbyterians for conferences and as a retreat. Visitors are welcome.

Back on US 59, continue south to the junction with SH 101, three miles north of Sallisaw. Turn east for seven miles to **Sequoyah's Home Site**. Enroute, the road passes the cemetery for the town of **Akins**. Buried here is gangster **Charles Arthur**

"Pretty Boy" Floyd. Born near Akins in 1904, "Pretty Boy" Floyd became a notorious gangster of the 1930s. Shortly after becoming involved in the June 17, 1933, Kansas City Massacre, in which four lawmen were murdered by Floyd and two others in their attempt to free Oklahoman Frank "Jelly" Nash from custody, Floyd became Public Enemy No. 1. Nash, one of the country's leading bank robbers, was being returned to Leavenworth from where he escaped in 1930. He also died in the

This was the cabin believed to have been built by Sequoyah in 1828. Sequoyah provided a written language for the Cherokee Indians.

hail of gun fire at Union Station in Kansas City. Floyd, who earned his notoriety as a bank robber, kidnapper and gunman, was killed on a farm near East Liverpool, Ohio, on October 22, 1934, by FBI agents led by Melvin Purvis.

SEQUOYAH'S HOME (NRHP, OHS and National Historic Landmark). Sequoyah (also known as **George Guess**) was born somewhere in the Appalachian region, possibly Tennessee, about 1775. He was the son of a Cherokee mother and a white trader father. As an adult he became fascinated with the fact white men could communicate with each other by writing messages and he began experimenting with a written alphabet for the Cherokee language. He worked on this project for over a decade despite the ridicule of many, including his wife who burned his tree bark notes at one point. In 1821 he completed his 86-character syllabary. The first person to learn to use it was his daughter **Ahyoka**.

In 1828 Sequoyah came to Indian Territory and it is believed built this one-room log cabin, now enclosed in a stone building for protection, soon after. In 1842 he traveled to Mexico looking for a band of Cherokees who had migrated there. He died in the summer of 1843 in Mexico and his burial place is unknown. Near the home site is the recently restored spring which Sequoyah lined with rock when he moved here. Logs in the nearby visitor center were hand cut by Sequoyah who had planned to use them to add another room to the cabin upon his return from Mexico. It is open from 9 a.m. to 5 p.m. Tuesday through Friday and from 2 to 5 p.m. weekends. Admission is free.

SALLISAW

Seat of Sequoyah County (named for its most famous resident) is SALLISAW (pop. 7,122) which began as **Childer's Station**, a trading post/camping site on the Fort Smith-Fort Gibson road. In 1888 the post office for a town named Sallisaw 11 miles north was moved to the Childer's Station location and the name of the town was changed to match the post office. Sallisaw is from the French word "salaison," meaning salt meat or salt provisions.

FOURTEEN FLAGS MUSEUM (NRHP) is located half block east of US 59/64 junction. Typical of the cabins of early settlers is this cabin built near Sallisaw in 1845 by **Franklin Faulkner**, a white man who came to Indian Territory as a teamster over the Cherokee "Trail of Tears." He served as judge of the Sequoyah District of the Cherokee Nation for 12 years.

The Hines Round Barn, on the NRHP, is located near Sallisaw.

Original furnishings and reproductions are in the museum. It is open from 8:30 a.m. to 4:30 p.m. daily. Admission is free.

HINES ROUND BARN (NRHP) can be seen east of US 59 before it goes under I-40 south of Sallisaw. Though it appears round it actually is 20-sided. It was built by **W. R. Hines** in 1912.

Twenty miles south is the junction of US 59 and US 271. Follow US 271 east for three miles to **Spiro** in the former Choctaw Nation.

SPIRO

It is generally believed SPIRO (pop. 2,146) was named for **Abram Spiro** of Fort Smith, Arkansas. Although the town wasn't established until 1895 with the arrival of the Kansas City Southern railroad, nearby were three of the earliest settlements in the state.

SPIRO MOUNDS STATE PARK (NRHP and OHS) is located 6.5 miles northeast of Spiro. The area was once an important trading and religious center in prehistoric America. Now an archaeological park, the area became a permanent settlement in approximately A.D. 600. It remained an important commercial, political, and religious center for several centuries until abandoned around A.D. 1400. The mounds left at Spiro are among the most important archaeological remains in the US. The 140-acre site includes 12 mounds with an interpretive center. Several walking tours are laid out. It is open from 9 a.m. to 5 p.m. Tuesday through Saturday, and from noon to 5 p.m. Sunday from May through October. November through April it is also closed on Tuesday. Admission is free.

SKULLYVILLE site is located a mile and a half east and less than a mile north of Spiro on US 271 (the post office spelled it Scullyville). The settlement began in 1832 when the US government established an agency here as a center for payment of annuities to the Choctaws being removed from the southeastern states into this area. In 1858, Choctaw Chief **Tandy C. Walker** took over the building for his home when the agency was moved to Fort Washita. In 1858 he used it as a stop **(Walker Station)** on the **Butterfield Overland Mail Route** through the territory. Although the building burned in 1947, the agency spring is still active with water flowing from a pipe near the road. The

The Craig Mound at Spiro Mounds State Park is 300 feet long, 115 feet wide, and 33 feet tall. Built in several stages over hundreds of years, it is actually four connected mounds. It is believed Craig Mounds were used for important burials by the Spiro people.

site is on the NRHP. Walker, reputed to be a friendly man, owned several hundred acres of land, taken care of by his many slaves. He fully approved of the mail line and personally cooperated in its operation. This was a breakfast stop and while the passengers were given a huge meal (75 cents) the horses were taken care of by Walker's slaves.

Of interest is the nearby **Skullyville Choctaw Burying Ground**. Here lie the remains of the **McCurtains, LeFlores, Folsoms, Walkers, Laniers**, and others, a Who's Who of the Choctaw Nation.

FORT COFFEE was established on June 16, 1834, to protect the newly arrived Choctaws. One and a half miles east of Spiro's Main Street on US 271 is a historical marker for Fort Coffee. The fort was named for **Gen. John Coffee**, of Tennessee. The site of the installation was high on a bluff overlooking the Arkansas River. The fort was abandoned in 1838 and in 1842 the site was selected by the Choctaw Council for the **Fort Coffee Academy for Boys**.

Return to US 59. It is five miles south to **Panama.** A historical marker just south of the SH 31 intersection notes the Butterfield Stage road crossed here.

PANAMA

Although PANAMA (pop. 1,528) wasn't established until 1895, just west was located the courthouse and jail for Skullyville County in the old Choctaw Nation. Remains of the old rock jail (NRHP), built in 1884, can still be seen about two miles west of town.

Two miles south of Panama is **Shadypoint.**

SHADYPOINT

SHADYPOINT (pop. 597) dates back to the 1890s but an earlier settlement called **Old Town** was located about a mile west. Both the military road from Fort Smith to Fort Towson and the Butterfield Stage route ran through this area. Travelers interested in the Butterfield and/or in exploring scenic back roads, might enjoy driving a winding country road stretching southwest from Shadypoint to **Latham** to **Red Oak.** The road, some 25 miles long, closely follows the Butterfield route through this part of Oklahoma.

BUTTERFIELD TRAIL–SIDE TRIP

Although the Butterfield Overland Mail Route only lasted for "2 years, 5 months, and 17 days" there are those who believe it was one of the greatest transportation achievements, not to mention adventures, of the 19th Century. By an act of Congress in 1857, the first transcontinental link between the Atlantic Seaboard and Pacific Coast was made possible. **John Butterfield**, an easterner who had never been farther west than Buffalo, New York, bid for and won a government contract to deliver the mail between St. Louis, Missouri, and San Francisco, California. For $600,000 he promised to accomplish this unheard of feat in 25 days. Passengers were permitted to travel along with the mail at a fare of $200 for a complete one-way journey or 10 cents a mile for shorter distances. The first regular mail delivery was made in 23 days, 23 hours, 30 minutes, well under the time promised.

The Butterfield route was laid out with official stations 12 to 18 miles apart generally. Coaches, pulled by four to six horse teams (usually mustangs) traveled three to five miles per hour, depending on the terrain. Since they traveled day and night the backs of the coaches could be let down to form a bed which could accommodate four to nine persons. It is doubtful much sleep was possible on these bumpy roads.

The Indian Territory leg of the trip was 197 miles. Twelve regular stations were situated along the route. Between Shadypoint and Red Oak were located two of these stations and one store which was a meal stop. Eight miles west of Shadypoint at Latham was **Trayhern's Station** (NRHP). A historical site marker can be found just east of the section line road going south to Latham Church. James Trayhern, a mixed-blood Choctaw, served as a member of the Supreme Court of the Choctaw Nation for several years. This stop was probably also a small trading center where Choctaw families in the neighborhood could buy staples and sell products such as meat, skins, and corn.

Next was the log **Edwards Store** and home (NRHP), which is still standing about seven miles northeast of Red Oak, north side of the road. The family cemetery is close by. Since the mail stage usually arrived at mealtime, Edwards set up a food station in the store and offered passengers a meal for 45 cents. The store was a separate building in front of the house and has long since been torn down.

Five miles west of the site is a small pass, about half a mile long known as "The Narrows." At the north end, **William Holloway** established his Butterfield Station (NRHP). Since the pass through the narrows was rocky and rugged, Holloway was allowed a permit to make this a toll road because of the maintenance work he had to do. A site marker is located here.

The next stop on the route was **Riddle's Station** near Wilburton (Section 13). Riddle, who was half Choctaw and half Irish, was granted a toll bridge permit because of the bridge he built next to his station across Big Fourche Maline Creek. Several Riddle family graves are located here as is a historical society site marker.

Back on US 59, it is six miles to **Poteau.**

POTEAU

Seat of **LeFlore County** (named for a prominent Choctaw family) is POTEAU (pop. 7,210), a Choctaw Record Town established in 1887. The town takes its name from the nearby Poteau River. Poteau means "post" in French. The Poteau River is the only major stream in Oklahoma which flows north.

KERR MUSEUM, six miles southwest on US 271, was established by a prominent Oklahoma politician. Two years before his death in 1962, **Robert S. Kerr**, U.S. Senator, Oklahoma governor, and a founder of the internationally known Kerr-McGee Corporation, finished building a home high atop a mountain near Poteau. It is now a museum with one room a reconstruction of the senator's Washington office. Other exhibits depict the history and development of Eastern Oklahoma. It is open daily from 1 to 4 p.m. An admission is charged.

Eleven miles south of the US 59/271 junction in Poteau is **Heavener.**

HEAVENER

A division point on the Kansas City Southern railroad HEAVENER (pop. 2,601) was named for townsite owner **Joe Heavener**, a white man who lived among the Choctaws. Two and a half miles east of town (watch for signs in town pointing the way) is the **Heavener Runestone.**

HEAVENER RUNESTONE PARK. Somewhat controversial are the strange symbols found carved (as early as 1830) on a large slab of rock on **Poteau Mountain.** There are three views as to what the symbols are and how they got there, if you count the group who think it is a hoax. A second group believes the eight mysterious characters were carved in the stone by a scholarly Swede who was in the area in the early 1700s with a colony of Germans. An even larger group believes these runes were carved by Vikings, possibly around 1012. Whatever the origin, the six to nine-inch figures are important enough to be listed on the NRHP.

The historic Peter Conser House west of Hodgen was built in 1894. The family graveyard is also on the grounds. Conser was chief of the Choctaw Lighthorsemen for many years. Today the house is open as a museum.

In 1986 this stone was studied by a runologist who was working on all known American runestones. He believes the message on the stone is not a date (November 11, 1012) as was previously thought. The new translation is "Glome Dal" which means "Valley owned by Glome," in other words it is a boundary marker or land claim. There have been at least five other authenticated runestones found in Oklahoma. The Heavener runestone is located in a ravine in the state park and can be seen daily from 8 a.m. until dark. Admission is free.

Five miles south on US 59 is the village of **Hodgen** and the turn-off to the **Peter Conser House**.

PETER CONSER HOUSE (NRHP and OHS) is located 3.5 miles west of Hodgen. Conser, half French, half Choctaw, was born about 1850 in present McCurtain County. He moved to this area after the Civil War. The house built in 1894 was the third at the site and he lived in it until his death in 1934. Conser was for many years chief of the **Choctaw Lighthorsemen**, a well-respected law enforcement group. This mounted police force for the Indian Nation rode all over the area to punish crimes and settle disputes. As captain of the Lighthorse for Moshulatubbee District, Conser's position can be compared to that of a chief of police or a county or high sheriff.

The restored home has many original furnishings and the barn displays farm equipment. It is open from 9 a.m. to 5 p.m. Tuesday through Friday, and from 2 to 5 p.m. weekends. Admission is free.

Eleven miles south of Hodgen, US 59 turns east to Arkansas and US 259 begins; we will follow it south. At five miles is the junction with SH 1, or the **Talimena Scenic Drive** (Section 13).

From SH 1 go south on US 259 five miles on a winding, mountainous road to **Big Cedar**, little more than a crossroads. Enroute is the **Three Sticks Monument**, honoring those who developed the natural resources in this area. In Big Cedar, at the junction of US 259 and SH 63, is a historical marker near the site where **President John F. Kennedy** gave a speech to dedicate the highway in 1966.

For the next 48 miles US 259 winds and curves over the ridges and valleys of the Ouachita Mountains. Turn at the entrance, SH 259A, to scenic **Beavers Bend State Park** in **McCurtain County** (named for a prominent Choctaw family).

BEAVERS BEND STATE PARK

The park is the site of an old Choctaw settlement along the

Three Sticks Monument near Big Cedar in the Kiamichi Mountains is dedicated to the people who developed the natural resources in this area.

Mountain Fork River and was named for **John T. Beavers,** a Choctaw intermarried citizen. There are others in this area who say this spot was not named for Beavers at all but for the many small animals early-day fur trappers found here along the river.

FOREST HERITAGE CENTER is a museum in the park in

which the history of forestry research is presented through
dioramas depicting the evolution of the forest from prehistoric
times to the present. It is open from 9 a.m. to 4:30 p.m. daily. An
admission is charged. The totem in front of the center was carved
by **Peter Toth** from a 450-year-old bald cypress.

Return to US 259 by the south park entrance. Broken Bow
is seven miles south.

*The totem outside the Forestry museum in Beavers Bend
State Park is the work of sculptor Peter Toth.*

BROKEN BOW

In 1911 the Dierks brothers, pioneer lumbermen, established BROKEN BOW (pop. 3,961) and named it for their home in Nebraska. Today the Dierks operations have been merged with Weyerhaeuser.

MEMORIAL INDIAN MUSEUM, located at Second and Allen, features a large collection of prehistoric Caddo Indian pottery, antique glass, paintings, sculptures, and rare books. It is open daily from 8 a.m. to 9 p.m., May through August, and 8 a.m. to 5 p.m., September through April. Admission is free.

GARDNER MANSION and EAGLETOWN, east of town on US 70, also are of interest (Section 15).

Located 11 miles south is **Idabel.**

IDABEL

First name for this county seat community of 6,957 was **Mitchell** but the name was changed to honor sisters **Ida and Belle Purnell.** The town was established in 1903 with the arrival of the Arkansas and Choctaw railroad. Four points of interest are listed below. For other historic spots in the area see Section 15.

MUSEUM OF THE RED RIVER is located at 812 E. Lincoln, south of town on the US 70 bypass. The museum features artifacts of American Indians and the archaeology of the Red River Basin. It is open from 9 a.m. to 5 p.m. Tuesday through Saturday, and from 1 to 5 p.m. Sunday. Admission is free.

MAGNOLIA MANSION (NRHP), 601 SE Adams, is a 1910 Colonial-style mansion with period furnishings. It is open by appointment, 405/286-3200. Admission is free.

BARNES-STEVENSON HOUSE (NRHP) is home of the McCurtain County Historical Society. The Victorian-style house at 35 E. Adams was completed in 1912 for the family of the county's first judge, **Thomas Jefferson Barnes.** The house remained in the family until 1974 when it was purchased by artist **Harold Stevenson Jr.**, a native of Idabel. It is open for tours.

MILLER COURTHOUSE historical marker is on US 259 north of the US 259/70 junction. On April 1, 1820, the government of Arkansas Territory created Miller County which included a large area of what is now southeastern Oklahoma. Oklahoma's first post office was established at the Miller County seat named Miller Courthouse, September 7, 1824. By treaty this area was ceded to the Choctaw Nation January 20, 1825.

This marker honors the CCC workers who helped build Beavers Bend State Park which was developed between 1935 and 1941. These workers were assigned to CCC Company 2815 and lived in a camp on the park site during those half dozen years. The company members built the park roads, trails and bridges, cleared brush, planted trees, constructed a bathhouse, cabins and other buildings.

SECTION 12
US 60

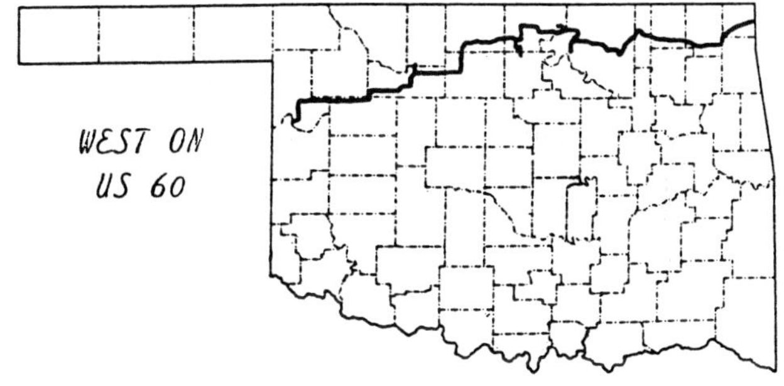

Two Osage Indian girls in The Osage pose in traditional dress of their tribe. Osage County, or The Osage, covered the Osage Indian Reservation during territorial days. Today, Osage County is Oklahoma's largest county.

SECTION 12
US 60

There is no possible way to prove it of course, but of all the numbered highways in Oklahoma US 60 is almost surely the one best qualified to represent the history and development of the all-important petroleum industry. Granted 70 plus of the state's 77 counties have produced some oil or gas over the years. And several of these, within an individual field or two, have from time to time dominated the scene. But consider this on behalf of US 60. The Nowata area in the extreme northeast first boomed about the time of statehood in 1907 on the strength of generous yields of extremely shallow sand, some as shallow as 30 to 35 feet. Recognized today as one of the world's largest shallow well fields, its 20,000 producing wells provide a giant laboratory for testing advanced secondary and tertiary production techniques. Meanwhile extreme western Oklahoma counties served by US 60, while waiting until the last half of the 20th century to boom, are now on yet another frontier. Here massive "deep test" drilling rigs are pushing holes five and six miles into geological formations hinting at unbelievably rich gas reserves. Along the way, on its course across the state's northern counties, the route has left in its wake northwestern Oklahoma's largest city (Enid) and two of its wealthiest, most progressive smaller cities, Bartlesville and Ponca City—cities long contributing more than their share of famous names to the petroleum (and thereby political) scene.

WEST ON US 60

This trip begins at the state line where US 60 enters Oklahoma from Missouri and will end at Arnett, 13 miles from the Texas Panhandle. The trip covers over 300 miles. Twice the tour leaves US 60 for a few miles travel on an alternate route. There are also three very short side trips offered for those with extra time to spend.

OTTAWA COUNTY

Just west of the state line in OTTAWA COUNTY (named for the Indian tribe) is a historical marker commemorating the old **Seneca Agency.** It was established July 4, 1832, for the Senecas, **Cayugas, Shawnees**, and the remnants of six other tribes that came to what is now Oklahoma from Ohio. Site of the original agency was located about 12 miles south along **Buffalo**

Creek. In 1838 the agency was moved to a new site near this marker and was known as the **Neosho Sub-Agency**. Later it was moved to Wyandotte near the **Seneca Boarding School.**

Four miles from the state line, south of the highway, is Wyandotte.

WYANDOTTE

The town of WYANDOTTE (pop. 366) is named for the small Indian tribe that came to this area in 1855 and then moved to the northeast corner of the state in 1867 when the Senecas gave up that region. Although no longer open, the **Seneca Indian School**, founded by the Quakers in 1869, was at one time the oldest Indian boarding school in the U.S. still in operation. Riverside in Anadarko (Section 8) now has that distinction.

It is 24 miles to **Vinita** (Section 5), county seat of **Craig County** (named for prominent Cherokee **Granville Craig**). It is 28 miles to **Nowata**, seat of **Nowata County** (named for the town).

NOWATA

The present town of NOWATA (pop. 3,896) began as a trading post soon after the Cherokees sold this area to the Kansas **Delawares** in 1868. The name comes from the word "no-we-ata," meaning "Welcome" or "We welcome you to come." The post office department changed the first town spelling of **Noweta** to the present Nowata.

NOWATA COUNTY HISTORICAL MUSEUM, 121 S. Pine, has exhibits of wood carvings, arrowheads, paintings, and rugs as well as articles and artifacts relating to the history of the county. Also included are artifacts from the Delaware and Cherokee Indian tribes. It is open from 1 to 4 p.m. Tuesday through Sunday. Admission is free.

NOWATA COUNTY COURTHOUSE (NRHP) was completed in 1912. The red brick and granite building is an unusual combination of architectural styles. Most distinctive is the octagonal, tiled roof cupola.

NOWATA POST OFFICE has a mural by the late, well-known Oklahoma Indian artist **Woody Crumbo**. "Rainbow Trail" was painted by Crumbo in egg tempera in 1943 as part of the New Deal art projects commissioned by the Federal government between 1933 and 1943. If not the last, this project was certainly one of the last approved by the Section of Fine Arts of the WPA for Oklahoma. In the early 1980s Crumbo was asked to do a little restoration on his original mural and he found it amusing that he was paid more than three times as much for the second job as he was for the first.

A few miles west of Nowata US 60 crosses into **Washington County** (named for **George Washington**). Approximately eight miles further is **Bartlesville**, county seat, and its smaller neighbor, **Dewey**, five miles north on US 75.

BARTLESVILLE

BARTLESVILLE (pop. 34,256) is named for **Jacob Bartles**, a trader and the third white man to move into the **Coo—wee—scoo—wee** District of the old Cherokee Nation. Married to the daughter of Delaware Chief **Charles Journeycake**, Bartles was an adopted citizen of the Cherokee Nation as the Delaware tribe had been granted equal rights in that nation. In 1875, Bartles bought out a grist mill which had been built on the **Caney River** in 1868 and opened a new trading post nearby. A historical marker on the north edge of Bartlesville is located near the site of the old mill. The first light bulb to glow in Oklahoma was lighted here by a dynamo Bartles hauled to his grist mill in 1878.

Another Oklahoma "first" occurred in the same area in 1897 when the **Nellie Johnstone No. 1**, the first commercial oil well in what was to become the state of Oklahoma came in on April 15. Two major oil companies had their birth in Bartlesville. The **Indian Territory Illuminating Oil Co.** later became Cities Service. The **Phillips Petroleum Co.**, founded by brothers **Frank** and **L. E. Phillips**, is still headquartered in Bartlesville.

Born here was Broadway dancer **Gretchen Wyler.** It is also the hometown of songwriter **Becky Hobbs** and comedian, newspaper columnist **Argus Hamilton III.**

BARTLESVILLE AREA HISTORY MUSEUM AND AR-CHIVES, located at 6th and Johnstone, include a local history of a three-county area with genealogy of local Indians and pioneers. It is open year-round from 9 a.m. to 6 p.m. Monday through Thursday, and from 9 a.m. to 5 p.m. Friday, and from 9 a.m. to 4 p.m. Saturday during the winter. It is closed Saturday during the summer. Admission is free.

FRANK PHILLIPS HOME (NRHP and OHS). The 26-room Greek Revival home of Frank Phillips, founder of Phillips Petroleum Company, is located at 1107 S. Cherokee. The home was built in 1908 but is restored with 1930s furnishings, a period when the house underwent a $500,000 remodeling. It is open from 9 a.m. to 5 p.m. Tuesday through Friday and from 2 to 5 p.m. weekends. Admission is free.

LAQUINTA FOSTER MANSION (NRHP), 2201 Silverlake Road, is a 32-room Spanish-style mansion built in 1939 and is located on the campus of **Wesleyan College**. It is open by appointment, 918/333-6151. Admission is free.

JOHNSTONE PARK, north of downtown on Cherokee Ave., contains three historical attractions. First is the Nellie Johnstone Well (NRHP). The oil rig structure is recreated on the original site. Nearby is the restored Hulah Santa Fe Depot originally located 15 miles north of town. It was built in 1923 on a Santa Fe feeder line to serve area cattle ranches. Also here is Santa Fe Engine No. 940, built in 1903.

CHEROKEE AVENUE WALKING TOUR. The Washington County Historical Society has mapped out a walking tour of historic Cherokee Avenue, near downtown Bartlesville. Included on the tour is **Price Tower** (NRHP) designed by architect **Frank Lloyd Wright**. Brochures are available at the Chamber of Commerce, 201 SW Keeler.

Five miles north on US 75 is the town of **Dewey**.

DEWEY

DEWEY (pop. 3,326) is named for **Admiral George Dewey** and was founded by Jacob Bartles (of Bartlesville). In 1898 the Santa Fe railroad came into the area from Caney, Kansas, 20 miles north. Bartles decided to move north of Bartlesville to meet the track, taking along with him a store and two houses. Because of the mud in the Caney River bottoms, it took five months to move the store building by oxen to the new site. Business was conducted as usual, however, as the building was inched north on log rollers to the new location.

DEWEY HOTEL (NRHP). First structure built by Jacob Bartles at the site of Dewey was the Dewey Hotel, completed in May, 1900. The architecture is Victorian and the hotel is one of the oldest buildings in Washington County. It is open from 10 a.m. to 5 p.m. Tuesday through Saturday and from 1 to 5 p.m. Sunday, from May through September. An admission is charged.

TOM MIX MUSEUM (OHS), 721 N. Delaware. Before he became a Hollywood cowboy movie star, Tom Mix was a bartender, band major, prize fighter, athletic coach, and trick roper, the latter for the Mulhall and later the Miller Brothers' 101 Wild West Shows (Section 6). In Dewey he was a crusading marshal. Displayed in the museum are the silent movie star's personal collection of saddles, pictures, records, clothing, and trophies. It is open from 9 a.m. to 5 p.m. Tuesday through Friday, and from

A replica of the Johnstone Oil Well is located in Johnstone Park in Bartlesville, the first commercial oil well in Oklahoma.

2 to 5 p.m. weekends. Admission is free.

PRAIRIE SONG VILLAGE is a re-creation of a pioneer village including a school, church, dance hall, general store, barn, home, and other buildings built with private funds on a ranch east of town. All contain period furnishings. It is open by appointment, 918/534-2662. An admission is charged.

The historical Dewey Hotel, built in 1900, is open for tours today.

Flat rocks from nearby fields are used as fence posts that are a common scene in Kay and Osage counties.

From Dewey take SH 123 back to the west edge of Bartlesville where you will enter **Osage County**, the largest county in Oklahoma. Its boundaries are the same as of the Osage Indian Reservation of territorial days and the area is still spoken of locally as **The Osage**. It is a land of timbered hills in the east and lush pastures in the central and western parts. It is a land of large cattle ranches, fabulous oil production, and rich Indians.

The Osage was a land that the Osages had chosen for themselves and they paid for it with tribal funds. They had hunted there for more than a century before they secured it for their reservation. When they moved here from Kansas in 1871-72, they were unaware of the rich pools of oil underground and they became possibly the richest per-capita group of people ever as a result of this good fortune.

Beginning in 1907 and ending in 1909, the reservation land was divided and the 2,229 Osages then on the tribal rolls each received 658 acres of land. The allotment applied to surface rights only and all mineral rights were reserved for the tribe as a whole. Each Osage on tribal rolls at that time received a headright (an equal share of all mineral income). A headright could not be sold but was passed on to the legal heirs at the death of its owner. In time some persons owned more that one headright, others less. At one time in the 1920s, a single headright paid its owner as much as $12,400 a year, about $150,000 in today's economy.

West of Dewey and Bartlesville is unincorporated **Okesa**. On August 21, 1923, **Al Spencer** and his gang, who had robbed several banks, stopped and robbed the Katy Limited on the Missouri, Kansas & Texas Railroad. The bandits took $20,000 in Liberty bonds and cash before making good their escape. The gang leader was tracked down later in the year in Coffeyville, Kansas, and killed in a hail of bullets as he attempted to escape. Spencer had planned many of his bank robberies in the Tulsa house owned by Ma Barker.

ALTERNATE ROUTE

From Bartlesville take SH 123 south and west 10 miles to the well-marked turn-off to **Woolaroc**.

WOOLAROC is owned and operated by the Frank Phillips Foundation, Inc. Begun in the 1920s by Frank Phillips as a relaxing retreat for himself, family, friends, and business associates, today WooLaRoc (WOOds, LAkes, ROCks) is a wildlife refuge and museum open for all to enjoy. Among the many interesting exhibits are the original entries in the contest to choose the sculptor for the **Pioneer Woman** statue in Ponca City (Section 6) and the airplane that won the "Dole Pineapple Race" between Oakland, California, and Honolulu, Hawaii, in 1927. It is open from 10 a.m. to 5 p.m. Tuesday through Sunday and all major summer holidays that fall on a Monday. An admission is charged.

Continue south on SH 123 eight miles to **Barnsdall.**

BARNSDALL

Originally named **Bigheart** for Osage Chief **James Bigheart**, the name of this town of 1,316 was changed to BARNSDALL in 1921 at the height of the Osage oil boom to honor the **Barnsdall Oil Company**. A historical marker by the highway just east of town marks the site of Bigheart's grave. The chief was influential in the **Osage Nation** from 1865 to 1908. He was instrumental in organizing the nation under a written constitution and was responsible for preserving the mineral rights of the land for members of the tribe when oil was discovered.

Born here was entertainer **Anita Bryant**. Actor **Clark Gable** once worked in the oil fields in this area.

BIGHEART HISTORICAL MUSEUM, 601 W. Main, is open from 1 to 5 p.m. Tuesday through Friday. Admission is free.

AMERICA'S ONLY MAIN STREET OIL WELL is located in the center of town at Eighth and Main St. Left here is a pump jack surrounded by a fence of white pipe. This well dates to the early 1900s.

To get to **Pawhuska**, seat of Osage County, go north and west out of Barnsdall on SH 11 for 10 miles, then north at the junction of SH 11/99 back to US 60 in Pawhuska.

PAWHUSKA

In addition to being county seat, PAWHUSKA (pop. 3,825) is the Osage Tribal Capital. The post office was established in 1876 and named for Osage Chief **Paw-Hu-Scah**. The word means "white hair." Tradition says Chief Paw-Hu-Scah received his name while a youth taking part in a battle fought during George Washington's administration. After wounding an officer, the young Indian grabbed for his victim's white hair to scalp him. To the youth's amazement the whole scalp (in reality a white, powdered wig) came off in his hand and the wounded soldier escaped. Because he believed the "scalp" possessed supernatural powers, the warrior always wore it fastened to his roach.

The town of Pawhuska has a look unlike most Oklahoma

The Pawhuska City Hall once served as the Osage Council House. The building is listed on the National Register of Historic Places.

The first Boy Scout troop in America was organized in Pawhuska in 1909 by the Rev. John Mitchell. This statue in the town commemorates the event. Bill Sowell was the sculptor.

The Osage Tribal Museum in Pawhuska has preserved the Osage Indian culture. The monument outside the museum provides a brief story about the Million Dollar Elm where the tribe held public auctions for oil leases on their lands.

towns in that the downtown business district sits at the foot of a high bluff. Three sets of steep steps are provided for hardy pedestrians wishing to take the shortest route up to the Osage County Courthouse and the Osage tribal buildings on the bluff.

In 1878, **Major Lahan J. Miles** became the Osage agent at Pawhuska and here he was visited during several summers by his young nephew, later **President Herbert Hoover**.

Pawhuska is the hometown of movie actor **Ben Johnson**, composer **Lemuel Jennings Childers, Gen. Clarence Tinker**, and former U.S. Treasurer **Maybelle Kennedy**. In the vicinity of Pawhuska live a number of artists, many of them Indian.

CHIEF FRED LOOKOUT. A historical marker on US 60 at the east edge of town honors Chief Lookout, last hereditary chief of the Osage and his wife, Julia, a descendant of Chief Paw-Hu-Scah. Turn north on Lynn Ave. in town and drive north and east to the memorial site, marked with a 10-foot tall granite stone.

OSAGE COUNTY HISTORICAL MUSEUM, in the Santa Fe Railway Depot at 700 N. Lynn Ave., features exhibits highlighting the area's Indian, western, pioneer, and oil heritage. It also provides details about the first Boy Scout troop in the United States, organized in Pawhuska in 1909 by **Rev. John Mitchell**, an English priest sent to St. Thomas Episcopal Church. On the grounds are a one-room schoolhouse, 1890s gazebo, and two railroad cars. It is open from 9 a.m. to 5 p.m. weekdays, and from noon to 5 p.m. weekends. Admission is free.

CATHEDRAL OF THE OSAGE is the title of one of 22 stained-glass windows in Immaculate Conception Church (NRHP), 1314 Lynn Ave., all crafted by artisans of the Bavarian Art Glass Company, Munich, Germany. This window depicts the coming of the Catholic faith to the Osage people and it was purchased in 1919 for $5,000 plus the cost of bringing the German workers to Pawhuska to install it. The 22 windows are valued at over $1 million. Inside the gothic styled church, built in 1916, are 12 wall-mounted stations of the cross crafted in Italy and recently restored by artist **Bill Sowell**. For a tour call 918/287-1414.

CONSTANTINE CENTER. This opera house, 110 W Main, originally opened in 1914 after the structure, built in the mid-1880s as the Pawhuska House Hotel, was renovated and redesigned. In 1986 the building once again underwent work to restore it to its former grandeur. The theater, by the way, comes with its own ghost. Information on upcoming events may be obtained from the Chamber of Commerce, 114 W. Main.

DOWNTOWN HISTORIC DISTRICT (NRHP). One of the more unusual buildings is the "Flatiron" or "Triangle" building, its shape chosen to fit the plot of land it stands on. The building is on the site of the town's original station for disbursing funds to the Osage tribe. The site once was enclosed with a hitching rail and was a watering site for horses. The triangle of land is now enclosed by streets on all three sides. The city hall building, located on the other side of US 60, was the original Osage Indian Council House (NRHP). In the post office is a WPA mural painted in 1938 by artist **Olive Rush** of Santa Fe, New Mexico. Entitled "Osage Treaty," it represents the treaty or agreement between the Osage Indians and the white man in Oklahoma's early history.

SUSPENSION BRIDGE. Turn south on Osage Ave. to the bridge located about five blocks away. This swinging bridge across **Bird Creek** was built in 1926; refurbished 1970.

OSAGE COUNTY COURTHOUSE (NRHP) is located on the

south point of the bluff on Grandview St., above the downtown. Work was begun on the building in 1912.

MILLION DOLLAR ELM. Just north of the courthouse stands the elm where the Osage Tribe held the first public auction sale for oil leases on Osage Reservation tracts in 1912. All the early sales were held here and over the years a number of 160-acre tracts have been leased for a total of more than $1 million each, thus the name for the tree.

OSAGE TRIBAL MUSEUM. Preserving the culture of the Osage tribe is this museum which features displays, crafts, and records covering all aspects of Osage life including home, religion, games, arts, crafts, food, and work. Of special interest are the examples of Osage fingerweaving by a former museum curator, the late **Maudie Cheshewalla**, recognized by the Smithsonian Institution as the "World Master Fingerweaver." It is open from 8 a.m. to 4:30 p.m. weekdays. Admission is free.

Just west of downtown and on the south side of the street stands the oldest house (NRHP) in Pawhuska, built for the tribal blacksmith.

Follow US 60 west from Pawhuska through an area of large cattle ranches which cover the hills as far west as the **Arkansas River**. The shallow soils are not suited to plowing but livestock are easily fattened on the nutritious grasses the soils produce. Note that windmills for pumping stock water are seldom seen. Used instead are artificial ponds behind earthen dams called "stock tanks."

In June, 1990, the **Nature Conservancy**, a private environmental organization, purchased the 30,000-acre **Barnard Ranch** as a nucleus of a 52,000-acre **Tallgrass Prairie Preserve** soon to be open to the public by road. Plans are to remove all livestock and most other signs of man and after letting the prairie rest a few years, a herd of bison will be introduced. The preserve lies northwest of Pawhuska and northeast of Shidler and tour information may be obtained from either chamber of commerce.

Twenty miles west of Pawhuska is the US 60/SH 18 junction.
A SIDE TRIP
Eight miles south on SH 18 is Fairfax.
FAIRFAX
Established in 1902, FAIRFAX (pop. 1,749) possibly was named to honor **Lord Fairfax** of Virginia. Except that they weren't born until much later, the town could have been named

This statue in Fairfax marks the grave site of Chief Ne-kah-wah-she-tun-kah, the last Osage chief to be provided the traditional tribal burial ceremony.

Tallchief to honor two local sisters, **Maria and Marjorie Tallchief**, two of the five Indian ballerinas from Oklahoma who achieved international acclaim during their careers.

CHIEF'S GRAVE (NRHP). In the cemetery on the southwest edge of town is the grave, marked by a statue, of Osage Chief **Ne-kah-wah-she-tun-kah**, last Osage to be given the tribe's traditional burial ceremony. Unfortunately this included placing a human scalp in the grave. A Wichita chief was selected for this "honor" and the taking of the scalp in 1923, understandably caused a rather nasty inter-tribal incident and the U.S. government banned any future scalp-hunting.

ALTERNATE ROUTE

Return north on SH 18 to US 60, then continue north another nine miles to SHIDLER (pop. 487), established by **E.S. Shidler** in 1922. Continue west on SH 11 toward **Kaw City**.

BURBANK OILFIELD

From about four miles south of Shidler to four miles west, the route passes through the heart of the giant **Burbank Oil Field**, still in limited production after 70 years. The discovery well, **Bertha Hickman No. 1**, began producing in May, 1920. It was drilled by **E.W. Marland** of the **Marland Oil Company**, future state governor and a U.S. Congressman. The Marland Oil Company later became **Conoco.** The field eventually expanded into eastern Kay County and covered about 33 square miles with 2,000 wells. At its peak in 1923 it was considered the largest daily producer of oil of any field in the world. Boom towns sprang up overnight. **Whizbang** was the first, near the discovery well, followed by **Webb City, Carter Nine, Cooper, Lyman,** and **Shidler** (the main survivor).

WHIZBANG

West of Shidler, 2.5 miles on SH 11, a public road extends south one mile to an intersection. This is the site of **Whizbang** (called **DeNoya** by the post office because they considered Whizbang too undignified). South from the intersection there are weed-covered sidewalks, store foundations, and steps. This was main street. On the west side one can see foundations of the old high school. Life was rough and tumble in Whizbang and shootings were frequent. The bank was robbed twice and it "wasn't safe for a woman to be on the streets at night." The name came from the popular magazine of the time, "Captain Billy's Whizbang." DeNoya was the surname of a prominent Osage.

Back on SH 11 it is 4.5 miles to **Kay County.** This section of

This is a photograph taken of Washunga School classes outside a Kaw Indian Agency building circa 1910.

the county, east of the Arkansas River, was the reservation of the **Kansa or Kaw Indians**, added to the rest of Kay County in 1904 and known locally as **Kaw Country**. Less than a mile inside the county line is a paved county road leading north. Travelers interested in Kaw Country should take this road which becomes gravel. It is five miles to **Washunga Bay Recreation Area** (site of the Kaw Agency).

A SIDE TRIP

The Kaws are close relatives of the Osage and obtained their reservation from the latter, arriving from Kansas in 1873. The **Kaw Agency** was soon established (post office 1880) consisting of four limestone buildings and a barn. When the reservation lands were allotted to the individual Kaws in 1902 the town of **Washunga** (for the chief) was platted across the road west from the Agency. The buildings and townspeople of Washunga were forced out in the 1970s when Kaw Lake was constructed and the townsite is now the primitive camping area of Washunga Bay.

KAW AGENCY (NRHP). One of the agency buildings used as a school, chapel, and tribal meeting room was moved and restored. From the entrance of the recreation area go .5 mile farther west on the county road. The building sits on a hilltop on

278

The Kaw Agency building was relocated and restored for tribal use after the creation of Kaw Lake and the removal of the town of Washunga.

the south side of the road.

Charles Curtis, who was a part-blood member of the Kaw tribe, served as Herbert Hoover's vice-president. Curtis owned land here that was allotted to him but spent most of his life in Kansas.

Back on SH 11 it is four miles to Kaw City.

KAW CITY

Although the land here was settled in the "run" of 1893, the town was not laid out until 1902 when the **Santa Fe railroad**

An interior view of the Kaw City Museum housed in the old Santa Fe depot.

built through. Many houses were moved in the early 1970s to a new townsite to make way for Kaw Lake. Today Kaw City has a population of 314. Best known citizens of old Kaw City were **I.M "Ike" and Laura Clubb,** ranchers who discovered oil and built a four-story hotel in the town. Mrs. Clubb collected art and displayed many paintings by world-famous artists in the hotel. In 1947, the best of the collection was given to the **Philbrook Art Center** in Tulsa (Section 3).

KAW CITY DEPOT MUSEUM (NRHP). This depot was moved from the old townsite and is typical of many small town stations built by the Santa Fe around the turn of the century. When the frame structure was put in place the old brick platform was relaid beside it. Also moved in to add authenticity—an outhouse near the southeast corner of the station. Exhibits depict small town and rural life in an area of oil and cattle; also Indian artifacts. It is open from 2 to 6 p.m. weekends in the summer, and from 9 a.m. to 5 p.m. Memorial and Independence Days. Other times ask at adjacent city hall. Admission is free.

Eleven miles west of Kaw City SH 11 joins US 77 just north of Ponca City (Section 6). When this stretch of highway was built in 1925 it was named "The Kaw City Scenic Highway" for its gentle hills and curves, rock ledges, wildflowers, and trees. Today the route is used mainly by boaters and campers who no doubt wish the "scenic drive" was a little straighter for pulling their boats and trailers.

At the SH 11/US 77 junction follow SH 11 north for three miles, then west 12 miles to **Blackwell**.

BLACKWELL

One of the towns that emerged with the opening of the **Cherokee Outlet** to settlement, September 16, 1893, was BLACKWELL (pop. 7,538). Townsite developer was **Andrew J. Blackwell**, an adopted member of the Cherokee Nation. There was another, earlier settlement in this area.

In 1884, **David L. Payne**, leader of the **Boomers**, and his followers established a tent city called **Rock Falls** across the **Chickaskia River** from present-day Blackwell. The Boomers were a sometimes militant group of mostly white, homeless agrarians who fought for the opening of the Unassigned Lands in Indian Territory as early as 1880. Here they printed their official newspaper, *The Oklahoma War Chief,* until they were chased back across the border into Kansas. The newspaper helped hasten the opening of Oklahoma to settlement in 1889.

ELECTRIC PARK PAVILION (NRHP) is located at 303 S. Main. This white Spanish-style brick and stucco building was

The Electric Light Pavilion, a community meeting place in Blackwell, also boasts a museum.

dedicated Easter Sunday, 1913. Its name comes from the many electric lights with which the builders outlined the dome and walls. It must have been an unusual and exciting showpiece for a small town in a relatively new state. The building, minus some of its original lights, is a community meeting place as it has been since it opened. It also houses a museum.

TOP OF OKLAHOMA MUSEUM, in the Electric Park Pavilion, features early pioneer history of the Cherokee Outlet. It is open from 1 to 5 p.m. Monday through Saturday. Admission is free.

MONUMENTS. On the pavilion grounds are two markers. One concerns the opening of the Cherokee Outlet (or Strip) in 1893. The other memorializes **Oklahoma Baptist College** which opened September 4, 1901, and closed August 12, 1913. It was located six blocks east.

SANTA FE ENGINE AND CABOOSE. A few blocks west of the museum is a small park with the restored engine and caboose, both sitting just a few feet from the old Santa Fe tracks. The engine, No. 1096, was built in 1902 and saw service for 50 years.

BLACKWELL ARMORY (NRHP). In Oklahoma 52 armories were built by WPA workers. In 1990, 34 of these were still being used as armories. Twelve of the original 52 structures are listed on the NRHP with five of these still serving as armories. The Blackwell armory, built in 1936, gained a certain measure of fame when it was used in a 1940 painting which was widely circulated. Entitled "Goodbye Dear, I'll Be Back in A Year," it depicted a national guard unit leaving for military duty while relatives and friends bid them farewell.

Follow SH 177 eight miles south out of Blackwell to US 60.

NEZ PERCE/TONKAWA INDIANS

In 1877 **Chief Joseph** and his band of Nez Perce were brought as prisoners from their home in Idaho first to Kansas, then in 1879 to a 91,000 acre reservation surrounding the present city of **Tonkawa**. Just west of the present town was the **Yellow Bull Crossing** of the **Salt Fork of the Arkansas**, named for **Chief Yellow Bull** who had a log cabin there. The Nez Perce suffered much sickness and death in this southern climate and were allowed to return home in May, 1885. Chief Joseph died in exile at Neslepem in Washington's Colville reservation on September 21, 1904.

The small Tonkawa tribe of 92 people were moved to Indian

Territory in 1884 from Fort Griffin, Texas. The next year they were permanently settled on the old Nez Perce reservation.

From US 177 exit onto US 60 East and go one mile to a granite historical marker on the south side of highway concerning Chief Joseph and the Nez Perce.

A few hundred feet beyond the marker turn south on a section line road. At one mile on the left is a small cemetery with many crosses. Here were reportedly buried the many Nez Perce babies and others who died during the short stay here. Just past the cemetery is the Tonkawa Tribal Complex.

TONKAWA TRIBAL MUSEUM, in the Tribal Housing Authority Building, features exhibits that include artifacts and original allotment records. It is open during business hours on weekdays. Admission is free.

TONKAWA

Established in 1894, a year after the opening of the Cherokee Strip, TONKAWA (pop. 3,127) is named for the tribe, a Waco word meaning "all stay together."

A.D. BUCK MUSEUM, 1300 block of E. North Ave., features historic artifacts and a diorama of prey animals in natural habitat. It is open by appointment 405/628-2581. Admission is free.

NORTHERN OKLAHOMA COLLEGE. At the east end of Grand is the picturesque campus of this small state college begun in 1901. Oldest building is Central Hall.

TONKAWA HISTORICAL MUSEUM, in the former Santa Fe Railway depot on east Grand, features exhibits reflecting the lifestyles of pioneers and other early settlers. It is open by appointment, 405/628-2203. Admission is free.

THREE SANDS MARKER. From main business corner of Tonkawa go south several blocks on US 77. Just before reaching the Salt Fork bridge, on the west side of street, is Ray See Park. In the park near the street is a granite marker for the **Three Sands Oil Field** which opened in June, 1921, seven miles south on US 77. At its peak this field was producing more than 100,000 barrels of oil a day from over 500 wells. Many foundations and other remains of the sprawling field can still be seen. Enroute, about four miles south on the east side of the road, is a granite marker. This stone marks the homestead of **Jim N. Stone**, one of the men who made the Run of '93.

Back on US 60 it is 30 miles to **Pond Creek**, then 18 miles south to **Enid** (both Section 10).

Central Hall was the first building constructed at Northern Oklahoma College in Tonkawa.

This marker relates the brief history of the Three Sands Oil Field located seven miles south of Tonkawa. This marker has been placed in Ray See Park in town.

For the next 25 miles US 60 passes through farming country (wheat) and from here on across the state most towns, large and small, will be marked with a grain elevator.

A SIDE TRIP

At the junction of US 60 and SH 8 near **Cleo Springs** turn north for six miles to the **Sod House** (NRHP and OHS) on the line between **Major** and **Alfalfa Counties**. The former is named for **John C. Major**, member of the Oklahoma Constitutional Convention and the latter for **William H. "Alfalfa Bill" Murray**, president of the constitutional convention and later a state governor (Section 15). **Murray County** also was named for him.

SOD HOUSE

In 1893, Marshal McCully took part in the land run which opened the Cherokee Outlet to homesteaders. McCully's first claim was disputed so he moved to this one where he built his soddy in 1894 while living in a dug-out. The sod house was used by the family from 1894 until 1909 when a two-story frame house was built. Over the years the soddy received a few refinements not usually found in this type of dwelling such as a wood floor and

The interior of Marshal McCully's sod house built in 1894. The soddy is located in Alfalfa county.

plaster on the inside walls. In 1963 the OHS acquired the building and set about preserving and protecting this bit of history that shouldn't have survived at all. Why it did is something of a mystery. It is open from 9 a.m. to 5 p.m. Tuesday through Friday and from 2 to 5 p.m. weekends. Admission is free.

Return south to US 60 and continue on to **Fairview**.

FAIRVIEW

Seat of Major County is FAIRVIEW (pop. 2,936). The name honors a nearby scenic attraction, the **Glass or Gloss Mountains**, gypsum hills which sparkle and gleam when the sun hits the millions of selenite crystals that cover the landscape. There is a debate of long-standing over the correct name for these gypsum hills. There is the theory that they were listed as "Gloss" on an 1880 survey by an English engineer. He was supposed to have spelled Glass the way he pronounced it— "Glaws." A pretty far-fetched theory it is, too, insist the local folks who say the name is and always has been "Gloss."

A few years ago the Major County Historical Society was donated 160 acres east of town. The group has begun a collection of early-day buildings here. Each summer they hold an old-fashioned threshing bee using steam and horse-powered machines to thresh grain and bale the straw. The wheat and oats used for the show are grown on Society property. Also featured at the three-day event is a large display of coal-fired steam and gasoline engines, all in working order.

It is 34 miles to Seiling in **Dewey County** (named for Adm. George Dewey).

SEILING

The town of SEILING (pop. 1,031) was established in 1894 and named for townsite developer **Louis A. Seiling.** The town has been home to two historical personages. **Amos Chapman**, Army scout, buffalo hunter, trader, and wagon train guide in the late 1800s, was a hero of the Buffalo Wallow battle in Texas where he lost a leg. This didn't slow him down much. He reportedly was equipped with a wooden leg which he held firmly in place while on horseback with a black cloth brought up from either side of the leg and tied in back of his neck. He spent many more years in the saddle, pursuing his line of work. Chapman spent his retirement years east of town and is buried in the family cemetery.

In the early 1900s **Carry A. Nation** and her husband **David** (preacher, lawyer, and editor) lived in a two-story log house west of town. A historical marker is located near the site of the cabin. It is said Carry (the family spelling rather than the often seen Carrie) would sometimes preach for her husband. In later years she would load her buggy with bricks and set off on one of her saloon smashing expeditions. There is no evidence she started the latter until she moved to Kansas. However, Carry was known to travel down to Oklahoma Territory to conduct some of her saloon raids.

It is 21 miles to **Vici** (pop. 751) where the landscape becomes more desert-like and yucca or soapweed plants make an appearance. The plant is called soapweed because the long, tough roots can be boiled to make a thick soap. Just west of Vici is the **Ellis County** line (named for **Albert H. Ellis**, vice-president of the Oklahoma Constitutional Convention). County seat is **Arnett**.

ARNETT

A post office was established at ARNETT (pop. 547) in 1902. The settlement was named for **A.S. Arnett**, a Fayetteville, West Virginia, minister.

COURTHOUSE (NRHP). Built in 1912, few changes have been made to this three-story brick building over the years. On the grounds is a log cabin built in 1893 from cedar trees and it features furnishings of the period. It is open by appointment 405/885-7680. Admission is free.

Arnett was not the first seat of Ellis County. That designation went to **Grand** (NRHP), 13 miles south on US 283, then two miles west.

GRAND

This settlement, which hasn't even been a town for 40 or more years, is often described as one of Oklahoma's liveliest ghosts. When the **Cheyenne-Arapaho Pastures** were thrown open to settlement in 1892, Grand grew up around **Upper Robinson Spring** near one of the best stands of native trees in western Oklahoma and close to the banks of the **South Canadian River**. In late 1893, the Territorial **Day County** courthouse burned at **Ioland** and it was voted to move the seat to Grand. Soon the town grew to include a hotel, two saloons, blacksmith shop, two newspapers, and four law offices. At statehood in 1907, Day County was divided with the part north of the Canadian River going to Ellis County and the part south to **Roger Mills County**. In 1908 Arnett won the Ellis County seat away from Grand and the one-story, wooden courthouse was jacked up and moved to its new site.

Among the well-known who lived in Grand were **Temple Houston** (son of Sam) who was a judge, **Will Rogers** who worked on the nearby **Ewing Ranch**, and primitive artist **Augusta Metcalfe**. Each July on the third Saturday this ghost county seat of a ghost county has a very successful reunion for former residents and their descendants. Not much remains of Grand except the spring, some of the trees, and a few ruins but visitors are welcomed by the family that now owns the property.

Across the river one can view the six irregular peaks of **Antelope Hills**, a landmark to travelers on the **California Trail**.

A modern-day cattle round-up in Oklahoma covers far less distance than the early-day roundups but it is still dusty, hard work.

SECTION 13
US 270

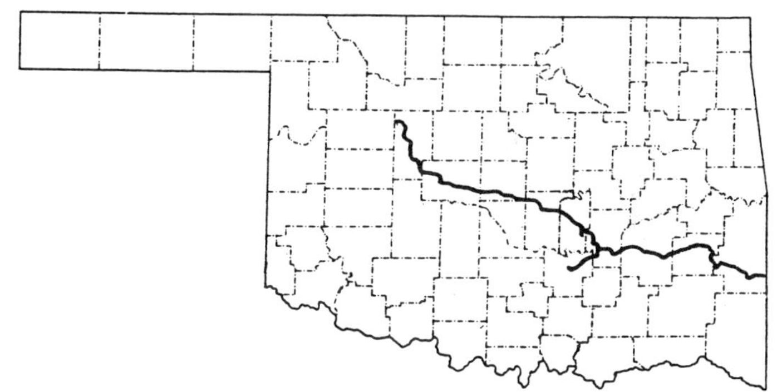

Cantonment on the Canadian River was established on the Cheyenne-Arapaho Indian Reservation in 1879 by Col. Richard Dodge, commanding the 23rd Infantry Regiment. The post was established to control hostile Indian raiders.

SECTION 13
US 270

US 270 is a solitaire, a loner, a maverick. The western half, at least, is a route with few historic or scenic features and the whole has no discernible theme or storyline, and little likelihood of inspiring a groupie craze like the Lincoln Highway or Route 66. In a word, US 270 is something of an ugly stepchild, a drone created in response to the need for a transportation link between Denver and New Orleans. When various attempts to provide such a link by rail failed this was one of the attempts to provide a highway link instead. In its own carefree way the route does pursue a southeast/northwest course across Oklahoma but it is not a recognizable New Orleans/Denver-Highway. It is, however, a pleasant cross-state route that offers a buffet of Sooner State staples, an unfolding display of geographical features, economic activities, social environments. From the Kansas line in northwestern Oklahoma to the Arkansas line in far southeast, US 270 passes from arid, virtually treeless High Plains to humid pine forestlands. Along the way it offers the traveler an ever changing panorama of sprawling cattle ranches, wheat fields, grain elevators, oil fields, and wooded mountains. All this and history, too. Maverick or not US 270 has its own rewards for the traveler trained to search out and appreciate the less obvious.

SOUTHEAST ON US 270

Covered in this tour is a midsection of the route stretching some 260 miles between **Canton** (a few miles east of US 270 on SH 51 in **Blaine County**) to the **Red Oak** vicinity in the southeast part of the state. At the end of the tour an optional side trip will be outlined from Red Oak to **Talihina** via SH 82, then east on SH 1 along the **Talimena Drive** to Mena, Arkansas. This part of SH 1 was one of the first scenic highways to be designated a **National Forest Scenic Byway** by the National Forest Service in 1989.

CANTON

The town of CANTON (pop. 632) was established in 1905 in Blaine County (named for **James G. Blaine**, Maine, an unsuccessful 1884 presidential candidate). The town name probably comes from the destination chalked on freight being sent there: "Cantonment on the Canadian River, Indian Territory." The site today is three miles northwest of the town on the banks of

Canton Lake, created in 1948.

CANTON AREA MUSEUM, 107 S. Washington, features historical memorabilia from the area. It is open from 1 to 4:30 p.m., Tuesday through Friday, and from 10 a.m. until noon Saturday. Admission is free.

CANTONMENT. This post was established on the Cheyenne-Arapaho Reservation on March 6, 1879, by **Col. Richard Dodge** and six companies of the 23rd Infantry. Purpose was for controlling and intercepting hostile Indians who were raiding into Kansas and Nebraska. The military considered the post important enough to need several stone buildings but the post was never designated as a fort. The post was abandoned in 1882 after the Northern Cheyenne were allowed to return to their old home in the northern plains. A school for children of the Plains Indians was established at the site and it was here Mennonite missionary **Rudolphe Petter** wrote his "Cheyenne Dictionary." Today one stone building (NRHP) is still standing and has been restored by the Cheyenne-Arapaho Tribal Council as an administrative headquarters and visitor center.

Leave Canton going south on SH 58 for 15 miles to join US 270, then east to **Watonga.**

WATONGA

Seat of Blaine County is WATONGA (pop. 3,408). The post office was established in 1892 and the name is for Arapaho Chief **Wa-ton-ghe** (Black Coyote). Watonga is the hometown of the late **Clarence Nash**, the voice of **Donald Duck** for 50 years.

ROMAN NOSE STATE PARK, six miles north on SH 8A, was named for the last warrior-chief of the Cheyenne, **Chief Henry Roman Nose.** The canyons and streams of the park were a favorite camping spot for the Cheyenne when they roamed freely through this area and the chief chose his 160 acres here when the tribal members received their allotments. His dugout was near the **Spring of Everlasting Water** which today feeds the park lake and rock-lined swimming pool. Soldiers following the military road which ran north of the park (from **Fort Reno,** Section 5, to Cantonment) often chose the spring as a camping site as did many early-day territorial outlaws.

FERGUSON HOME (NRHP and OHS), 519 N. Weigel, was built in 1901 by newspaper publisher **Thomas Benton Ferguson,** territorial governor 1901-05. An '89er who later moved to Watonga, Ferguson published the *Watonga Republican* until his death in 1921 when his wife, **Elva Shartel**

Ferguson, took over and continued as publisher until 1943. Author **Edna Ferber** began her novel "Cimarron" while a guest in this house. The experiences of the main character were based on those of Mrs. Ferguson. It is open from 9 a.m. to 5 p.m. Tuesday through Saturday and from 1 to 5 p.m. Sunday. From

Novelist Edna Ferber was once a guest in the historic Ferguson House in Watonga.

The historic Blaine County Courthouse dates back to 1906.

November through April also closed Tuesday. Admission is free.

WPA POST OFFICE MURAL, downtown. Of the 31 murals placed in Oklahoma post offices as part of a WPA project in the 1930s and early 1940s, this one probably received the most publicity. The fame came not because of the artist, **Edith Mahier**, or the subject, "Roman Nose Canyon," but because of the reaction Cheyenne Chief **Red Bird** had when he first saw the mural. He publicly announced: "It Stinks." This news, of course, received national coverage. Some say it was all a setup to get a little notice for Watonga but setup or not (as others say) it did bring a flurry of attention to the town.

Red Bird's list of objections included: "Roman Nose's breech-clout too short, makes him look like a Navajo jelly-bean...ponies Indian riding look like hobby horses with swan necks, Roman Nose's baby look like a stumpy pig...Roman Nose's clothes look Navajo. No Good."

The artist took this criticism from one of Roman Nose's descendants with good humor.

"I think a mural should cause the interest of the people; that above all else," she remarked.

COUNTY COURTHOUSE (NRHP). This attractive, domed building was completed in 1906.

TRAIN RIDE. At the present time there are no passenger trains in Oklahoma so opportunities to experience train travel, even for a couple of hours, are considered a treat in the state. Two groups concerned with history are currently providing visitors and homefolks with a chance to experience train travel. **The Central Oklahoma Chapter** of the **National Railway Historical Society** runs the train in Watonga (down the track to **Greenfield** and back) on alternate weekends in the spring and fall. To date in 1991 the group has restored a diner, coach, and two cabooses and dinner trips are available. Schedules, ticket information and reservations may be obtained by calling Midwest Travel in Oklahoma City, 405/732-0566. The state's other train is the Hugo Heritage Railroad (Section 15), a project of the Choctaw County Historical Society. The same telephone number will provide information and ticket prices for these weekend train rides.

Nine miles southeast is **Greenfield**. Two miles past the small settlement look for signs pointing the way to the **Jesse Chisholm Grave** about seven miles.

CHISHOLM GRAVE (NRHP). On a knoll near the North Canadian River is **Raven Spring** renamed **Left Hand Spring** because it was selected by Arapaho Chief Left Hand as part of his allotment. It was here Chisholm died on March 4, 1868, during a visit to the camp of his friend Left Hand while checking on the line of trading posts he operated in what is now central Oklahoma. Curiously, although his name was carried by the most famous of all cattle trails Chisholm was not a cattleman but a trader.

Jesse Chisholm, who developed the trail that bears his name while trading in the Indian Territory for nearly four decades, is buried in a grave northeast of Geary.

The northern section of the Chisholm Trail simply followed the route previously scratched into the prairie sod by Chisholm wagons bringing in supplies from Kansas to stock his trading posts.

Eight miles southwest of the grave, on US 270, is **Geary**.

GEARY

The town of GEARY (pop. 1,347) was established in 1898 with arrival of the Choctaw Oklahoma & Gulf Railroad (Rock Island beginning in 1902.) The name is believed to be a corruption of that of Ed Guerrier, a French-Canadian scout on the southern Plains who married an Indian woman and settled in the area.

PUBLIC WATER TROUGH (NRHP). Dating from 1901 this concrete trough at the east end of Main St. was designed so a team of horses could drink comfortably while still in harness.

CANADIAN RIVERS HISTORICAL SOCIETY MUSEUM (NRHP), Broadway and Main. Exhibits include the area's first log jail and a Rock Island train caboose. It is open from 1 to 4 p.m. Friday and by appointment, 405/884-2505. Admission is free.

At the east edge of town, US 270 enters Canadian County (named for the river). Two miles east the road tops a shoulder of **Coyote Hill** (left), a dolomite butte that figured prominently in the Arapaho ceremonials relating to the Ghost Dance craze that swept the area in the 1890s.

From here it is ten miles to Calumet.

CALUMET

Another Rock Island (CO&G) railroad town established in 1898, CALUMET (pop. 560) was named for the "chalumet," the name of the Indian ceremonial pipe.

Five miles south, US 270 joins I-40. It is 75 miles east to Shawnee. For points of interest to see along the way check El Reno (Section 5) and Oklahoma City (Section 2).

SHAWNEE

Seat of **Pottawatomie County** (named for the Indian tribe) is SHAWNEE (pop. 26,017), named for yet another tribe. Pottawatomie is a Chippewa term signifying "people of the place of fire" and Shawnee is from the Algonquian "shawun" meaning southerners. The town is very near the geographic center of the main body of the state. A post office called **Shawneetown** was at this site from 1876 to 1892. The settlement began in 1872 as a trading post near the **West Shawnee Cattle Trail.** The present town was laid out in 1892 with the opening of the Shawnee Indian lands to non-Indian settlement. Shawnee received a major advantage over its rival to the south, Tecumseh, when the CO&G chose to build through Shawnee in 1895 and located its division-point, yards, and locomotive and coach repair shops here. In 1902 CO&G became part of the Rock Island railroad.

Born in Shawnee was **Lt. Col. L. Gordon Cooper,** the first

astronaut to be sent into space twice. A granite historical
monument is located on US 177 north of Shawnee.

Wilbur Underhill, known as the "Tri-State Terror," robbed
dozens of banks in Oklahoma, Kansas, and Arkansas during the
1920s and '30s. During the fall of 1933, he with others robbed the
bank in Coalgate and Okmulgee as well as others in Arkansas
and Kansas. One of their biggest hauls was the $13,000 robbery
of the Okmulgee bank on November 2, 1933. Shortly after this
robbery, Underhill married his childhood sweetheart and moved
to Shawnee. Federal agents surrounded their honeymoon cottage
on New Year's Day 1934. In the gunfight that ensued Underhill
was badly wounded and after his capture was taken to a hospital
in McAlester where he died on January 6, 1934.

National Register properties include the **Beard Cabin**, first
residence in Shawnee at Woodland Park near downtown; **Kerfoot
House**, 740 N. Beard, built by **E. O. Nelson** in 1903 to resemble
a Mississippi steamboat; and **Billington Building**, 23 E. Ninth.

HIGLEY GRAVE. In Fairview Cemetery, on N. Harrison, is
the grave of **Dr. Brewster Higley**, a Kansas surgeon who wrote
the frontier ballad, "Home on the Range." He wrote the words to
his famous song, initially titled "My Western Home," while

*Dr. Brewster Highley, who wrote the famous ballad "Home
on the Range," is buried in Fairview Cemetery in Shawnee.*

homesteading near Athol, Kansas, in 1872. The words were set to music by Daniel E. Kelley. Originally from Ohio, he moved his family to Shawnee in 1886. He died here in 1911. A historical marker is located near the grave.

ST. GREGORY ABBEY/COLLEGE (NRHP), 1900 N. MacArthur Dr. The college was moved here in 1915 from **Sacred Heart Mission**, located eight miles east of Asher in this county. The mission, often called the "Cradle of Catholicism in Oklahoma," was established by the Benedictines in 1876. Restored sections of two minor buildings and two cemeteries of the old mission are located near Sacred Heart Church on SH 39. On the Shawnee campus is the **Mabee-Gerrer Museum** featuring European paintings dating from 1300 to the present and over 500 artifacts from Egyptian tombs. It is open from 1 to 5 p.m. Tuesday through Sunday. Admission is free.

SANTA FE DEPOT MUSEUM (NRHP) 614 Main. This grey limestone building completed in 1903 is one of the few large Romanesque Revival style depots surviving in the southwest. The tower was patterned after a Scottish lighthouse. Exhibits in the recently restored building include county and railroad

The old Santa Fe depot houses a museum in Shawnee. The depot has been placed on the National Register.

memorabilia. It is open from 8 a.m. to 4 p.m. weekdays. Admission is free.

WHEELS-DEALS-ANTIQUES, SH 18 north of I-40 contained 110 vehicles built between 1903 and 1941 including the car belonging to actress **Carol Lombard** and her husband, **Clark Gable**. In September, 1991, the cars were packed up and shipped to Japan to be part of a museum there.

POTTAWATOMIE INDIAN MUSEUM, 1901 S. Gordon Cooper Dr., features headdresses, beadwork, and feather flag of the tribe. Nearby is the **Shawnee Friends Mission** (NRHP), currently undergoing restoration. It is a frame meetinghouse built in 1885 by the Society of Friends who arrived in 1871 to minister to the Absentee Shawnees, the tribal band living in this area, one of three Shawnee groups in the state. Also nearby is the **Bourbonnais Log House** built in 1882 and moved close to the mission when the village of Shawneetown was abandoned during the Run of 1891. The museum is open from 8 a.m. to 5 p.m. weekdays. Admission is free.

Five miles south of Shawnee is **Tecumseh**.

TECUMSEH

Seat of Pottawatomie County, twice, was TECUMSEH (pop. 5,750). The town began with the opening of the Pottawatomie Indian lands in 1891 and the name honors the renowned Shawnee Indian war chief. County government was located here until February 26, 1909, and again from February 13, 1913, to December 19, 1930.

Thirteen miles east is Seminole.

SEMINOLE

SEMINOLE (pop. 7,071) was first called **Tidmore** for the man who built **Mekasukey Mission**, a school for Seminole boys opened in 1891 southeast of town. In February, 1906, the name was changed to that of the county in which it is located. Seminole, an Indian tribe, is a Creek word meaning "runaway" as in emigrants. Seminole remained a quiet town of less than 800 people until July 16, 1926, when the **Fixico No. 1** oil well blew in at three in the afternoon. Within a year there were 35,000 people in town. A replica of the well stands in Municipal Park.

The Seminole oil region covers almost 1,300 square miles and contains five huge oil pools. It is this concentration of large producing pools that made the **Greater Seminole Oil Field** unique. In the 25 years after discovery this field produced almost 154 million barrels of oil.

The Shawnee Friends Mission on SH 18 south of Shawnee was built in 1871 to minister to the Absentee Shawnees, the tribal band living in this area.

It is nine miles to the turnoff, east, then three miles on US 270 Business to **Wewoka**, seat of Seminole County.

WEWOKA

When the Seminole Indians began their removal to Indian Territory from Florida in 1845, they first agreed to share the land with and live under the general government of the Creeks

These remains are all that are left of the Sacred Heart Mission, established by the Benedictines in 1876. The mission is currently undergoing restoration.

although with their own town government. This never proved satisfactory and in 1856 the Creek ceded a part of their nation to the Seminole. In 1866, the Seminoles purchased their new land and established WEWOKA (pop. 4,050). The name is a Creek word meaning "barking waters." The nation was abolished with statehood and the only remaining tie is a pecan tree on the county courthouse lawn which was the tribal whipping post from 1899-1907. None of the tribal government buildings are still standing. Whites moved into the area after the arrival of the railroad in 1895. When oil was found in 1926, the population doubled in 60 days.

Pro golfer **Gil Morgan** is from Wewoka.

SEMINOLE NATION MUSEUM, 524 S. Wewoka. Featured are exhibits preserving the heritage of both the Seminoles and pioneers. Also on display is a replica of an early drilling rig. It is open from 1 to 5 p.m. Tuesday through Sunday. Admission is free.

Five miles south of town on SH 56 is a historical marker for **Emahaka Mission** established in 1894 as a school for Seminole

Indian girls. The school was closed in 1914 and the building burned in 1927. A few ruins remain 30 yards northeast of the marker.

It is nine miles from Wewoka to **Holdenville**, both county seats and nearest to each other of any in Oklahoma.

HOLDENVILLE

Hughes County seat is HOLDENVILLE (pop. 4,792). The county is named for **W. C. Hughes**, member of the Oklahoma Constitutional Convention, and the town for **J. F. Holden**, general manager of the CO&G railroad. The town was established in 1890 as Fentress for the son of Indian agent **D. M. Wisdom**. The name was changed to Holdenville a few months later but Fentress still got a town. In 1895 another settlement some 35 miles northeast was given his name but it disappeared in 1908.

Born in Holdenville were financier **J. Paul Getty**, oilman **T. Boone Pickens**, and actor **Clu Gulager**. It is also hometown to baseball brothers **Jerome "Dizzy"** and **Paul "Daffy" Dean**, pitchers of the famed Gashouse Gang of St. Louis.

ALTERNATE ROUTE

Two early historical locations were near present Holdenville, south on SH 48.

Fort Holmes was about five miles south, near the historical marker on SH 48. The actual site is marked with a small white stone shaft some distance northwest. It was established in 1834 by **Lt. Theophilus H. Holmes**, who served as a lieutenant general in the Confederate Army during the Civil War. The post served as an advance base for troops stationed at **Fort Towson** (Section 15).

Edwards Store (not to be confused with Edwards Store on the Butterfield Stage road near Red Oak) was about a mile west of Fort Holmes on the west side of Little River about three miles from its mouth. Traders Edwards and Shelton established the busy stop on the **California Trail**, a road west to the gold fields blazed in 1849 from **Fort Smith**. A daughter of Edwards married **Jesse Chisholm** and he ran the store and trading post at one time.

Continue down SH 48 to SH 1.

At Atwood take SH 1 west for 25 miles to Oklahoma's other "crossword puzzle clue" town, **Ada**, sometimes a Town in Oklahoma, sometimes An Oklahoma Palindrome. The other crossword clue town is Enid.

Somewhere in the area between this turnoff and Ada, during

303

gold rush days, was a Shawnee Indian settlement called **Shawnee Town**. This is only one of several "Shawnee Towns" which have appeared and disappeared in various locations in the state. The main route of the **California Trail** ran through here and some of the travelers made side trips north across the South Canadian River to Edwards Store for supplies. Some of them went west from there on the alternate trail north of the river but the main trail continued south of the river, passing the present site of Ada.

ADA

ADA (pop. 15,820) is the seat of **Pontotoc County**, which also was a county in the old Chickasaw Nation. The name means "cattails growing on the prairie" and came from a Chickasaw settlement in northern Mississippi.

Jeff Reed, a pioneer mail carrier, put up the first building at this spot in 1889, a combination log store and house. When he got his post office in 1891, he named it for his daughter. The town began to grow with the coming of the Frisco railroad in 1900 and soon earned a well-deserved reputation for lawlessness.

In 1908 there were 36 murders in and around Ada. Finally, in 1909, the townspeople became indignant over a particularly spectacular ambush slaying. A vigilante group broke into the jail "one April night and took four men charged with the killing to a nearby livery stable and strung them up from convenient rafters. The quadruple lynching, still a record for Oklahoma, had the desired salutary effect on local law and order," wrote the late historian, **Kent Ruth**.

Natives of Ada include newsman **J. Douglas Edwards**, evangelist **Oral Roberts**, poet **Welborn Hope**, and U.S. Senator and Oklahoma governor, **Robert S. Kerr**. Trumpeter **Harry James** attended school in Ada.

EAST CENTRAL STATE UNIVERSITY was created in 1909 as a two-year teacher training school. It became a four-year school in 1919. For many years on the campus has been the stump of a fossilized tree, five feet in diameter, dating back 350 million years. Southeast of town at one time was a large area of petrified trees which many people can still remember going to see. Probably in the early 1930s the land owner sold this petrified wood believed to have been taken to Oklahoma City and sold for mantels and other decorations in homes. It is probable there are still Oklahoma City homes with bits of the petrified wood.

KERR CABIN. Birthplace of Robert S. Kerr, governor from 1943-1947 and probably the state's best known and most powerful U.S. Senator, was this log cabin. It is located in a small park two miles south of town and his gravesite is nearby. Kerr was responsible for the **Arkansas Navigation Project** which links Tulsa by water with the Gulf of Mexico (Section 5).

LITTLE RED SCHOOLHOUSE, in Winterset Park on East 18th, was built in 1907 as the one-room **Jones Chapel Schoolhouse**. It has been moved here and restored.

FRISCO DEPOT, downtown, is being restored (1991) by the Ada Chamber of Commerce for its offices. In the parking lot is the first water trough used in Ada.

CHICKASAW CULTURAL CENTER MUSEUM, 520 E. Arlington, contains items and artifacts pertaining to the history of the Chickasaw tribe. It is open from 8 a.m. to 5 p.m. weekdays and from 10 a.m. to 4 p.m. Saturday between June 1 and September 1. Admission is free.

Return to the SH 48/SH 1 junction, then go east on SH 1 five miles to rejoin US 270 at **Calvin.** It is 30 miles to **McAlester** (Section 7) and its near neighbor **Krebs** on the north side of US 270. Both are in **Pittsburg County** (named for the city in Pennsylvania, but spelled differently). This is coal country. From west of McAlester to **Wilburton** and beyond, the countryside is dotted with relics of towns and ghost towns brought into being and supported by coal mining. There are still coal deposits but the demand faded when oil and natural gas were produced in large quantities in the state.

KREBS

The town of KREBS (pop. 1,955) was settled in 1871 when the Missouri, Kansas, and Texas (Katy) railroad first reached this rich coal mining area. The town was named for a Choctaw, **Judge Edmond F. Krebs**.

Listed on the NRHP are **St. Joseph's Catholic Church**, off SH 31, and **Hokey's Drug Store**, Main and Washington. The latter was established in 1888 and during Indian Territory days many victims of mine injuries were treated here, since there were no hospitals.

Near Krebs the first commercial underground mine in Indian Territory was opened in 1872 by the Osage Coal and Mining Company. Krebs was the scene of the state's worst mining disaster on January 7, 1892, when approximately 100 miners died in an explosion in the No. 11 mine. The victims are buried

This memorial commemorates the approximately 100 coal miners who lost their lives in an explosion at the Number 11 mine in Krebs in 1892. Some of those killed are buried in a common grave at a McAlester cemetery.

in a common grave, with marker (NRHP) in St. Joseph's Cemetery in McAlester.

It is 12 miles to two more mining towns, the twins of **Haileyville** and **Hartshorne.**

HAILEYVILLE AND HARTSHORNE

Both were established with the arrival of the **Choctaw Coal and Railway Company**, later the Rock Island, and both were settled in about 1890 with coal mining as the principal industry.

HAILEYVILLE (pop. 918) was named for **Dr. David Hailey** who assisted in sinking the first mine shaft in the McAlester district.

HARTSHORNE (pop. 2,120) was named for **Dr. Charles Hartshorne**, a railroad official and early settler. Hartshorne is the hometown of former national league pitcher **Warren Spahn.**

STS. CYRIL AND METHODIUS ORTHODOX CHURCH, Modoc and 3rd, Hartshorne. This Russian Orthodox Church with its onion domes was built in 1917 by the Carpatho-Russians from Galicia who came to work the mines. It replaced a less elaborate wooden church built in 1897. Services are still held here.

Six miles north of Hartshorne on a county road is the near-ghost town of **Adamson**, scene of another mining disaster, September 14, 1914. A white granite monument near the abandoned Adamson school is close to the entrance to the sealed-off Union Coal Company's No. 1 mine. It is a memorial to the 14 miners entombed in the cave-in.

Back on US 270 it is 15 miles to **Wilburton** in **Latimer County** (named for **James S. Latimer**, member of the Oklahoma Constitutional Convention).

WILBURTON

Seat of Latimer County is WILBURTON (pop. 3,092), named for **Elisha Wilbur**, president of the **Lehigh Valley Railroad**. It began as yet another mining camp along the Choctaw Coal and Railway. **Eastern Oklahoma State College of Mines and Metallurgy** (now Eastern Oklahoma Junior College) was established here in 1909. **Mitchell Hall** on the campus is listed on the NRHP.

ROBBERS CAVE STATE PARK, six miles north of town on SH 2. It is said outlaws (including Frank and Jesse James) and

Early day outlaws are said to have once used these caves in Robbers Cave State Park as hideouts. The park is located near Wilburton.

gang members used the caves in the park for hideouts and hiding places for their stolen loot. There also may be a ghost—"Fiddlin Jim," a swain of **Belle Starr**, who was shot one night by a jealous rival as he sat playing his fiddle at the mouth of the cave. When the harvest moon shines it is said a weird melody is sometimes heard near the mouth of the cave- -"Fiddlin Jim's" last tune.

VETERAN'S MUSEUM. Nine miles south on SH 2 is the only colony established in the United States as a retirement place for veterans of the Spanish American War. Founded in 1936, the colony now welcomes veterans and their families from all wars. The park pavilion is listed on the NRHP. The museum is open by appointment, 918/465-2607. Admission is free.

LUTIE COAL MINERS MUSEUM, 2.5 miles east of Wilburton on US 270. **Lutie** was once a town in its own right, three miles east of Wilburton. It began as **Ola**, post office May 1, 1886, changed to Lutie October 4, 1901. Today it pretty well merges with its larger neighbor. Museum features coal mining in early-day Latimer County and surrounding area. It is open from 10 a.m. to 4 p.m. Saturday and from 1 to 4 p.m. Sunday. Admission is free.

RIDDLE'S STATION SITE (NRHP), 3 miles east of Wilburton, south side of US 270 in the southeast corner of Lutie Cemetery below the hill. Riddle's Station, just east of Big Fouche Maline Creek, was a stop and blacksmith shop on the Butterfield Stage Line (Section 11). A historical site marker and several Riddle family graves are in this area.

It is 14 miles to **Red Oak**.

RED OAK

Post office for RED OAK (pop. 602) was established in 1868. The name was taken from the big red oak tree which stood for many years in the center of town and was used as a whipping post under Choctaw Nation law.

Although this is officially the end of the US 270 tour, nearby is the 54-mile-long **Talimena Scenic Drive** linking **Talihina** with Mena, Arkansas. US 270 continues east and at Heavener joins US 59 (Section 11).

A SIDE TRIP

Talihina is 18 miles south of Red Oak down winding, hilly SH 82.

TALIHINA

The town of **TALIHINA** (pop. 1,297) was a small unnamed missionary settlement in 1887 when the Frisco Railroad came across the **Winding Stair Mountain** from Fort Smith, Arkansas. The name Talihina celebrated this event as it is a Choctaw word meaning "iron road." For several years it was mainly a lumber town and almost inaccessible except by rail. The town is at the western edge of the **Ouachita National Forest** (the French way to spell the sound of the Indian word Washitaw, meaning "good hunting ground.")

SCENIC DRIVE

Scenic SH 1 begins seven miles northeast of town off of US 271 and follows the crest of **Winding Stair Mountain** and **Rich Mountain** to Mena. The information booth here sells mile-by-mile guides of the road which add to the enjoyment of the trip as some of the historic sites are difficult to locate especially in summer when the undergrowth is lush.

OLD MILITARY ROAD is located .8 of a mile from the information booth. A bronze tablet near the picnic area marks the crossing of an old wagon road built in 1832. The road, built by soldiers from Fort Towson, ran from Fort Smith to Tuskahoma to Fort Towson. The road was used until about 1930. A nearby spring made it a good camping spot. One can walk on the old road down the north side of the mountain.

LENOX VISTA, about 11 miles, overlooks the village of **Lenox** on SH 63 and the **Lenox Mission Church** founded in 1853 by **S. L. Hobbs**, possibly the first white man to settle in the **Kiamichi River Valley.**

HORSE THIEF SPRINGS, mile 16.1. The old spring was enclosed by rock walls built by CCC workers during the early 1930s. The area near the springs was used as a campground in the late 1800s and early 1900s by people moving horses from Texas to market in Missouri. Horse thieves were common along the trail.

ONE ROOM HOUSE. Remains of this rock house is 17 miles farther. It was used by an Arkansas man who ran hogs on **Rich Mountain.** The four-foot high walls of the house were covered with a tarp and served as his camp when he came to Oklahoma to check on his hogs.

PIONEER HISTORICAL SITE. For the next half mile there were two homesteads including log houses and barns, rock fences, spring, fields, flower gardens, and a grave. Very little remains today as the last man to live on Rich Mountain in Oklahoma lived there alone until 1942 when he was called into the army.

STATE LINE is at mile 37. Here on June 7, 1970, President Johnson's daughter, **Luci Baines Johnson**, cut a ribbon opening the scenic drive. A path from the parking area leads down to an iron survey marker put in place in 1877 by a crew marking the line between Arkansas and the Choctaw Nation. This was mile 48. Along the state line ran a trail, probably made by the survey crew, used until the 1930s, mainly for the purpose of transporting "moonshine whiskey" to the settlements across the mountains from the Kiamichi Valley.

This is the old Military Road between Fort Smith and Fort Towson.

SECTION 14
US 183

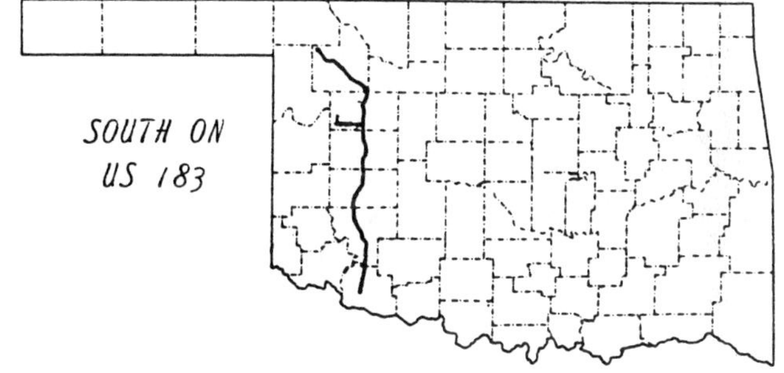

This monument in the small town of Bessie honors a local banker who was killed in the 1920s while giving chase to bank robbers.

SECTION 14
US 183

Of all the tours laid out in this book, US 183 is undoubtedly the most lightly traveled–today, that is. That's all to the good for the motorist. It leaves more time to relax; to let the mind wander back over the years when conditions were considerably different. First non-Indian American of note to appear was Lt. Col. George Armstrong Custer. In 1868, he came to establish a base for his winter campaign that ended with the Black Kettle Massacre near present Cheyenne. Camp Supply lingered on for some 25 years serving as a hub for frontier trails until the coming of the railroads. Meanwhile, this route was being introduced to a different kind of traffic as millions of cattle moved up the Great Western Trail. In 1892, the vast Cheyenne and Arapaho reservation was thrown open to settlement by land run. In 1901 it was the Kiowa and Comanche lands by lottery. Western Oklahoma tends to differ from the rest of the state. There are the topography (plains) and climate (high temperature, low humidity, more wind, less rain). There are less obvious differences, too. Tardy emergence from the frontier, a challenging environment, physical isolation. . . .all have tended to breed a certain spirit of independence in the average western Oklahoman. US 183 travelers will have time to look for evidence of these differences as they glide along through open country. Comfortably conforming but with a difference. That's US 183.

SOUTH ON US 183

US 183 begins at the Kansas state line in northern **Harper County** and leaves the state some 200 miles south when it crosses the **Red River** south of **Davidson**. This historical tour of the highway will begin at **Fort Supply**, 32 miles south of the Kansas line, and end at **Frederick**, 175 miles away.

FORT SUPPLY

In November, 1868, **Lt. Col. George A. Custer** led 11 companies of the Seventh Cavalry to northwestern Indian Territory to establish a supply base for a campaign against the Plains Indians. With them came five companies of infantry, a 450-vehicle wagon train, and **Lt. Col. Alfred Sully**. It was Sully's job to select a provisioning point and he placed the "camp of supply" a little above the spot where **Wolf Creek** and **Beaver River** meet to become the **North Canadian**.

The guardhouse at Fort Supply was restored in the early 1990s for its historical significance. Below is the teamsters' cabin, also at Fort Supply.

Although this was to be a temporary Post on November 8, 1868, maybe five months or so, Camp Supply remained an important frontier post for more than a quarter of a century. It was designated Fort Supply on December 30, 1878. The main body of troops were withdrawn from the post on October 6, 1894, leaving a detachment to garrison it until February 25, 1895. Also of note, the last great herd of buffalo in Indian Territory was reportedly seen near Camp Supply in 1877. West of the town of Fort Supply (pop. 559), is a DAR marker designating the crossing here of a military road from Dodge City, Kansas, to Fort Elliott, Texas.

FORT SUPPLY HISTORIC DISTRICT (NRHP and OHS) is now part of the Western Hospital and Key Correctional Center Campus. Five original and well preserved buildings remain dating from 1870 to 1892. Included are the **Custer House**, **Sheridan House**, and the **teamster's cabin**, built in the vertical "picket post" style and believed to be the oldest structures remaining. This historic site is currently undergoing reconstruction and preservation (1991) but visitors are welcome.

It is 15 miles to **Woodward**.

WOODWARD

Seat of **Woodward County** is the town of WOODWARD (pop. 13,781). The county was named for the town but there is still some difference of opinion as to which of several Woodward families was so honored. The town was born in April, 1887, when a railroad being built from Kansas to the Texas Panhandle via Fort Supply missed the mark by 12 miles. The depot for Fort Supply was left in this spot since a military road from Fort Reno crossed the line here and it was decided provisions could be moved by wagon the remaining few miles.

Al Jennings and his three brothers, Frank, Ed, and John, were roustabout cowboys who lived at Kiowa Creek near Woodward. Al fell into bad company and was goaded into several awkward attempts at robbery. At first, Al and his brothers, posing as U.S. marshals, levied tolls against some of the gullible ranchers driving cattle through the area. They soon tired of this and tried to rob two trains near Woodward. The engineer on the first train they attempted to flag down ignored the would-be robbers. The second attempt was just as futile because the engineer thought the cowboys riding alongside his train firing their pistols were just being friendly. They finally robbed the express car from a train stopped to take on wood at a water stop.

The robbery netted the Jennings brothers $60. Al and his brother Frank were captured the next day without a shot being fired. The other two Jennings brothers ran into the famed lawman Temple Houston, goaded him into a fight and he shot them both. Ed was killed and John was wounded. Al and Frank Jennings were sentenced to life imprisonment for their absurd robbery. Al was freed in five years; Frank in seven. Al Jennings, the bank robber, ran for governor of Oklahoma in the 1914 Democratic primary. He placed third in the balloting.

One of the state's worst tornadoes occurred in Woodward on April 9, 1947, when a funnel cloud ripped through town killing more than 100 people and destroying 200 city blocks.

PLAINS INDIANS AND PIONEERS MUSEUM, 2009 Williams Ave. Featured are exhibits of ranching, pioneer, and Indian life in this area. From 1893 to his death in 1905, **Temple Houston** practiced law in Woodward. The youngest son of Sam Houston, he was born in the governor's mansion in Austin, Texas. The museum has a collection of artifacts owned by him. It is open from 10 a.m. to 5 p.m. Tuesday through Saturday and from 1 to 4 p.m. Sunday. Admission is free.

Temple Houston's father died when he was not quite 3 and his mother when he was 7. He seemed to spend the rest of his life running from the famous names of these parents he barely knew yet he became a famous person himself. He was practicing law in Canadian, Texas, when he decided to move his law office to Woodward. Houston had a quick temper, a flamboyant manner, and he enjoyed a drink more than he should have. His colorful courtroom dramatics coupled with two highly publicized gun-fights brought a measure of glamour and recognition to the town of Woodward. It also brought fame to Houston and made him one of the most sought-after lawyers in the southwest. He died in August, 1905, at the age of 45 and is buried in Woodward.

WOODWARD THEATER, downtown, recently has been restored and made available for live stage productions.

BOILING SPRINGS STATE PARK, east of town on SH 34C. This has historically been a popular recreation spot in a High Plains area where water is not always readily available.

At 34 miles from Woodward on US 183, cross US 60. **Seiling** is two miles east (Section 12).

WESTERN CATTLE TRAIL

Most of US 183 is never too far from the path of this cattle trail (especially true from Seiling south) which began when traffic on the Chisholm Trail to the east began to dry up. First fences began to appear along the Chisholm as more formal ranching operations got under way. When per-head levies were collected from trail herds the virtually free transportation system was no long free so owners swung their herds into the western third of Oklahoma. Precise figures are impossible to come by but total number of cattle thought to have used the Western Trail during its relatively short life during the 1870s and '80s are estimated well into the millions. It is generally agreed that during 1881 and 1882, the peak years, that as many as a third of million cattle went north on this route.

It is eight miles to **Taloga**.

TALOGA

Smallest of the 77 county seats is TALOGA (pop, 446), located in a scenic setting on the south bank of the **South Canadian River. Dewey County** was organized as "D" County in 1891 when the Cheyenne-Arapaho Reservation was surveyed for settlement prior to opening to non-Indian settlement in 1892. The county was named for Admiral George Dewey. It is believed Taloga is from a Creek word meaning "rock in water" having reference to the original boundary of the Creek Nation which was in this area.

COURTHOUSE (NRHP). Of all the courthouses in Oklahoma, this one has the most "Southwest" look about it though it wasn't built in that style in 1926. The design is an adaptation of neo-classical architecture with cut-stone trim and quoins on the corners of the building. In recent years the building has been painted white. The pilasters framing the main entry, the quoins, and other trim has been painted brown resulting in the distinctive look the building now has.

One museum which reflects the life in this part of the state is at **Leedey**. Go 15 miles south on US 183 to the junction with SH 47.

A SIDE TRIP

Twenty-two miles west, then two miles back north at SH 34 is **Leedey**.

LEEDEY

Established in 1900, this western Oklahoma farming-ranching community (pop. 499) was named for the first postmaster, **Amos Leedey**. On May 31, 1947, the town was almost destroyed by a tornado.

BOSWELL MUSEUM, Main and Broadway. Examples of

pioneer transportation, day-to-day living, photographs, documents, and assorted antiques representing life in Western Oklahoma can be found here. It is open from 1 to 4 p.m. Tuesday through Saturday from June through August. It is closed in winter. Admission is free.

Back on US 183 it is 18 miles to **Arapaho**, another small county seat town.

ARAPAHO

While Taloga has had little trouble remaining the seat of government for its county, ARAPAHO (pop. 851), post office established March 23, 1892, has had to fight to remain the seat of **Custer County**. Between 1908 and 1933 there were five bitterly fought attempts to move the county seat to Clinton (Section 4), a large neighbor to the south. Neither town, however, won the legally mandated vote needed to get the county seat. After the last vote a governor's proclamation finally settled the matter in Arapaho's favor. Arapaho was named the seat of "G" County after the Cheyenne-Arapaho Reservation survey. On the day of the run, April 19, 1892, about 400 people staked lots in this new townsite. When the Choctaw Railroad built through in 1901 it missed Arapaho by about four miles. In 1903, a new town (Clinton) began forming along the railroad and Arapaho's growth began to decline.

Custer County is named for Maj. Gen. George A. Custer (his brevet Army rank achieved during the Civil War; he held the rank of lieutenant colonel in the Regular Army at the time of his death at Little Big Horn) and Arapaho is named for the tribe, a word from the Pawnee term "larapihu" meaning "he buys or trades."

COURTHOUSE (NRHP). While this courthouse, built in 1935, then added on to, is not an especially unusual building for its type, it is unusual for its location. The courthouse square with its neat and impressive buildings, up on a slight rise, completely dominates this small town.

Nineteen miles south is **Cordell**.

CORDELL

Second seat of **Washita County** (named for the river) is CORDELL (pop. 3,301) officially named New Cordell as the town is several miles west of the original townsite. The seat of Territorial Washita County was won from nearby **Cloud Chief** in a special election in 1900. However, it took special federal legislation to accomplish the transfer.

On the north edge of town is a historical marker for **Cordell Academy**, opened by the Dutch Reformed Church in 1906. Purpose was to provide a guarded and thorough education for boys and girls to the end "that they may become useful American citizens, and maintain the building of individual Christian character." The institution was closed in 1911.

COURTHOUSE. Completed in 1910, and among the state's most attractive, this is one of 17 state courthouses designed by the architect firm of **Solomon Andrew Layton**, often called the "Father of Oklahoma Courthouses." One of the special features is the large dome with its four clocks, a rather pretentious nicety for a raw frontier area less than a decade removed from Indian reservation.

WPA MURAL. At the Cordell Post Office is one of two Oklahoma post office murals painted by **Ila McAfee Turner** under the auspices of the WPA. The second one is in Edmond (Section 4). Called "The Scene Changes," the mural depicts the Indian and buffalo being displaced by the white man and his cattle. The artist painted the mural at her White Horse Studio in Taos, New Mexico, in 1938, then traveled to Cordell to display it. Thirty years later she cleaned and restored her original work.

WASHITA COUNTY MUSEUM is located at 106 E. First. Featured are items, photographs, and manuscripts relating to the settlement of Washita County and Oklahoma. It is open from 1 to 4 p.m. Friday. Admission is free.

Enroute to the turn off to Hobart, 22 miles south, make another turn-off eight miles down the road to **Bessie**, a mile west. In this tiny community is an impressive monument to banker **Bill Kiehn** who was killed in the 1920s while pursuing bank robbers.

Hobart is two miles west of US 183 on SH 9.

HOBART

Kiowa County seat is HOBART (pop. 4,735). The county is one of 15 in the state named for an Indian tribe. The town was named for Vice President **Garrett A. Hobart** in the McKinley administration.

OLD CITY HALL THEATER (NRHP), Main and Third. The old Hobart city hall, built in 1912, has been restored and is now the home of the Shortgrass Theater. It is open by appointment, 405/726-3415. Admission is free.

COURTHOUSE (NRHP). This building, completed in 1903, is the only building ever used to house Kiowa County govern-

This monument marks the site of the Babbs Switch School fire in 1924 in which 35 persons lost their lives while attending a Christmas party in a one-room frame school house. A school was rebuilt on this site as a memorial and a model to point the way to safer county schools. The school was discontinued in 1943, was dismantled and sold.

ment. The county was organized in 1901 after the openings of the Kiowa-Comanche-Apache and Caddo-Wichita reservations to non-Indian settlement. On the grounds are two military figure statues which were cast in 1929 and restored in 1979. They stood for many years on a war memorial bridge on SH 9 west of town. The two matching figures (another soldier and sailor) are in downtown Granite (Section 8).

HOBART PUBLIC LIBRARY, one of four in the state listed on the NRHP. This library, opened in September, 1912, was built with a grant from the Andrew Carnegie Foundation at a cost of $9,000. The remaining $1,000 was used for furnishings and books. The library is still open and serving the community.

Six miles south on US 183 is a large granite marker (on the left) in a small roadside park.

BABBS SWITCH. On December 24, 1924, 35 men, women, and children lost their lives when a fire destroyed the one-room frame schoolhouse that stood here. The fire started when a Christmas tree was ignited by one of the lighted candles used for decoration. The tragedy led to laws and design changes which made schools throughout the United States safer. The school was named for the nearby railroad switch that had been named for Edith "Babbs" Babson. She delivered the first load of wheat to the elevator at the switch.

It is 12 miles to **Roosevelt** (pop. 323) and south of it, **Great Plains Park**. On the north edge of the park are the remains of the ghost town of **Wildman** (named for mining developer Frank W. Wildman) and the old Gold Belles Mine.

As early as the 1600s there had been rumors of "lost" gold mines in the Wildman area but until August 6, 1901, when the Indian lands were opened for settlement, this area had been closed to the gold-seeking non-Indians. The discovery of silver just to the west and a mini-gold rush in 1895 to the north only served to make the Wichita Mountain area even more appealing as a prospective mining site. It is said that more than 5,000 miners and prospectors came from all over the country in 1901 and among the many mining towns which quickly sprang up was Wildman. The "gold fever" died almost as quickly as it began and by 1905 most of the miners had moved on. Although traces of gold, silver, copper, and other minerals were discovered, the hard granite apparently was too difficult to smelt. About all that remains of Wildman are the stone piers of the old smelter, the entrance to the mine and a cemetery.

The Gold Belle Mine and Milling Company was formed near the rough mining town of Wildman. The Gold Belle Company erected a 50 ton cyanide mill to process the gold ore. The gold rush here was short-lived.

One mile north of **Mountain Park** (pop. 473), south of Tom Steed Lake in the state park, is a historical marker for an early army post.

CAMP RADZIMINSKI was established in September, 1858, by **Capt. Earl Van Dorn** who named it for a lieutenant in his regiment who had died. The post was abandoned on December 6, 1859 when **Fort Cobb** construction was completed. During its brief history, Camp Radziminski was in continuous action against hostile Indians.

Snyder (Section 7) is three miles south of Mountain Park. It is 17 miles to **Frederick**.

FREDERICK

Seat of **Tillman County** (named for Benjamin W. Tillman of South Carolina) is FREDERICK (pop. 6,153). The county was created at statehood from parts of the territorial counties of Kiowa and Comanche. Frederick was established in 1901 and

322

A large party of gold seekers enroute to California camped near here on May 28, 1849, with a military escort commanded by Capt. R. B. Marcy. The California Road, as this route became known, was used for more than 50 years. East of here about four miles are traces of the Western Cattle Trail to Dodge City, Kansas.

named for the son of a St. Louis railroad promoter. In 1905, Frederick received nation-wide publicity for hosting President **Theodore Roosevelt** on his famous "wolf hunt" into the **Big Pasture**. This was a 488,000 acre area owned by the Comanches and Kiowas and leased to cattlemen under the direction of the Secretary of the Interior. The Big Pasture was opened to homesteaders in 1906 by sealed bids.

TILLMAN COUNTY MUSEUM. This complex includes a restored one-room schoolhouse and a large red barn. The Horsecreek School, built in 1902, was used until 1946. Exhibits include school-related items as well as dolls, baseballs, and war memorabilia. In the barn are antique farm tools and equipment and displays relating to "A Woman's World, 1900-1935." One unusual attraction in the museum is the 30-foot length of knotted hemp that served as the official State of Oklahoma "hanging rope" for some ten years. The museum is open from 2 to 4 p.m. Wednesday and weekends. Admission is free.

RAMONA THEATER (NRHP) has been restored recently as a community theater.

The remains of an old mining community near Roosevelt, Wildman is a ghost town today. Oklahoma has several such ghost towns.

SECTION 15
US 70

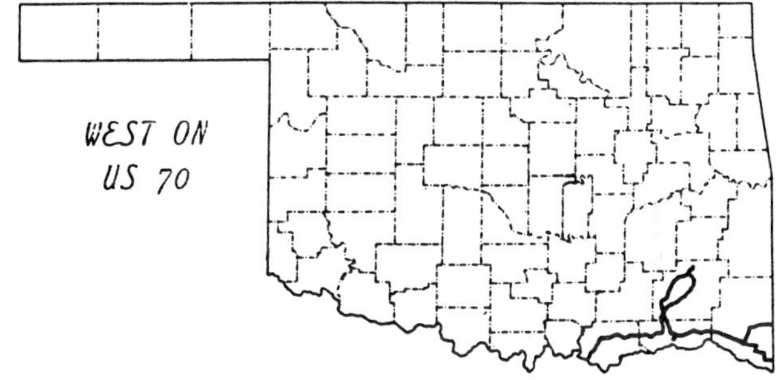

This stone marks the grave of Isaac Levi Garvin (1832-1880), principal chief of the Choctaw Nation, 1878-1880. This marker is in the Waterhole Cemetery near Idabel. The cemetery was rescued and restored by the McCurtain County Historical Society.

SECTION 15
US 70

US 70 offers a number of important historical sites and events on its 300-mile route along the Red River in southeastern and south-central Oklahoma. They relate for the most part to the Choctaw Indians and to the friendly Chickasaws with whom they shared the western section of their new homeland. Uprooted from Mississippi in the 1830s, they roughly followed the present course of US 70 as they pushed westward to build new homes and villages, lay out new farmlands, orchards, and gardens; re-establish schools, churches, and other institutions abandoned in their forced exodus west. Settlements are for the most part modest, the land relatively flat as the pine-covered Ouachita Mountains of southeastern Oklahoma give way to hardwood, rolling uplands then to fertile Red River bottomlands. A steady procession of roadside markers fills in the history of the region for those with time and will to search for sites with surviving relics of once busy days.

WEST ON US 70

Although US 70 runs most of the way across the southern part of the state this trip will begin near the Oklahoma-Arkansas state line and end 195 miles west at Durant. A 100-mile circle side trip to Antlers and Tuskahoma is offered those interested in learning more of the history of the Choctaws.

McCURTAIN COUNTY

The most southeastern county in Oklahoma is also one of the state's most forested and mountainous. Created at statehood, it is named for a prominent Choctaw family that produced four chiefs, a father and three sons. A mile inside the state line is a historical marker for the **Harris Family Cemetery**.

HARRIS CEMETERY. Members of several Harris families, Choctaws, traveled by flatboat down the Mississippi River and up the Red River to Fulton, Arkansas, before continuing overland to the Choctaw Nation at this point in 1836. The Harrises operated a cotton gin, grist mill, salt works, and tannery and eventually farmed 800 acres with slave labor. The cemetery contains family members as well as slaves. The Harris wives were daughters of a prominent Choctaw couple **Major John and Sophia Folsom Pitchlynn**. The cemetery is located southeast of the marker about a quarter of a mile, through a gate and down a dirt track. A sign points the way.

It is five miles to **Eagletown**. Turn south at the gas station/store to the stop sign, then back east, following the curve of the road to the business area.

EAGLETOWN

One of the oldest towns in Oklahoma is EAGLETOWN, named for the eagles nesting in the swamps along the **Mountain Fork River**. The community was established about 1820 when the area was still part of Arkansas Territory. The post office was one of the first in Indian Territory, established July 1, 1834, and a sign on the outside of the present building proclaims it "Oldest Post Office in Oklahoma." Originally known as Eagle Town, the settlement was located first on the west side of the Mountain Fork rather than the east side.

Just south of the present settlement was **Stockbridge Mission**, established in 1836. There the superintendent, **Rev. Cyrus Byington**, compiled his "Dictionary of the Choctaw Language." The Choctaw General Council established **Iyanubbe Seminary** for Choctaw girls in this same area in 1842.

OLD EAGLE TOWN is located between the Mountain Fork and an open field just west of the **Gardner Mansion**, north of US 70. Tracks of the old military road from the east to **Fort Towson** and **Doaksville** are still visible in the field. The settlement was at the site of **Bethabara Mission**, established by the Presbyterians in 1832. The mission grounds served as the seat of **Eagle County** of the Choctaw Nation from 1850 until 1907.

GARDNER MANSION (NRHP). A two-story log house built in 1884 by Choctaw **Chief Jefferson Gardner** is still standing, though not in its original configuration. A model inside the house shows the way it looked and the way the present owners hope it will look again as time and money permits. Today, visitors approach the back of the house as it was built to face the town located to the north and west. Displayed inside the home are items relating to the area including many prehistoric and historic Indian artifacts from eastern Oklahoma. It is open from 10 a.m. to 5 p.m. Monday through Saturday in winter and from 8 a.m. to 6 p.m. in summer. Sunday hours are from 1:30 to 5 p.m. in winter and until 6 p.m. in summer. An admission is charged.

GIANT CYPRESS TREE. When the Choctaws were forcibly moved from Mississippi to Indian Territory this tree marked the end of their "Trail of Tears" journey between 1831-34. In May, 1982, lightning struck this 2,000-year old tree and killed it. It is still standing, though, and is part of the Gardner House tour.

CHIEFS' MARKERS. About .2 of a mile past the Gardner House turnoff, look for a roadside park to the south of US 70. Here are historical markers to three prominent Choctaw chiefs, **George Hudson**, **Peter Pitchlynn**, and **Jefferson Gardner**.

It is six miles to Broken Bow, then 13 miles south to **Idabel** (both Section 11).

A SIDE TRIP

From Idabel follow SH 3 for 11 miles through the **Ouachita** (pronounced wash-a-taw) **National Forest** to the village of **Haworth** (pop. 293). Five miles further is the home of prominent Choctaw leader **Henry Harris**.

HARRIS HOUSE (NRHP) was built in 1867 and features period furnishings and "Trail of Tears" memorabilia. It is open by appointment, 405/245-1129. Admission is free.

Eleven miles farther, past the village of **Tom**, can be seen the remnants of the large Garland plantation. A historical marker points the way, a short distance north on a dirt road, then back west.

GARLAND FAMILY CEMETERY. Graves includes those of **Samuel Garland**, a principal chief of the Choctaws; his wife **Mary Pitchlynn**, and mother-in-law Sophia Folsom Pitchlynn, mother of another principal chief, Peter Pitchlynn. Mrs. Pitchlynn, as a widow, came to the Choctaw Nation in 1837 bringing her slaves to help work her son-in-law's plantation. She died at age 98 and her birthdate on her tombstone, December 27, 1773, is thought to be the oldest date on a tombstone in Oklahoma.

Back on US 70 in Idabel, go west for 11 miles to **Millerton**.

MILLERTON

Also among the oldest communities in the Choctaw Nation MILLERTON (pop. 234) dates from about 1832. From March 21, 1845, until May 3, 1895, the post office was known as **Wheelock** for nearby **Wheelock Academy**, a seminary for girls established by the Choctaw Council in 1842. The academy was open until 1955 and many of its buildings still stand. A historical marker about the academy and **Wheelock Mission Presbyterian Church** is located 1.5 miles east of Millerton at the junction of US 70 and Wheelock Road.

WHEELOCK MISSION AND ACADEMY (both on the NRHP). The mission is the oldest church building in Oklahoma, dating back to 1846, and it is still used for church services. The mission was established in 1832 by **Rev. Alfred Wright**, a physician, translator of the New Testament into Choctaw, and missionary to the tribe for 33 years. The building, the only structure in Indian Territory to be used for a **Currier and Ives** print, is a mile north and .2 mile west of the marker. It can be viewed at any time as can the nearby cemetery which contains Wright's grave. Note the inscription on his stone. The academy is passed on the way to the church. Visitors are welcome to drive through the grounds, which are now owned by the Choctaw tribe.

Back on the highway it is five miles to **Valliant**. East of town is a historical marker for **Clear Creek Water Mill**, the remnants of which are located two miles south on Clear Creek. The mill was near the site of **Clear Creek Academy for Choctaw Boys**, (1836-42). The mill was first operated as a grist mill and was used by Caddo Indians and whites as early as 1819.

VALLIANT

Originally called Fowlerville, the name of this town was changed to VALLIANT (pop. 873) in 1902 to honor the chief engineer for the **Arkansas and Choctaw Railway** (later Frisco),

The Choctaw Chiefs House northeast of Swink was first built in 1832. The present structure is basically a re-creation.

F. W. Valliant. In 1886, the Presbyterians established a chapel school here called **Hill School**, later **Oak Hill Industrial Academy**, to educate the children of slaves freed by the Choctaws following the Civil War. In 1912, the name was changed to the **Alice Lee Elliott Memorial School**, when her husband gave the institution funds for a new dormitory in his wife's memory. Before the school was closed in 1934, hundreds of black students received training here.

Three miles west of town the highway enters **Choctaw County** (named for the tribe). It is two miles to **Swink** and the turnoff to what many believe to be the oldest house in Oklahoma, located .5 mile north, 1.5 miles east, and .3 mile back south of the Swink grocery store.

CHOCTAW CHIEF'S HOUSE (NRHP and OHS) was built for the chief of the **Apukshunnubbee District** of the Choctaw Nation as provided in the 1830 Treaty of Dancing Rabbit Creek. First chief to live in the house, built in 1832, was **Thomas LeFlore**. He owned a thousand-acre plantation around the log house and lived there until the early 1850s when he was forced to give it up. In 1960, what was left of the crumbling house was given to the Oklahoma Historical Society which has rebuilt and restored it close to the way it may have been when owned by the LeFlores. The garden and orchards also are being gradually restored. It is open from 9 a.m. to 5 p.m. Tuesday through Friday and from 1 to 5 p.m. weekends. Admission is free.

Back on US 70, it is 3.5 miles west to the turn-off to military **Fort Towson**.

FORT TOWSON (NRHP and OHS) was established in May, 1824, by **Col. Matthew Arbuckle**. Original site was about five miles south where it remained until the fort was closed in 1829. A year later it was reactivated and at the time the unhealthy location in the bottoms of the **Red River** was abandoned and the post moved to the present location. Purpose of the fort was to protect the peaceful Choctaws from the raiding Plains tribes to the west as well as from the outlaws who headquartered along the north bank of the Red River. It was abandoned in 1854 and the buildings used for the Choctaw Indian Agents. At the outset of the Civil War, it was taken over by the Confederacy and in 1864 was headquarters for **Gen. S. B. Maxey**. Featured are ruins as well as a reconstruction of the old Sutlers Store. Artifacts are displayed in the visitor center/museum. It is open from 8 a.m. to 5 p.m. weekdays and

A young tourist enjoys a close look at one of the canons on display at Fort Towson.

from 1 to 5 p.m. weekends. Admission is free.

Return to the highway and drive through the town of Fort Towson (pop. 568) to the west side of town. Turn north at a corner grocery and drive on a winding road for about two miles to the **Doaksville Cemetery** and a historical marker.

DOAKSVILLE CEMETERY contains graves of many early-day (pre-Civil War) white and Indian citizens including several Choctaw leaders. In the black section is believed to be the graves of **Uncle Wallace** and **Aunt Minerva Willis**. These two slaves, from a large plantation near Doaksville, were hired out to work for the missionaries at Spencer Academy, also located in the area. It was here they were heard to sing the spirituals "Swing Low Sweet Chariot," "Steal Away to Jesus," and "Roll, Jordan, Roll." The words and music were copied by academy superintendent Rev. Alexander Reid who sent the transcriptions to the Jubilee Singers at Fisk University in Nashville. The group liked the tunes so well they sang them on a tour of the United States and Europe including a concert for Queen Victoria. At the north side of the cemetery are steps leading to the old townsite.

DOAKSVILLE HISTORIC SITE (NRHP and OHS). The settlement of Doaksville began in 1821 when the fur-trading

In the top photo are some of remains of Fort Towson and below is the Doaksville Site Cemetery.

Doaks brothers migrated west ahead of the Choctaws who had signed the Treaty of Doak's Stand, paving the way for their ultimate removal from Mississippi. Original site of the store was a few miles southeast but with establishment of Fort Towson, the brothers and other early day settlers living near the store for protection from raiding Indians from the west, resettled to the present townsite near the fort. Many of the Choctaws moving to Indian Territory in the early 1830s settled in and around Doaksville, making it one of the three most important towns in the Choctaw Nation. Doaksville was the capital of the Choctaw Nation from 1850 until 1863. In June, 1865, Indian Confederate **General Stand Watie** rode into town and surrendered his troops, two months after the official end of the Civil War. He was the last Confederate general to surrender (note historical marker). **Pine Ridge School** for Choctaw girls, opened in 1845, was located near here.

Six miles west of Fort Towson on the west side of the **Kiamichi River** bridge is a historical marker for **Goodwater Female Academy** which was six miles south of the marker. Opened in 1837, it closed at the beginning of the Civil War and never reopened.

Seven miles west of the bridge and one mile south is the site of **Rose Hill Plantation**.

ROSE HILL CEMETERY (OHS). Rose Hill was the home of **Capt. Robert M. Jones**, who was the first millionaire of the Choctaw Nation. A half-blood Choctaw, Jones had many successful enterprises including three stores and a string of plantations along the Red River worked by 500 slaves. To carry his produce to market and to stock his stores, Jones also owned and operated two steamboats. The opulent house at Rose Hill, abandoned and falling into decay, burned in 1912 and only a few trees remain to mark its site. Located nearby is the family cemetery protected by a picturesque rock wall.

Back on the highway, it is two miles to **Hugo**.

HUGO

HUGO (pop. 5,978) is the seat of Choctaw County. The town was named for French novelist **Victor Hugo**, favorite author of **Mrs. W. H. Darrough**, wife of the man who surveyed the original townsite. Hugo is the birthplace of journalist **Bill Moyers**. It also is the hometown of **Ed Ansley**, better known as the portrayer of **Buster Brown**, who, with his dog Tige, "lives in a shoe."

For many years Hugo has been the winter quarters for the **Carson Barnes Circus** as well as, at times, various lesser known shows. The Carson Barnes Show is the last large (five ring) circus still performing outdoors under a big top. Of special interest to circus fans is a section of **Mount Olivet Cemetery**.

MOUNT OLIVET CEMETERY. The Showman's Rest section, with its many unique headstones, was opened in 1960 following the death of circus man **Kelly Miller**. It is the only burial area in the southwest exclusively for show people. The entrance is marked by a large granite shaft picturing a circus tent and a performing elephant and the inscription "In Tribute To All Showmen Under God's Big Top." A sign on the east side of town on US 70 points the way to the cemetery.

HUGO FRISCO DEPOT MUSEUM (NRHP) is along US 70 on the west side of town. The railroad alongside the depot was one of the earlier ones in Indian Territory, completed in 1887 as a main line between St. Louis, Missouri, and Texas. The two-story red brick building contains many exhibits pertaining to early days in the area. The upstairs has been furnished, in part, as it was when lived in by the **Harvey Girls** who worked in the Fred Harvey Restaurant downstairs. It is open from 10 a.m. to 4:30 p.m. weekends. Admission is free.

HUGO HERITAGE RAILROAD. Every weekend an engine with two restored passenger cars leaves the Hugo station for a two and a half hour train ride. The mystery is which direction will the train go. It depends on freight traffic on the **Kiamichi Railroad** which sponsors this project with the **Choctaw County Historical Society**. There are four options open and all provide a scenic trip. Prior to the trip the refurbished **Harvey House** restaurant is open for meals as it was during the time Fred Harvey operated his famous restaurant chain. For information and reservations call 405/732-0566, the same number for the train in Watonga (Section 13).

GOODLAND PRESBYTERIAN CHILDREN'S HOME is south and west of Hugo. A historical marker, two miles south at the corner of US 271/SH 2A, is at the turn to the home two miles west. Started in 1848 as a mission in the Choctaw Nation, for many years it had the distinction of being the oldest school in continuous operation in Oklahoma. It is the oldest Protestant home for Indian children in the United States. Two structures to view are the Presbyterian Church, built in 1850, and the nearby log cabin office of **Basil LeFlore**, governor of the Choctaw Nation, 1859-60. It is open by appointment, 405/326-7568. Admission is free.

Back on US 70 and two miles west of Hugo is the **Indian Nation Turnpike**, turn-off for travelers wishing to take the side trip to **Antlers** and **Tuskahoma**.

A SIDE TRIP

The route begins with a 16-mile swing north on the turnpike to the Antlers exit. From here it follows SH 2, a scenic drive along the course of the Kiamichi River, northeast to a junction with US 271 in **Clayton** (pop. 636). Follow US 271 six miles to **Tuskahoma** and the well marked turnoff to the **Choctaw Council House**. For different scenery on the return trip follow US 271 south from Clayton to US 70, five miles west of Hugo.

ANTLERS

ANTLERS (pop. 2,524) is the seat of **Pushmataha County**, named for **Chief Pushmataha**, noted Choctaw leader who fought in the War of 1812. Antlers was well-known in pre-Civil War days as a camping area called **Beaver's Station**. It was the Indian custom to mark a spring with a set of antlers fastened to a nearby tree and it is thought this is how the present-day town received its name. Site of the spring is a block south of Main Street between the railway depot (soon to be a museum as of 1991) and the county courthouse. Signs point the way.

TUSKAHOMA

Tuskahoma is one-half mile south of US 271. Although the area was already well settled, the post office at TUSKAHOMA was not established until February 27, 1884. Until 1891 the official spelling was **Tuska Homma**, a Choctaw word meaning "red warrior." The first Choctaw tribal council meeting was held at **Jack's Fork**, 1.5 miles northwest, in 1834 for the purpose of drawing up a new constitution for the Nation. In 1837, a spacious log council house was built at the site and called **Nanih Waiya** after the tribe's sacred mound in Mississippi. A historical marker is located on US 271, .5 miles north and 1.5 mile west of Tuskahoma. This marker is about 200 feet west of the site of Nanih Waiya.

In 1850, the capital was removed to Doaksville, then to Chata Tamaha, but in 1883 the tribal government was returned to the Tuskahoma area. The handsome red brick council house 2.5 miles north of town served as the capitol until statehood in 1907. Various agencies of the Choctaw Tribal Government still hold meetings in the building.

The Choctaw Council House (capitol) is still used for tribal business. A museum has also been established here to house Choctaw artifacts.

CHOCTAW COUNCIL HOUSE MUSEUM (NRHP). Restored in recent years, the museum now houses Choctaw artifacts, paintings, and photographs. It is open from 11 a.m. to 3 p.m. weekdays. Admission is free.

CEMETERY. Many well-known Choctaws are buried in the nearby cemetery. These include **Jackson McCurtain**, chief of the Nation when the council building was constructed, and his wife, **Jane**, the most prominent of the few Choctaw women who took an active part in politics.

Jane Austin McCurtain received her education at Wheelock Academy and Edgeworth Seminary, Pittsburgh, Pennsylvania, as it was the custom for the Choctaws to send their brightest, most talented daughters to schools in the East. She became a schoolteacher and taught until she met and married Capt. Jackson McCurtain of the First Choctaw Regiment during the Civil War. Jackson served the Choctaw Nation as a senator, president of the senate and principal chief. Jane, in addition to her domestic duties and rearing five children, was his secretary, speech writer, and close advisor.

The couple's home in Tuskahoma was a gathering place for officers and legislators where affairs of the Nation were discussed. After Jackson's death in 1885, Jane remained a force in tribal affairs. Her home became a meeting place for tribal leaders who sought her counsel. In later life she served as superintendent of **Jones Academy** for boys, one of two academies she helped found. Jane McCurtain died in 1924.

After a return to US 70 proceed west 15 miles to **Boswell**.

BOSWELL

The town of BOSWELL (pop. 643) was originally located two miles north and was named **Mayhew** after the Mayhew Presbyterian Mission in Mississippi. The post office was established February 5, 1845, and continued until 1902 when the town was moved two miles south to the railroad which was building through the area. The town was renamed for territorial civic leader **A. V. Boswell**. Of interest is the **Mayhew Cemetery** with graves dating from the 1850s.

It is 10 miles to **Bennington**. Enroute the highway passes into **Bryan County** (named for **William Jennings Bryan,** three-time nominee of the Democratic Party for United States president).

BENNINGTON

Located south of US 70, BENNINGTON (pop. 251) grew up around a church established at this location in 1848 by the Presbyterian Mission Board. The town was named by a descendant of **Gen. John Stark,** who chose to commemorate the Revolutionary War battle in Vermont. The church and its accompanying burying ground are still located here but the church has been greatly altered through the years.

BOKCHITO

The name of BOKCHITO (pop. 576) is a Choctaw word

meaning "big creek." The town began in the 1890s but the area was an important location in the Choctaw Nation from the early days. A historical marker on the east edge of town points the way to the site, three miles northeast, of Armstrong Academy.

ARMSTRONG ACADEMY SITE (NRHP). On weekends neighborhood or Saturday and Sunday schools were held here to give Indian adults instruction in reading, writing, and arithmetic as well as religion. Friday evenings the families would begin arriving by wagon from over the district and would camp out until classes ended Sunday evening. Classes for Choctaw boys continued at the school until 1919. In 1921 the buildings burned. Although a cemetery and a few piles of rock remain, the site is presently on private property and not open to the public.

CHATA TAMAHA (Choctaw Town). For 20 years (1863-1883) the main hall of Armstrong Academy was the meeting place for the Choctaw National Council. During the Civil War, Chata Tamaha, the name of the settlement around the academy, hosted the delegates of the United Nations of Indian Territory (Cherokee, Choctaw, Seminole, Creek, Chickasaw, and Caddo) in alliance with the Confederacy. In 1883 the capital was moved to Tuskahoma.

It is 13 miles to **Durant**.

DURANT

The county seat of Bryan County, DURANT (pop. 12,823), is named for a family that settled the land in 1870. A historical marker north of town on US 69/75 honors another, though later, prominent resident, **Robert Lee Williams**, member of the Oklahoma Constitutional Convention, Chief Justice of the Oklahoma Supreme Court, and governor of the state from 1915-1919.

Durant sometimes calls itself the "City of Magnolias" because of magnolia trees growing there. It is also known as the "Peanut Capital of Oklahoma."

BRYAN COUNTY COURTHOUSE was completed in 1917. On the grounds is an imposing statue to "Our Gallant Confederate Soldiers" placed there by a chapter of the Daughters of the Confederacy.

BIG PEANUT MONUMENT. Located in the next block east of the city hall is a monument billed as "The World's Largest Peanut." The peanut, of course, isn't a nut at all but a member of the legume family.

THREE VALLEY MUSEUM (NRHP), 16th and Elm, is

located in one of the buildings that once housed **Durant Presbyterian College**, (originally **Calvin Institute** and, when closed in 1960, **Presbyterian College for Girls**). Many of the exhibits pertain to the college, but others relate to the history of the town and surrounding area. It is open from 2 to 4:30 p.m. weekdays. Admission is free.

FAIRCHILDS GALLERY, 401 Denison St., has exhibits relating to the Navajo Indians including paintings, bronzes, dolls, rugs, and jewelry. It is open from 1 to 5 p.m. weekdays. Admission is free.

SOUTHEASTERN OKLAHOMA STATE UNIVERSITY, originally Southeastern Normal School, was opened in 1909 as one of six teachers colleges in the state. The campus is located on the northwest side of town.

Also of interest in the area are a number of historic sites described in Section 7. South of Durant, 16 miles on US 69, is the historic **Colbert's Ferry** site.

COLBERT'S FERRY (NRHP), on the Red River, is where the old **Texas Road** left Indian Territory to enter Texas. **B. F. Colbert** established the first ferry here on his plantation in 1853. From 1858-61 he operated a station on the Butterfield Stage Route next to the ferry, the last stop in Indian Territory heading toward the west coast. Colbert eventually turned his ferry charter over to the Texas Toll Bridge Co. which operated a toll span near the site until 1931. A historical marker is located at Burney St. and Moore Ave. in Colbert (pop. 1,043). The ferry site is south and east of town on private property. A stone site marker is just inside the fence of the home there.

TOLL BRIDGE WAR. This toll span played a prominent role in an incident in 1931 called **"The Red River Bridge War."** In 1929 Texas and Oklahoma received consent from Congress to build a free bridge over the river. The stockholders of the toll bridge obtained an injunction in federal district court to stop the opening of the "free" bridge and the governor of Texas ordered barricades across the south end of it. On July 23, 1931, Oklahoma's governor, William H. "Alfalfa Bill" Murray, ordered the Oklahoma National Guard to clear the bridge to permit traffic over it. He had learned that a previous Supreme Court decision had declared both banks of the river belonged to Oklahoma. He went further when he ordered the highway leading to the Oklahoma end of the toll bridge plowed up and the paving removed. The free bridge remained open.

William H. Murray was one of Oklahoma's most colorful governors. He came from Texas and opened a law practice in Tishomingo (Section 7). He served as president of the Oklahoma Constitutional Convention in 1906, was elected a representative to the first state legislature, was the speaker of the state house in 1907 and 1908, and was elected to the U.S. House in 1912. He ran for governor twice before being elected in 1930. Murray identified with the middle class and rural voters, describing them as "lying between the privilege seeking and idle rich and the hopeless, indolent poor." In one campaign speech he promised, if elected, to plow up the ground around the governor's mansion in Oklahoma City and plant potatoes. He hinted he didn't much care for wasting all that good land with fancy, big city lawns. He won an easy victory but didn't do too well in the cities with his casual manners and rumpled clothes.

During his term he worked hard to help the people of the state through the Depression but also enjoyed some of the authority and power of the office. Use of the National Guard became almost a trademark of his four-year administration. He called out the "Guard" 34 times. Some of his dramatics brought him national media attention and in 1932 he was put forth as a candidate for the Democratic nominee for president.

Two counties in Oklahoma are named for him, Alfalfa and Murray. His son, **Johnston Murray**, was elected governor of Oklahoma in 1951. "Alfalfa Bill" died in 1956.

This memorial in the Showman's Rest Section of Mount Olivet Cemetery is a tribute to deceased circus performers. It was established in 1960 in Hugo.

Index

Sherman, Gen. William T. 51
Shidler, E. S. 277
Shidler 277
Shirley, Glenn 105
Shotgun Houses 109
Shoulders, Jim 170
Sibley, George C. 199
Sill, Brig. Gen. Joshua W. 47
Silver City 222, 223, 227, 228
Simmons, Del 105
Sinclair Oil & Gas Company 198
Skedee 193
Skeleton Creek 218
Skelly, William 34
Skullyville 251, 252
Skullyville Choctaw Burying Ground 252
Skullyville Jail 252
Slick, Tom B. 108
Smallwood, Norma 34, 40
Smith, Maj. John L. 8
Smith, Laverne 203
Smotherman, Michael 89
Snyder, Bryan 178
Snyder 8, 178
Society of Friends (Quakers) 59, 176, 199, 264, 300, 301
Sod House 285
"Sooner" 2, 15
Soucek, Apollo and Zeus 214
South Canadian River 118, 143, 222, 227, 287, 304, 317
Southeastern Oklahoma State University 340
Southern Plains Indian Museum 175
Southwestern Oklahoma State University 85
Sowell, Bill 22, 272, 274
Spahn, Warren 306
Spanish American War 220, 308
Spavinaw Creek 6
Speed, Dick 105
Spencer Academy 332
Spiro, Abram 250
Spiro (town) 250
Spiro Mounds Archaeological Park 238, 250, 251
Splitlog, Mathias 241, 243
Splitlog Indian Mission Church 241, 243
Spradlin, G. D. 18
Spring Creek 245
Spring of Everlasting Water 292
Stafford, Thomas P. 10, 85
Star House 53, 54, 177, 178
Starr, Belle 2, 70, 144, 145, 308
Starr, Henry 70
Starr, Sam 144
State Capital Publishing Museum 114
State Seal 16, 17
Stella Friends Academy 199
Stephens, John A. 231
Stephens, Jennie "Little Breeches" 195
Stephens County 231
Stephens County Historical Museum 233
Stevenson, Harold Jr. 259
Stidham (town) 144
Stillwater 102, 103, 105
Stillwater Creek 103
Stilwell 156, 195, 246, 247
Stockbridge Mission 328
Stone, Jim N 283
"Stone City" 202
Stone Museum 134
Strawn, George 136
Stroud, James J. 70